Fodor
Bern

Fodor's Travel Publications, Inc.
New York • Toronto • London • Sydney • Auckland

Fodor's Bermuda

Editor: Larry Peterson
Contributors: Andrew Collins, John DeMers, Honey Naylor, Peter Oliver, Marcy Pritchard, Judith Wadson
Creative Director: Fabrizio LaRocca
Cartographer: David Lindroth
Illustrator: Karl Tanner
Cover Photograph: Andrew McKim/Masterfile
Design: Vignelli Associates

Contents

Maps

Foreword

For their help in preparing this guide, we would like to thank the Bermuda National Trust; Connie Dey; Elsbeth Gibson; Stephen Martin of Bermuda Small Properties; David Mitchell for the Bermuda Collection; Jacqueline Pash of Porter/Novelli; Judy Blatman of Princess Hotels; Vivian Guerrero of Trust House Forte; Charles Webbe and Pam Wissing of the Bermuda Department of Tourism; Lisa Weisbord and Georgetta Lordi of Hill & Knowlton; and Jim Zuill of the Bermuda Book Store.

While every care has been taken to assure the accuracy of the information in this guide, the passage of time will always bring change, and consequently, the publisher cannot accept responsibility for errors that may occur.

All prices and opening times quoted here are based on information supplied to us at press time. Hours and admission fees may change, however, and the prudent traveler will avoid inconvenience by calling ahead.

Fodor's wants to hear about your travel experiences, both pleasant and unpleasant. When a hotel or restaurant fails to live up to its billing, let us know and we will investigate the complaint and revise our entries where the facts warrant it.

Send your letters to the editors of Fodor's Travel Publications, 201 E. 50th St., New York, NY 10022.

Highlights '94 and Fodor's Choice

Highlights '94

In 1992 **United Airlines** cancelled its service to Bermuda. However, in early 1993 **USAir** began nonstop service to Bermuda from Boston. The airline will operate 151-passenger Boeing 727 aircraft for the new service, which will depart Boston at 9:05 AM and arrive in Bermuda at 12:15 PM. The return flight departs Bermuda at 1:15 PM and touches down in Boston at 2:30 PM. USAir's other nonstop flights to Bermuda are from New York (La Guardia) and Philadelphia. Other airlines serving the island are Air Canada, American, Continental, Delta, and Northwest.

In December 1992 **Celebrity Cruises** did not renew its option, and its 1,354-passenger MV *Horizons* will not sail to Bermuda. The cruise ship had been doing seven-day cruises to the island between April and October, with stops at St. George's and Hamilton. At press time, negotiations were still under way with other cruise-ship companies for a replacement. According to local newspaper reports, Bermuda tourism officials are looking for a ship that would stop only in St. George's, with service beginning in the 1994 season.

Visitors to Bermuda can now pay the $15 **airport departure tax** when booking through a travel agent or when checking out of their hotel. In either case they will receive a voucher, which they will present at the airport upon departure. The tax can also be charged against American Express, Visa, or MasterCard at the airport.

In early 1992 the government passed the **Hotel Refurbishment Tax** Act, and the results can be seen in even the smallest properties. Prior to the new legislation the tax on imported goods was more than 30%. The tax act, which will be in effect until the end of 1993, cut the duty to 5%, and hoteliers all over the island have been taking advantage of the break to make improvements.

The **Elbow Beach Hotel,** which changed ownership in 1991 and began a five-year, multimillion-dollar, top-to-bottom renovation, announced plans for other phases of development. According to John Jefferis, managing director of the Elbow Beach Hotel Development Company, 22 "super-luxury" one-bedroom executive suites are to be added in 1993, at a cost of some $4 million. The suites will be on the hillside below the pool. The hotel's controversial plan for "palace suites" and a convention center on the beach have been scuttled, following strong opposition from the Bermuda National Trust and neighboring hoteliers. The latter complained that the six-story beach property would obstruct the view from their hotels. Elbow Beach's future plans call for a 42,000-square-foot European spa, the island's largest;

a river/pool waterway cascading through the property; four new tennis courts; and a small tennis stadium.

Bermuda has not traditionally been noted as a great vacation place for **children.** In fact, many properties would not accept children as guests (some still don't), and if they did come with their parents there was little for them to do. All that is changing. Several hotels now have full-fledged daycare and/or activities programs. Among the hotels with good plans for young children are the Belmont Hotel, Southampton Princess, Sonesta Beach, Grotto Bay Beach Hotel, and Willowbank.

The U.S.–Bermuda treaty that allows U.S. businesses holding **conventions** in Bermuda the same tax advantages they'd receive if the meeting were held in the United States has inspired a flurry of meeting-room activity around the island. The larger hotels have convention services—the Sonesta has a separate convention center—and even the smallest can boast some sort of meeting space. If called for, the Surf Side can convert its video-game room for small business meetings. Cambridge Beaches has a new 900-square-foot boardroom that contains a 28-foot-by-7-foot cherry table.

Spas and health clubs are springing up all over the island. The Southampton Princess and Sonesta Beach have long had European-style spas, and the Elbow Beach plans to construct the island's largest such facility. Cambridge Beaches also has a new, posh European-style spa. These properties offer attractive spa packages. As for health clubs, all of the aforementioned properties have them (as does Marriott's Castle Harbour), and, for the 1993 season, health clubs were added at the Reefs (whose guests have access to the spa at the Sonesta), Grotto Bay Beach, and the Hamilton Princess.

Bermudians are justly proud of the **Bermuda National Gallery,** which opened in March 1992. Located in the east wing of the city hall in Hamilton, the climate-controlled art gallery houses the Masterworks Bermudiana Collection, which showcases paintings of the island by local artists, as well those by Georgia O'Keeffe and Winslow Homer, among others. The gallery collection also includes paintings from the 15th to the 19th centuries by a host of artists that includes Thomas Gainsborough and Sir Joshua Reynolds.

Fodor's Choice

No two people will agree on what makes a perfect vacation, but it's fun and helpful to know what others think. We hope you'll have a chance to experience some of Fodor's Choices yourself in Bermuda. For detailed information about each entry, refer to the appropriate chapter.

Beaches

Chaplin Bay
Horseshoe Bay
Somerset Long Bay
Warwick Long Bay

Favorite Outdoor Activities

Offshore wreck diving
Snorkeling at Church Bay
Golfing at Port Royal Golf & Country Club
Running or riding through the dunes at South Shore Park

Favorite Sights

Pink-and-white cottages dotting the island
Pipers going at full tilt on the green at Ft. Hamilton
The children's room at Verdmont
The astonishing blues and greens of the sea
Statues by Desmond Fountain
Pastel Hamilton from the deck of a ferry
The narrow alleys in St. George's
The view from Gibbs Hill Lighthouse

Lodging

Cambridge Beaches (*Very Expensive*)
Horizons & Cottages (*Very Expensive*)
The Reefs (*Very Expensive*)
Newstead (*Expensive–Very Expensive*)
The Princess (*Expensive*)
Rosedon (*Expensive*)
Waterloo House (*Expensive*)
Little Pomander Guest House (*Moderate*)
Oxford House (*Moderate*)
Pretty Penny (*Moderate*)
Salt Kettle House (*Inexpensive*)

Restaurants

Waterlot Inn (*Very Expensive*)
Plantation (*Expensive*)

Black Horse Tavern (*Moderate*)
Colony Pub (*Moderate*)
Once Upon a Table (*Moderate*)
Dennis's Hideaway (*Inexpensive*)

Special Moments

The ferry ride from Hamilton to Somerset
Driving around the island in a London cab
Browsing through the Bermuda Book Store
Watching the Gombey Dancers
Swimming and sunning at Horseshoe Bay

Taste Treats

A Dark and Stormy (or two or three) at Casey's Bar
Diet destroyers at Fourways Pastry shops
Burgers at the Ice Queen at 3 AM
A rum swizzle at the Swizzle Inn
Shark hash at Dennis's Hideaway

Bermuda

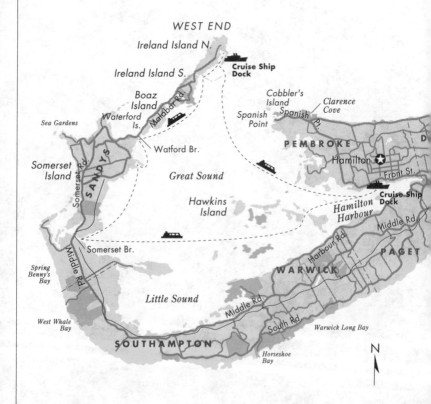

ATLANTIC OCEAN

WEST END
Ireland Island N.
Cruise Ship Dock
Ireland Island S.
Boaz Island
Waterford Is.
Cobbler's Island
Clarence Cove
Spanish Point
Spanish Pt.
Sea Gardens
Watford Br.
PEMBROKE
Somerset Island
Great Sound
Hamilton ★
Front St.
SANDYS
Hawkins Island
Cruise Ship Dock
Hamilton Harbour
Middle Rd.
Somerset Br.
Spring Benny's Bay
Little Sound
WARWICK
PAGET
West Whale Bay
Middle Rd.
Middle Rd.
South Rd.
Warwick Long Bay
SOUTHAMPTON
Horseshoe Bay

N

World Time Zones

Numbers below vertical bands relate each zone to Greenwich Mean Time (0 hrs.).
Local times frequently differ from these general indications,
as indicated by light-face numbers on map.

Algiers, **29**

Anchorage, **3**

Athens, **41**

Auckland, **1**

Baghdad, **46**

Bangkok, **50**

Beijing, **54**

Berlin, **34**

Bogotá, **19**

Budapest, **37**

Buenos Aires, **24**

Caracas, **22**

Chicago, **9**

Copenhagen, **33**

Dallas, **10**

Delhi, **48**

Denver, **8**

Djakarta, **53**

Dublin, **26**

Edmonton, **7**

Hong Kong, **56**

Honolulu, **2**

Istanbul, **40**

Jerusalem, **42**

Johannesburg, **44**

Lima, **20**

Lisbon, **28**

London (Greenwich), **27**

Los Angeles, **6**

Madrid, **38**

Manila, **57**

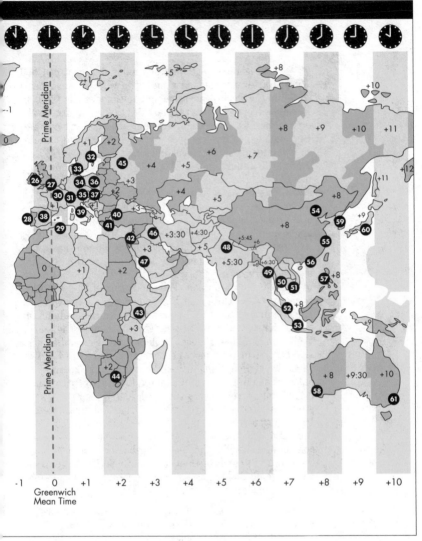

Introduction

Basking in the Atlantic 508 miles due east of Cape Hatteras, Bermuda is one of the wealthiest countries in the world—average per capita income is $20,000. Bermuda has no income tax, no sales tax, no slums, no unemployment, and no major crime problem. Don't come to Bermuda expecting a tropical paradise where laid-back locals wander around barefoot drinking piña coladas. On Bermuda's 20 square miles, you will find neither towering mountains, glorious rain forests, nor exotic volcanos. Instead, pastel cottages, quaint shops, and manicured gardens are indicative of a more staid, suburban way of life. As a British diplomat once said, "Bermuda is terribly middle-age"—and in many ways he was right. Most of the island is residential; the speed limit is 20 mph; golf and tennis are popular pastimes; the majority of visitors are over 40 years old; restaurants and shops are expensive; and casual attire in public is frowned upon. The population of 58,000 is 61% black and 39% white, but Bermudians speak the Queen's English in the Queen's own accent. White Bermudians, in particular, have strived to create a middle-class England of their own. And like almost all colonies, the Bermudian version is more insular, more conservative, and more English than the original. Pubs, fish-and-chips, and cricket are just outward manifestations of a fierce loyalty to Britain and everything it represents (or used to represent). A self-governing British colony, with a Parliament that dates to 1620, Bermuda loves pomp and circumstance, British tradition, and Bermudian history. Great ceremony attends the convening of Parliament; marching bands parade through the capital in honor of the Queen's official birthday; regimental bands and bagpipers reenact centuries-old ceremonies; and tea is served each afternoon.

Bermuda wears its history like a comfortable old coat—land is too valuable to permit the island's legacy to be cordoned off for mere display. A visitor need only wander through the 17th-century buildings of St. George's, now home to shops and private residences, to realize that Bermudian history remains part of the fabric of life, with each successive generation adding its own thread of achievement and color. Indeed, the island's isolation and diminutive size have forged a continuity of place and tradition almost totally missing in the United States. Walk into Trimingham's or A. S. Cooper & Son department stores, and you are likely to be helped by a descendant of the original founders. The same names from history keep cropping up—Tucker, Carter, Trott—and a single lane in St. George's can conjure up centuries of memories and events. Even today, the brief love affair in 1804 between Irish poet Thomas Moore and the married Hester Tucker—the "Nea" of his odes—is gossiped about with a zeal usually reserved for the transgressions of a neighbor. Bermuda's attachment to its history is more than a product of its size, however. Through its past, Bermuda invokes its own sense of identity and reinforces its relationship with Britain. Otherwise, cast off in the Atlantic more than 3,445 miles from London (yet only 508 miles from the United States), Bermuda would probably have succumbed to American cultural influences long ago.

Since the very beginning, the fate of this small colony in the Atlantic has been linked to that of the United States. The crew of the *Sea Venture*, whose wreck on Bermuda during a hurricane in 1609 began the settlement of the island, was actually on its way to Jamestown in Virginia. Indeed, the passenger list of the *Sea Venture* reads like a veritable *Who's Who* of early American history. Aboard were Sir Thomas Gates, Deputy Governor of Jamestown; Christopher Newport, who had led the first expedition to Jamestown; and John Rolfe, whose second wife was Princess Pocahontas. In succeeding centuries, Bermuda has been a remarkable barometer of the evolving relationship between the United States and Britain. In 1775, Bermuda was secretly forced to give gunpowder to George Washington in return for the lifting of a trade blockade that threatened the island with starvation. In the War of 1812, Bermuda was the staging post for the British fleet's attack on Washington, DC. And with Britain facing a national crisis in 1940, the United States was given land on Bermuda to build a Naval Air Station in exchange for ships and supplies. As recently as 1990, Prime Minister Thatcher and President Bush held talks on the island.

The fact that Bermuda—just two hours by air from New York—has maintained its English character through the years is obviously part of its appeal for the more than half-million Americans (89% of all tourists) who flock here each year. More importantly, however, Bermuda means sun, sea, and sand. This bastion of Britain boasts a mild climate year-round, pink beaches, turquoise waters, coral reefs, 17th-century villages, and splendid golf courses (Bermuda has more golf courses per square mile than anywhere else in the world).

Bermuda did not always seem so attractive. After all, more than 300 wrecks lie submerged on those same reefs where divers now frolic. William Strachey, Secretary-elect for Virginia and a passenger on the *Sea Venture* in 1609, wrote that Bermuda was "a place so terrible to all that ever touched on them—such tempests, thunders and other fearful objects are seen and heard about those islands that they are called The Devills Islands, feared and avoided by all sea travellers above any place in the world." For the crew of the *Sea Venture*, however, the 181 small islands that comprise Bermuda meant salvation. Contrary to rumor, the islands proved to be unusually fertile and hospitable, supporting the crew during the construction of two new ships, in which they departed for Jamestown on May 10th, 1610.

Shakespeare drew on the accounts of the survivors in *The Tempest*, written in 1611. The wreck of the *Sea Venture* on harsh yet beneficent Bermuda—"these infortunate (yet fortunate) islands," as one survivor described them—contained all the elements of Shakespeare-an tragicomedy: That out of loss something greater is often born. Just as Prospero loses the duchy of Milan only to regain it and secure the kingdom of Naples for his daughter, Admiral Sir George Somers lost a ship but gained an island. Today, Bermuda's motto is "Quo Fata Ferunt" (Whither the Fates Carry Us), an expression of sublime confidence in the same providence that carried the *Sea Venture* safely to shore.

That confidence has largely been justified over the years, but concerns have recently been raised about congestion, overfishing, reef damage, and a declining quality of life. Nearly 600,000 visitors a year are the golden eggs that many Bermudians feel are now killing the goose. In the face of such an influx of tourists, the behavior of some service employees, particularly bus drivers and young store clerks, has become sullen and rude. Traffic jams leading into Hamilton, the island's capital, are no longer a rarity, despite the fact that families can only have one car and car rentals are prohibited. In 1990, the government restricted the number of cruise-ship visits to four per week, citing the large numbers of passengers who add to the congestion but contribute little to the island's coffers. Instead, the Bermuda Department of Tourism hopes to attract a wealthier clientele (Bermuda's tourists are already among the most affluent anywhere), preferably during the less-frequented winter season, when golf and tennis are the island's major attractions.

When all is said and done, however, Bermuda's problems stem from a surfeit of advantages rather than a dearth, and almost every island nation would gladly inherit them. The "still-vexed Bermoothes" is how Shakespeare described this Atlantic pearl, but the author of *The Tempest* may have changed his tune if he had had a chance to swim at Horseshoe Bay, or hit a mashie-niblick to the 15th green at Port Royal. Who knows, instead of referring to a storm-wracked island, *The Tempest* might have been Shakespeare's reaction to a missed putt on the 18th.

1 Essential Information

Before You Go

Government Information Offices

Tourist Information The **Bermuda Department of Tourism** has offices in the following locations:

In the United States 310 Madison Avenue, Suite 201, New York, NY 10017, tel. 212/818–9800 or 800/223–6106, fax 212/983–5289; 245 Peachtree Center Ave., Suite 803, Atlanta, GA 30303, tel. 404/524–1541, fax 404/586–9933; 44 School Street, Suite 1010, Boston, MA 02108, tel. 617/742–0405, fax 617/723–7786; Randolph-Wacker Building, Suite 1070, 150 North Wacker Drive, Chicago, IL 60606, tel. 312/782–5486, fax 312/704–6996; Tetley/Moyer & Associates, 3075 Wilshire Boulevard, Suite 601, Los Angeles, CA 90010–1293, tel. 213/388–1151 or 800/421–0000, in CA 800/252–0211, fax 213/487–5467.

In Canada 1200 Bay Street, Suite 1004, Toronto, Ont. M5R 2A5, tel. 416/923–9600 or 800/387–1304, fax 416/923–4840.

In the United Kingdom **Bermuda Tourism,** BCB Ltd., 1 Battersea Church Road, London SW11 3LY, tel. 071/734–8813, fax 071/352–6501.

U.S. Government Travel Briefings The U.S. Department of State's **Citizens Emergency Center** issues Consular Information Sheets, which cover crime, security, and health risks as well as embassy locations, entry requirements, currency regulations, and other routine matters. For the latest information, stop in at any U.S. passport office, consulate, or embassy; call the interactive hotline (tel. 202/647–5225); or, with your PC's modem, tap into the Bureau of Consular Affairs' computer bulletin board (tel. 202/647–9225).

Tours and Packages

Should you buy your travel arrangements to Bermuda packaged or do it yourself? There are advantages either way. Buying packaged arrangements saves you money, particularly if you can find a program that includes exactly the features you want. You also get a pretty good idea of what your trip will cost from the outset. Usually you have two options: fully escorted tours and independent packages. However, because the island is small (just 16 miles long) and easy to explore on foot, by bicycle or moped, or via taxi, there are no escorted packages to Bermuda. If you do want an all-inclusive package, you should look into a cruise. Independent packages allow plenty of flexibility. They generally include airline travel and hotels, with certain options available, such as sightseeing and excursions.

While you can book directly through tour operators, you will pay no more to go through a travel agent, who will be able to tell you about tours and packages from a number of operators. Whatever program you ultimately choose, be sure to find out exactly what is included: taxes, tips, transfers, meals, baggage handling, ground transportation, entertainment, excursions, sports or recreation (and rental equipment if necessary). Ask about the level of hotel used, its location, the size of its rooms, the kind of beds, and its amenities, such as pool, room service, or programs for children, if they're important to you. Find out the operator's cancellation penalties. Nearly everyone charges them, and the only way to avoid them is to buy trip-cancellation insurance (*see* Trip Insurance, *below*). Also ask about the single supplement, a surcharge assessed to solo travelers. Some operators do not make you pay it if you agree to be matched up with a roommate of the same sex, even if one is not found by departure time. Remember that a program that has features you won't use may not be the most cost-wise choice for you.

Independent Packages Independent packages, which travel agents call FITs (for foreign independent travel), are offered by airlines, tour operators who may also do escorted programs, and any number of other companies from large, established firms to small, new entrepreneurs.

Contact **American Airlines Fly AAway Vacations** (tel. 800/321–2121), **Cavalcade Tours** (450 Harmon Meadows Blvd., Secaucus, NJ 07096, tel. 201/346–9061 or 800/356–2405), **Delta Dream Vacations** (tel. 800/872–7786), **Friendly Holidays** (1983 Marcus Ave., Lake Success, NY 11042, tel. 516/358–1200 or 800/221–9748), **Globetrotters** (139 Main St., Cambridge, MA 02142, tel. 617/621–9911 or 800/999–9696), **Gogo Tours** (book through your travel agent), **Haley/TNT Tours** (2 Charlesgate W, Boston, MA 02215, tel. 617/262–0123 or 800/232–5565), **Travel Impressions** (465 Smith St., Farmingdale, NY 11735, tel. 516/845–8000 or 800/284–0044), and **United Airlines' Vacation Planning Center** (tel. 800/328–6877).

Their programs come in a wide range of prices based on levels of luxury and options—in addition to hotel and airfare, sightseeing, transfers, admission to local attractions, and other extras. Note that when pricing different packages, it sometimes pays to purchase the same arrangements separately, as when a rock-bottom promotional airfare is being offered, for example. Again, base your choice on what's available at your budget for the destinations you want to visit.

When to Go

Bermuda has a remarkably mild climate that seldom sees extremes of either heat or cold. During the winter (December–March), temperatures range from around 55°F at night to 70°F in the early afternoon. High, blustery winds can make the temperature feel cooler, however, as can

Bermuda's high humidity. The hottest part of the year is between May and mid-October, when temperatures range from 75°F to 85°F; 90°F is not uncommon in July and August. The summer months are somewhat drier, but rainfall is spread fairly evenly throughout the year. Bermuda depends solely on rain for its supply of fresh water, so residents usually welcome the brief storms. In August and September, hurricanes moving northward from the Caribbean sometimes batter the island.

During summer, the island teems with activities. Hotel barbecues and evening dances complement daytime sightseeing excursions, and the public beaches are always open. The pace during the off-season slows considerably. A few of the hotels and restaurants close, some of the sightseeing boats are dry-docked, and only the taxis and the St. George's minibus operate tours of the island. The majority of hotels remain open, however, slashing their rates by as much as 40%—similar rates apply during shoulder seasons (March–April and October–November). The weather at this time of year is perfect for golf and tennis, and visitors can still rent boats, tour the island, and take advantage of the special events and walking tours offered (*see* Festivals and Seasonal Events, *below*).

Climate What follows are average daily maximum and minimum temperatures for Bermuda.

Jan.	68F	20C	**May**	76F	24C	**Sept.**	85F	29C
	58	14		65	18		72	22
Feb.	68F	20C	**June**	81F	27C	**Oct.**	79F	26C
	58	14		70	21		70	21
Mar.	68F	20C	**July**	85F	29C	**Nov.**	74F	23C
	58	14		74	23		63	17
Apr.	72F	22C	**Aug.**	86F	30C	**Dec.**	70F	21C
	59	15		74	23		61	16

Information Sources For current weather conditions for cities in the United States and abroad, plus the local time and helpful travel tips, call the **Weather Channel Connection** (tel. 900/932–8437; 95¢ per minute) from a touch-tone phone.

Festivals and Seasonal Events

Precise dates and information about the events listed below are available from the Bermuda Department of Tourism (*see* Tourist Information, *above*).

January **Jan. 1: New Year's Day** is a public holiday.
ADT International Marathon & 10K Race, in which top international runners participate, is open to all. Contact Race Committee (Box DV 397, Devonshire DV BX, tel. 809/238–2333, fax 809/297–8045).

January–February **Bermuda Festival** attracts internationally known artists for concerts, dances, and theatrical performances (Bermuda

Festival Ltd., Box HM 297, Hamilton HM AX, Bermuda, tel. 809/295–1291; *see* Chapter 10).

February **Golden Rendezvous Month** includes special events designed for older travelers.

Bermuda International Open Chess Tournament, open to visitors and residents, takes place at one of Bermuda's major hotels. Contact Bermuda Chess Association (Box HM 1705, Hamilton HM GX, tel. 809/293–8077).

Annual Regional Bridge Tournament is held at a major hotel (contact Bermuda Bridge Club, 7 Pomander Rd., Paget PG 05, tel. 809/236–0551).

Lobster Pot Tournament is an annual Pro-Am Invitational played at one of the island's golf courses; **Bermuda Valentine's Mixed Foursomes,** open to all golfers, is played at the St. George's Golf Club and the Port Royal Golf Course. Contact Tournament Chairman (Bermuda Golf Company, Box GE 304, St. George's GE BX, tel. 809/297–8067).

Bermuda Rendezvous Bowling Tournament, open to all bowlers, is sanctioned by ABC and WIBC. Cash prizes are awarded. Contact Warwick Lanes (Box WK 128, Warwick WK BX, tel. 809/236–5290).

Bermuda Golf Festival, a two-week event at six courses, includes tournaments for all. Contact the Bermuda Golf Festival (NYT Event/Sports Marketing Inc., 5520 Park Ave., Box 395, Trumbull, CT 06611–0395, tel. 203/373–7154 or 800/282–7656).

March **Bermuda All Breed Championship Dog Shows & Obedience Trials** draw dog lovers from far and wide to the Botanical Gardens in Paget. The same event also takes place in November.

Street Festival on Front Street in Hamilton includes marching bands, Gombey Dancers, and a variety of activities.

Bermuda Super Senior Invitational Tennis Championship is held at the Coral Beach & Tennis Club in Paget (Coral Beach Tennis Shop, tel. 809/236–6495).

Bermuda Horse & Pony Association Spring Show features jumping, driving, and Western and flat classes at the Botanical Gardens in Paget or the National Equestrian Centre in Devonshire.

Bermuda Amateur Golf Championship for Men is played at the Mid Ocean Club in Tucker's Town (The Secretary, Bermuda Golf Association, Box HM 433, Hamilton HM BX, tel. 809/238–1367).

Bermuda Diadora Youth Soccer Cup attracts teams from United Kingdom, the United States, Canada, and several Caribbean nations.

March–April **Palm Sunday Walk** is an annual stroll organized by the Bermuda National Trust.

Good Friday is a public holiday and traditionally a kite-flying day.

Easter Rugby Classic features international competitions at the National Sports Club in Devonshire (National Sports Club, Middle Rd., Devonshire, tel. 809/236–6994).

Bermuda Easter Lily Pro-Am Golf Tournament for Ladies takes place at St. George's Golf Club. Contact the Tournament Chairman (Bermuda Golf Company, Box GE 304, St. George's GE BX, tel. 809/297–8067).

Bermuda College Weeks, an annual spring break fling for American college students includes beach parties, dances, free lunches, boat cruises, calypso, rock bands, limbo shows, and a steel-band concert. Admission to all events is free with a complimentary "College Week Courtesy Card," issued to all college students with student ID. Dates vary to coincide with U.S. college vacation periods.

Harvard's Hasty Pudding Club has presented its satirical theatricals in Bermuda for some 30 years; it's the club's only performance outside the U.S. (City Hall Theatre, Hamilton, tel. 809/292–2313).

April **Agricultural Exhibition,** similar to a county or state fair, takes place at the Botanical Gardens in Paget.

The Peppercorn Ceremony celebrates, amid great pomp and circumstance, the payment of one peppercorn in rent to the government by the Lodge of St. George No. 200 of the Grand Lodge of Scotland for their headquarters in the Old State House in St. George's.

April–May **Open Houses and Gardens Tours,** sponsored by the Bermuda Garden Club, give visitors the chance to walk through many of Bermuda's historic homes; most are closed to the public during the rest of the year.

International Race Week pits sailors from around the world against Bermudians in a series of races on the Great Sound. Sunfish and sailboard races are held in Shelly Bay.

April–November **Beat Retreat Ceremony** is performed twice monthly by the Bermuda Regiment Band, the Bermuda Isles Pipe Band with Dancers, and members of the Bermuda Pipe Band. The historic ceremony is performed alternately on Front Street in Hamilton, King's Square in St. George's, and Dockyard in the West End. No performances are given in August.

May **Bermuda Heritage Month** features a host of cultural, commemorative, and sporting activities. The highlight is Bermuda Day, a public holiday that includes a parade at Bernard Park, a half-marathon (13 miles) for Bermuda residents only, and a Bermuda dinghy race in St. George's Harbour.

June **Sailing.** A host of watery events take place in June, some of them alternating between odd- and even-numbered years. Races that attract powerhouse yachtsmen during even-numbered years include the spectacular Newport to Bermuda Ocean Yacht Race, and the Bermuda Ocean Race (contact the Royal Bermuda Yacht Club, tel. 809/293–9553). Events in alternate years include the Bermuda 1-2

Single-Handed Race, from Newport to Bermuda and back (contact St. George's Dinghy & Sports Club (tel. 809/297–1612), and the Marion (MA)–Bermuda Cruising Yacht Race (contact the Royal Hamilton Amateur Dinghy Club (tel. 809/236–5432).

Queen Elizabeth II's Birthday is celebrated in mid-June with marching bands parading down Front Street in Hamilton.

July **Marine Science Day** at the Bermuda Biological Station for Research (11 Biological La., Ferry Reach, St. George's, tel. 809/297–1880) gives visitors an opportunity to learn about marine research from the perspective of a mid-ocean island. **Independence Day Celebrations.** On July 4, the United States Naval Air Station on St. David's Island hosts festivities that include fireworks displays. (Contact USNAS Public Affairs Office, tel. 809/293–5815).

July or August **Cup Match Cricket Festival** is a public holiday, with matches between East and West End cricket clubs. Held at the Somerset Cricket Club (Broome St., Sandys, tel. 809/234–0327) or the St. George's Cricket Club (Wellington Slip Rd., St. George's, tel. 809/297–0374), the match is one of the most festive occasions of the year, attracting thousands of fans who gather to picnic, chat, and dance.

August **Non-Mariners Race.** Landlubbers in homemade contraptions compete in this hilarious spectacle on Mangrove Bay.

September **Labour Day** is a public holiday featuring a wide range of activities, including a march from Union Square in Hamilton to Bernard Park.

October **Columbus Day Regatta Weekend,** sponsored by the Royal Bermuda Yacht Club, features keel boats competing in the Great Sound.

October–November **Omega Gold Cup International Match Race Tournament** is an exciting series of one-on-one yacht races in Hamilton Harbour. **The Convening of Parliament** is preceded by the arrival of His Excellency The Governor, in plumed hat and full regalia, at the Cabinet Building on Front Street in Hamilton.

November **Early Nov.: Guy Fawkes Night** (from a plot to blow up the Houses of Parliament in Great Britain) is celebrated with music, the burning of the Guy Fawkes effigy, food, and a half-hour fireworks display. Festivities take place in the Keepyard of the Bermuda Maritime Museum in the Royal Naval Dockyard. **World Rugby Classic** pits former international rugby players against the best players from Bermuda in a match at the National Sports Club (Middle Rd., Devonshire). **Remembrance Day** is a public holiday in memory of Bermuda's and its allies' fallen soldiers. A parade, with Bermudian, British, and U.S. military units, the Bermuda Police, and veterans' organizations, begins at Front Street in Hamilton.

December   **Hamilton Jaycees Santa Claus Parade** brings Father Christmas to Front Street, along with bands, floats, majorettes, and other seasonal festivities. St. Nick also appears at the West End Junior Chamber Santa Claus Parade and the St. George's Junior Chamber Silver Bells Santa Comes to Town Parade.

Bermuda Goodwill Tournament for Men is played on four courses.

Bermuda Goodwill Professional Championship (Golf) for junior and senior divisions, is played at one of the island's golf courses.

Dec. 24: Christmas Eve is celebrated with midnight candlelight services in churches of all denominations.

Dec. 25: Christmas is a public holiday.

Dec. 26: Boxing Day is a public holiday when Bermudians visit their friends and family. A variety of sports activities are also held, and the Bermuda Gombey Dancers can turn up anytime, anywhere.

What to Pack

Clothing   Bermudians are more formal than most Americans when it comes to dress. Although attire tends to be casual during the day—Bermuda shorts are acceptable, even for businessmen—cutoffs, short shorts, and halter tops are inappropriate. Swimsuits should not be worn outside pool areas or off the beach; you'll need a cover-up in the public areas of your hotel. Joggers may wear standard jogging shorts but should avoid appearing on public streets without a shirt. Bare feet and hair curlers in public are also frowned upon. In the evening, almost all restaurants and hotel dining rooms require that men wear a jacket and tie and that women dress comparably. Recently, some hotels have been setting aside one or two nights a week for "smart casual" attire, when jacket-and-tie restrictions are loosened. For women, tailored slacks with a dressy blouse or sweater are fine, although most Bermudian women wear dresses or skirts and blouses. Bermudian men often wear Bermuda shorts (and proper knee socks) with a jacket and tie.

During the cooler months, you should bring lightweight woolens or cottons that you can wear in layers, depending on the vagaries of the weather; a few sweaters and a lightweight jacket are always a good idea, too. Regardless of the season, you should pack a swimsuit, a cover-up, sunscreen and sunglasses, as well as an umbrella and raincoat. Comfortable walking shoes and a bag for carrying maps and cameras are a must. If you plan to play tennis, be aware that many courts require proper whites and that tennis balls in Bermuda are extremely expensive—bring your own balls if possible.

Miscellaneous Pack light, because porters and luggage trolleys can be hard to find. Bring an extra pair of eyeglasses or contact lenses. If you have a health problem that may require you to purchase a prescription drug, pack enough to last the duration of the trip, or have your doctor write a prescription using the drug's generic name, since brand names vary from country to country. And don't forget to pack a list of the addresses of offices that supply refunds for lost or stolen traveler's checks.

Luggage Free baggage allowances on an airline depend on the air-
Regulations line, the route, and the class of your ticket. In general, on domestic flights you are entitled to check two bags—neither exceeding 62 inches, or 158 centimeters (length + width + height), or weighing more than 70 pounds (32 kilograms). A third piece may be brought aboard as a carryon; its total dimensions are generally limited to less than 45 inches (114 centimeters), so it will fit easily under the seat in front of you or in the overhead compartment. There are variations, so ask in advance. The single rule, a Federal Aviation Administration safety regulation that pertains to carry-on baggage on U.S. airlines, requires that carryons be properly stowed and allows the airline to limit allowances and tailor them to different aircraft and operational conditions. Charges for excess, oversize, or overweight pieces vary, so inquire before you pack.

Safeguarding Your Before leaving home, itemize your bags' contents and their
Luggage worth; this list will help you estimate the extent of your loss if your bags go astray. To minimize that risk, tag them inside and out with your name, address, and phone number. (If you use your home address, cover it so that potential thieves can't see it.) At check-in, make sure that the tag attached by baggage handlers bears the correct three-letter code for your destination. If your bags do not arrive with you, or if you detect damage, do not leave the airport until you've filed a written report with the airline.

Taking Money Abroad

In Bermuda, most shops and some restaurants accept credit cards, but most hotels on the island insist on other forms of payment, such as cash or traveler's checks. Some take personal checks by prior arrangement (a letter from your bank is sometimes requested).

Traveler's Checks Although you will want plenty of cash when visiting small cities or rural areas, traveler's checks are usually preferable. The most widely recognized are **American Express, Barclay's, Thomas Cook,** and those issued by major commercial banks such as **Citibank** and **Bank of America.** American Express also issues *Traveler's Cheques for Two*, which can be counter-signed and used by you or your traveling companion. Some checks are free; usually the issuing company or the bank at which you make your purchase charges

1% of the checks' face value as a fee. Be sure to buy a few checks in small denominations to cash toward the end of your trip, when you don't want to be left with more foreign currency than you can spend. Always record the numbers of checks as you spend them, and keep this list separate from the checks.

Getting Money from Home

Cash Machines Automated-teller machines (ATMs) are proliferating; many are tied to international networks such as **Cirrus** and **Plus.** You can use your bank card at ATMs away from home to withdraw money from an account and get cash advances on a credit-card account (providing your card has been programmed with a personal identification number, or PIN). Check in advance on limits on withdrawals and cash advances within specified periods. Ask whether your bankcard or credit-card PIN number will need to be reprogrammed for use in the area you'll be visiting—a possibility if the number has more than four digits. Remember that on cash advances you are charged interest from the day you get the money from ATMs as well as from tellers. And note that, although transaction fees for ATM withdrawals abroad will probably be higher than fees for withdrawals at home, Cirrus and Plus exchange rates tend to be good.

Be sure to plan ahead: Obtain ATM locations and the names of affiliated cash-machine networks before departure. For specific Cirrus locations, call 800/424–7787; for Plus locations, consult the Plus directory at your local bank.

American Express Cardholder Services The company's **Express Cash** system lets you withdraw cash and/or traveler's checks from a worldwide network of 57,000 American Express dispensers and participating bank ATMs. You must *enroll first* (call 800/227–4669 for a form and allow two weeks for processing). Withdrawals are charged not to your card but to a designated bank account. You can withdraw up to $1,000 per seven-day period on the basic card, more if your card is gold or platinum. There is a 2% fee (minimum $2.50, maximum $10) for each cash transaction, and a 1% fee for traveler's checks (except for the platinum card), which are available only from American Express dispensers.

At AmEx offices, cardholders can also cash personal checks for up to $1,000 in any seven-day period; of this $200 can be in cash, more if available, with the balance paid in traveler's checks, for which all but platinum cardholders pay a 1% fee. Higher limits apply to the gold and platinum cards.

Wiring Money You don't have to be a cardholder to send or receive an **American Express MoneyGram** for up to $10,000. To send one, go to an American Express MoneyGram agent, pay up to $1,000 with a credit card and anything over that in cash, and phone a transaction reference number to your intended recipient, who needs only present identification and the reference number to the nearest MoneyGram agent to pick up the cash. There are MoneyGram agents in more than 60 countries (call 800/543–4080 for locations). Fees range from 5% to 10%, depending on the amount and how you pay. You can't use American Express, which is really a convenience card—only Discover, MasterCard, and Visa credit cards.

You can also use **Western Union**. To wire money, take either cash or a check to the nearest office. (Or you can call and use a credit card.) Fees are roughly 5%–10%. Money sent from the United States or Canada will be available for pick up at agent locations in Bermuda within minutes. There are approximately 20,000 agents worldwide (call 800/325–6000 for locations).

What It Will Cost

Since Bermuda imports everything from cars to cardigans, prices are high; the most common complaint of visitors to Bermuda is the high cost of a vacation on the island. At an upscale restaurant, for example, be prepared to pay as much for a meal as you would in New York, London, or Paris. The average cost of dinner in a chic restaurant is $50–$70 per person—$100 with drinks and wine. Upscale restaurants, however, are not your only option. The island abounds with coffee shops, where locals and thrift-minded tourists can eat hamburgers and french fries for about $4. The same meal at a restaurant costs about $12.

Hotels add a 6% government tax to the bill and most add a 10% service charge or a per diem dollar equivalent in lieu of tips. Other extra charges include a 5% "energy surcharge" at small guest houses and a 15% service charge at most restaurants.

Sample Costs A cup of coffee costs between 80¢ and $2.50; a mixed drink $3–$5; a bottle of beer $1.75–$5; and a can of Coke about $1. A 15-minute cab ride will set you back about $20 including the tip, and a pack of Kodak 110 cartridge film, with 12 exposures, costs about $3.95. A 36-exposure roll of 35mm film will set you back about $8.50. Smokers pay $3.75 to $4 for a pack of cigarettes.

Currency

The Bermudian dollar is on a par with the U.S. dollar, and the two currencies are used interchangeably. American money can be used anywhere, but change is often given in Bermudian currency. Try to avoid accumulating large amounts of this money, which is difficult to exchange for U.S. dollars in Bermuda and expensive to exchange in the United States.

Passports and Visas

U.S. Citizens You do not need a passport or visa to enter Bermuda if you plan to stay less than six months, although you must have onward or return tickets and proof of identity (original birth certificate with raised seal or voter's registration card, along with photo ID; a driver's license is unacceptable). If you have a passport, bring it to ensure quick passage through immigration and customs. You can pick up new and renewal application forms at any of the 13 U.S. Passport Agency offices and at some post offices and courthouses. Although passports are usually mailed within two weeks of your application's receipt, it's best to allow three weeks for delivery in low season, five weeks or more from April through summer. Call the Department of State Office of Passport Services' information line (1425 K St. NW, Washington, DC 20522, tel. 202/647–0518) for fees, documentation requirements, and other details.

Canadian Citizens Canadians do not need a passport to enter Bermuda, though a passport is helpful to ensure quick passage through customs and immigration. A birth certificate or a certificate of citizenship is required, along with a photo ID. Passport applications are available at 23 regional passport offices as well as post offices and travel agencies. Whether applying for a first or subsequent passport, you must apply in person. Children under 16 may be included on a parent's passport but must have their own passport to travel alone. Passports are valid for five years and are usually mailed within two weeks of an application's receipt. For fees, documentation requirements, and other information in English or French, call the passport office (tel. 514/283–2152).

U.K. Citizens Citizens of the United Kingdom need a valid passport to enter Bermuda for stays of up to 30 days. Applications for new and renewal passports are available from main post offices as well as at the six passport offices, located in Belfast, Glasgow, Liverpool, London, Newport, and Peterborough. You may apply in person at all passport offices, or by mail to all except the London office. Children under 16 may travel on a parent's passport when accompanying them. All passports are valid for 10 years. Allow a month for processing.

A British Visitor's Passport is valid for holidays and some business trips of up to three months to Bermuda. It can include both partners of a married couple. Valid for one year, it will be issued on the same day that you apply. You must apply in person at a main post office.

British travelers stopping over in the United States before returning to the U.K. will need a U.S. re-entry visa; contact the **U.S. Embassy Visa and Immigration Department** (5 Upper Grosvenor St., London W1A 2JB, tel. 071/499–3443 for a recorded message or 071/499–7010).

Customs and Duties

On Arrival In addition to personal effects, visitors entering Bermuda may bring in duty-free up to 50 cigars, 200 cigarettes, and one pound of tobacco; one quart of wine and one quart of liquor; 20 pounds of meat; and other goods to the value of $30. You may not import plants, fruits, vegetables, and animals without an import permit from the **Department of Agriculture, Fisheries and Parks** (Box HM 834, Hamilton HM CX, tel. 809/236–4201; fax 809/236–7582). Remember, though, that merchandise and sales materials for use by conventions must be cleared with the hotel concerned before you arrive.

Returning Home Provided you've been out of the country for at least 48 hours
U.S. Customs and haven't already used the exemption, or any part of it, in the past 30 days, you may bring home $400 worth of foreign goods duty-free. So can each member of your family, regardless of age; and your exemptions may be pooled, so one of you can bring in more if another brings in less. A flat 10% duty applies to the next $1,000 worth of goods; above $1,400, the rate varies with the merchandise. (If the 48-hour or 30-day limits apply, your duty-free allowance drops to $25, which may not be pooled.) Please note that these are the *general* rules, applicable to most countries, including Bermuda.

Travelers 21 or older may bring back 1 liter of alcohol duty-free, provided the beverage laws of the state through which they reenter the United States allow it. In addition, 100 non-Cuban cigars and 200 cigarettes are allowed, regardless of your age. Antiques and works of art more than 100 years old are duty-free.

Gifts valued at less than $50 may be mailed duty-free to stateside friends and relatives, with a limit of one package per day per addressee (do not send alcohol or tobacco products, nor perfume valued at more than $5). These gifts do not count as part of your exemption, unless you bring them home with you. Mark the package "Unsolicited Gift" and include the nature of the gift and its retail value.

For a copy of "Know Before You Go," a free brochure detailing what you may and may not bring back to the United States, rates of duty, and other pointers, contact the **U.S. Customs Service** (Box 7407, Washington, DC 20044, tel. 202/927–6724).

Canadian Once per calendar year, when you've been out of Canada for
Customs at least seven days, you may bring in $300 worth of goods duty-free. If you've been away less than seven days but more than 48 hours, the duty-free exemption drops to $100 but can be claimed any number of times (as can a $20 duty-free exemption for absences of 24 hours or more). You cannot combine the yearly and 48-hour exemptions, use the $300 exemption only partially (to save the balance for a lat-

er trip), or pool exemptions with family members. Goods claimed under the $300 exemption may follow you by mail; those claimed under the lesser exemptions must accompany you on your return.

Alcohol and tobacco products may be included in the yearly and 48-hour exemptions but not in the 24-hour exemption. If you meet the age requirements of the province through which you reenter Canada, you may bring in, duty-free, 1.14 liters (40 imperial ounces) of wine or liquor *or* two dozen 12-ounce cans or bottles of beer or ale. If you are 16 or older, you may bring in, duty-free, 200 cigarettes, 50 cigars or cigarillos, and 400 tobacco sticks or 400 grams of manufactured tobacco. Alcohol and tobacco must accompany you on your return.

Gifts may be mailed to friends in Canada duty-free. These do not count as part of your exemption. Each gift may be worth up to of $60—label the package "Unsolicited Gift—Value under $60." There are no limits on the number of gifts that may be sent per day or per addressee, but you can't mail alcohol or tobacco.

For more information, including details of duties on items that exceed your duty-free limit, ask the Revenue Canada Customs and Excise Department (Connaught Bldg., MacKenzie Ave., Ottawa, Ont., K1A OL5, tel. 613/957–0275) for a copy of the free brochure "I Declare/Je Déclare."

U.K. Customs From countries outside the EC such as Bermuda, you may import duty-free 200 cigarettes, 100 cigarillos, 50 cigars or 250 grams of tobacco; 1 liter of spirits or 2 liters of fortified or sparkling wine; 2 liters of still table wine; 60 millileters of perfume; 250 millileters of toilet water; plus £36 worth of other goods, including gifts and souvenirs.

For further information or a copy of "A Guide for Travellers," which details standard customs procedures as well as what you may bring into the United Kingdom from abroad, contact HM Customs and Excise (New King's Beam House, 22 Upper Ground, London SE1 9PJ, tel. 071/620–1313).

Traveling with Cameras, Camcorders, and Laptops

About Film and Cameras The cost of film in Bermuda is exorbitant, so bring all the film you need with you from home. If your camera is new or if you haven't used it for a while, shoot and develop a few rolls of film before leaving home. Pack some lens tissue and an extra battery for your built-in light meter, and invest in an inexpensive skylight filter, to both protect your lens and provide some definition in hazy shots. Store film in a cool, dry place—never in the car's glove compartment or on the shelf under the rear window.

Films above ISO 400 are more sensitive to damage from airport security X-rays than others; very high speed films, ISO 1,000 and above, are exceedingly vulnerable. To protect your film, don't put it in checked luggage; carry it with you in a plastic bag and ask for a hand inspection. Such requests are honored at American airports, up to the inspector abroad. Don't depend on a lead-lined bag to protect film in checked luggage—the airline may very well turn up the dosage of radiation to see what you've got in there. Airport metal detectors do not harm film, although you'll set off the alarm if you walk through one with a roll in your pocket. Call the Kodak Information Center (tel. 800/242–2424) for details.

About Camcorders Before your trip, put new or long-unused camcorders through their paces, and practice panning and zooming. Invest in a skylight filter to protect the lens, and check the lithium battery that lights up the LCD (liquid crystal display) modes. As for the rechargeable nickel-cadmium batteries that are the camera's power source, take along an extra pair, so while you're using your camcorder you'll have one battery ready and another recharging.

About Videotape Unlike still-camera film, videotape is not damaged by X-rays. However, it may well be harmed by the magnetic field of a walk-through metal detector. Airport security personnel may want you to turn the camcorder on to prove that that's what it is, so make sure the battery is charged when you get to the airport.

About Laptops Security X-rays do not harm hard-disk or floppy-disk storage. Most airlines allow you to use your laptop aloft but request that you turn it off during takeoff and landing so as not to interfere with navigation equipment. Make sure the battery is charged when you arrive at the airport, because you may be asked to turn on the computer at security checkpoints to prove that it is what it appears to be. If you're a heavy computer user, consider traveling with a backup battery. For international travel, register your laptop with U.S. Customs as you leave the country, providing it's manufactured abroad (U.S.-origin items cannot be registered at U.S. Customs); when you do so, you'll get a certificate, good for as long as you own the item, containing your name and address, a description of the laptop, and its serial number, that will quash any questions that may arise on your return. If your laptop is U.S.-made, call the consulate of the country you'll be visiting to find out whether it should be registered with customs in that country upon arrival. Some travelers do this as a matter of course and ask customs officers to sign a document that specifies the total configuration of the system, computer and peripherals, and its value. In addition, before leaving home, find out about repair facilities at your destination.

Staying Healthy

Sunburn and sunstroke are problems for summer visitors to Bermuda. On a hot, sunny day, wear a long-sleeve shirt, a hat, and long pants or a beach wrap. These are essential for a day on a boat, but are also advisable for midday at the beach. Carry sunscreen for your nose, ears, and other sensitive areas. Drink liquids and, above all, limit the amount of time you spend in the sun until you become acclimatized.

The Portuguese man-of-war is an occasional visitor to Bermuda's waters. These nasty sea critters are not numerous hereabouts but show up usually in summer or whenever the water is particularly warm. They are recognizable by a purple, balloonlike float sack of perhaps 8 inches in diameter, below which dangle 20- to 60-inch tentacles armed with powerful stinging cells. Contact with these stinging cells causes immediate, severe pain. A serious sting can put a person in shock, and medical attention should be sought immediately. Even if you don't think the sting is severe, you should still go to a doctor. In the meantime—or if getting to a doctor will take a while—liberally treat the affected area with ammonia (the traditional and preferred island remedy is, in fact, urine). Although usually encountered in the water, Portuguese men-of-war may also wash up on shore, and if you spot one on the sand, steer clear—the sting isn't diminished just because they're out of the water.

Bermuda poses no unusual health risks to visitors, and no shots are required for entry. If you have a health condition that may require purchasing prescription drugs in Bermuda, have your physician write a prescription for the drug using its generic name, as brand names can vary. Although the air quality in Bermuda is quite good, and there's virtually no smog, there is pollen, and those with hay fever or any allergic condition should take the same precautions they would when traveling anywhere.

Insurance

For U.S. Residents Most tour operators, travel agents, and insurance agents sell specialized health-and-accident, flight, trip-cancellation, and luggage insurance as well as comprehensive policies with some or all of these features. But before you make any purchase, review your existing health and homeowner policies to find out whether they cover expenses incurred while travelling.

Health-and-Accident Insurance Supplemental health-and-accident insurance for travelers is usually a part of comprehensive policies. Specific policy provisions vary, but they tend to address three general areas, beginning with reimbursement for medical expenses caused by illness or an accident during a trip. Such policies may reimburse anywhere from $1,000 to $150,000 worth of medical expenses; dental benefits may also be included. A second common feature is the personal-accident, or death-and-dismemberment, provision, which pays a lump sum to your beneficiaries if your die or to you if you lose one or both limbs or your eyesight. This is similar to the flight insurance described below, although it is not necessarily limited to accidents involving airplanes or even other "common carriers" (buses, trains, and ships) and can be in effect 24 hours a day. The lump sum awarded can range from $15,000 to $500,000. A third area generally addressed by these policies is medical assistance (referrals, evacuation, or repatriation and other services). Some policies reimburse travelers for the cost of such services; others may automatically enroll you as a member of a particular medical-assistance company.

Flight Insurance This insurance, often bought as a last-minute impulse at the airport, pays a lump sum to a beneficiary when a plane crashes and the insured dies (and sometimes to a surviving passenger who loses eyesight or a limb); thus it supplements the airlines' own coverage as described in the limits-of-liability paragraphs on your ticket (up to $75,000 on international flights, $20,000 on domestic ones—and that is generally subject to litigation). Charging an airline ticket to a major credit card often automatically signs you up for flight insurance; in this case, the coverage may also embrace travel by bus, train, and ship.

Baggage Insurance In the event of loss, damage, or theft on international flights, airlines limit their liability to $20 per kilogram for checked baggage (roughly about $640 per 70-pound bag) and $400 per passenger for unchecked baggage. On domestic flights, the ceiling is $1,250 per passenger. Excess-valuation insurance can be bought directly from the airline at check-in but leaves your bags vulnerable on the ground.

Trip Insurance There are two sides to this coin. **Trip-cancellation-and-interruption insurance** protects you in the event you are unable to undertake or finish your trip. **Default** or **bankruptcy insurance** protects you against a supplier's failure to deliver. Consider the former if your airline ticket, cruise, or package tour does not allow changes or cancellations. The amount of coverage to buy should equal the cost of your trip should you, a traveling companion, or a family member get sick, forcing you to stay home, plus the nondiscounted one-way airline ticket you would need to buy if you had to return home early. Read the fine print carefully; pay attention to sections defining "family member" and "preexisting medical conditions." A characteristic quirk of default policies is that they often do not cover default by travel agencies or default by a tour operator, airline, or cruise line if you bought your tour and the coverage directly from the firm in question. To reduce your need for default insurance, give preference to tours packaged by members of the United States Tour Operators Association (USTOA), which maintains a fund to reimburse clients in the event of member defaults. Even better, pay for travel arrangements with a major credit card, so that you can refuse to pay the bill if services have not been rendered—and let the card company fight your battles.

Comprehensive Policies Companies supplying comprehensive policies with some or all of the above features include **Access America, Inc.,** underwritten by BCS Insurance Company (Box 11188, Richmond, VA 23230, tel. 800/284–8300); **Carefree Travel Insurance,** underwritten by The Hartford (Box 310, 120 Mineola Blvd., Mineola, NY 11501, tel. 516/294–0220 or 800/323–3149); **Tele-Trip** (Mutual of Omaha Plaza, Box 31762, Omaha, NE 68131, tel. 800/228–9792), a subsidiary of Mutual of Omaha; **The Travelers Companies** (1 Tower Sq., Hartford, CT 06183, tel. 203/277–0111 or 800/243–3174); **Travel Guard International,** underwritten by Transamerica Occidental Life Companies (1145 Clark St., Stevens Point, WI 54481, tel. 715/345–0505 or 800/782–5151); and **Wallach and Company, Inc.** (107 W. Federal St., Box 480, Middleburg, VA 22117, tel. 703/687–3166 or 800/237–6615). These companies may also offer the above types of insurance separately.

U.K. Residents Most tour operators, travel agents, and insurance agents sell specialized policies covering accident, medical expenses, personal liability, trip cancellation, and loss or theft of personal property. Some policies include coverage for delayed departure and legal expenses, winter-sports, accidents, or motoring abroad. You can also purchase an annual travel-insurance policy valid for every trip you make during the year in which it's purchased (usually only trips of less than 90 days). Before you leave, make sure you will be covered if you have a preexisting medical condition or are pregnant; your insurers may not pay for routine or continuing treatment, or may require a note from your doctor certifying your fitness to travel.

For advice by phone or a free booklet, "Holiday Insurance," that sets out what to expect from a holiday-insurance policy and gives price guidelines, contact the **Association of British Insurers** (51 Gresham St., London EC2V 7HQ, tel. 071/600–3333; 30 Gordon St., Glasgow G1 3PU, tel. 041/226–3905; Scottish Provincial Bldg., Donegall Sq. W, Belfast BT1 6JE, tel. 0232/249176; call for other locations).

Student and Youth Travel

Like other travelers, students arriving in Bermuda must have confirmation of hotel reservations, a return plane ticket, a photo ID, and proof of citizenship, such as a passport, birth certificate, or a signed voter's registration card. There are no youth hostels, YMCAs, or YWCAs on the island. During Bermuda College Weeks (*see* Festivals and Seasonal Events, *above*), however, special student rates are offered at hotels and guest houses, restaurants, pubs, and nightclubs.

Travel Agencies The foremost U.S. student travel agency is **Council Travel**, a subsidiary of the nonprofit Council on International Educational Exchange. It specializes in low-cost travel arrangements, is the exclusive U.S. agent for several discount cards, and, with its sister CIEE subsidiary, **Council Charter**, is a source of airfare bargains. The Council Charter brochure and CIEE's twice-yearly *Student Travels* magazine, which details its programs, are available at the Council Travel office at CIEE headquarters (205 E. 42nd Street, New York, NY 10017, tel. 212/661–1450) and at 37 branches in college towns nationwide (free in person, $1 by mail). The **Educational Travel Center** (ETC, 438 N. Francis St., Madison, WI 53703, tel. 608/256–5551) also offers low-cost rail passes, domestic and international airline tickets (mostly for flights departing from Chicago), and other budgetwise travel arrangements. Other travel agencies catering to students include **Travel Management International** (TMI, 18 Prescott St., Suite 4, Cambridge, MA 02138, tel. 617/661–8187) and **Travel Cuts** (187 College St., Toronto, Ont. M5T 1P7, tel. 416/979–2406).

Discount Cards For discounts on transportation and on museum and attractions admissions, buy the **International Student Identity Card** (ISIC) if you're a bona fide student, or the **International Youth Card** (IYC) if you're under 26. In the United States the ISIC and IYC cards cost $15 each and include basic travel accident and sickness coverage. Apply to **CIEE** (*see* address *above*, tel. 212/661–1414; the application is in *Student Travels*). In Canada the cards are available for $15 each from **Travel Cuts** (*see above*). In the United Kingdom they cost £5 and £4 respectively at student unions and student travel companies, including Council Travel's London office (28A Poland St., London W1V 3DB, tel. 071/437–7767).

Traveling with Children

Publications *Family Travel Times,* published 10 times a year by Travel
Newsletter With Your Children (TWYCH, 45 W. 18th St., 7th Floor Tower, New York, NY 10011, tel. 212/206–0688; annual subscription $55), covers destinations, types of vacations, and modes of travel.

Books *Great Vacations with Your Kids,* by Dorothy Jordon and Marjorie Cohen ($13; Penguin USA, 120 Woodbine St., Bergenfield, NJ 07621, tel. 800/253–6476) and *Traveling with Children—And Enjoying It,* by Arlene K. Butler ($11.95 plus $3 shipping per book; Globe Pequot Press, Box 833, Old Saybrook, CT 06475, tel. 800/243–0495; in CT, 800/ 962–0973) help plan your trip with children, from toddlers to teens. From the same publisher is *Recommended Family Resorts in the United States, Canada, and the Caribbean,* by Jane Wilford with Janet Tice ($12.95).

Tour Operators **GrandTravel** (6900 Wisconsin Ave., Suite 706, Chevy Chase, MD 20815, tel. 301/986–0790 or 800/247–7651) offers international and domestic tours for grandparents traveling with their grandchildren. The catalogue, as charmingly written and illustrated as a children's book, positively invites armchair traveling with lap-sitters aboard. **Rascals in Paradise** (650 5th St., Suite 505, San Francisco, CA 94107, tel. 415/978–9800 or 800/872–7225) specializes in programs for families.

Getting There On domestic flights, children under 2 not occupying a seat
Air Fares travel free, and older children currently travel on the "lowest applicable" adult fare. Caribbean routes are considered neither international nor domestic and have other rules; check with the airline for details.

Baggage The adult baggage allowance applies for children paying half or more of the adult fare. Check with the airline for particulars.

Safety Seats The FAA recommends the use of safety seats aloft and details approved models in the free leaflet "**Child/Infant Safety Seats Recommended for Use in Aircraft**" (available from the Federal Aviation Administration, APA–200, 800 Independence Ave. SW, Washington, DC 20591, tel. 202/267–3479). Airline policy varies. U.S. carriers must allow FAA-approved models, but because these seats are strapped into a regular passenger seat, they may require that parents buy a ticket even for an infant under 2 who would otherwise ride free.

Facilities Aloft Airlines do provide other facilities and services for children, such as children's meals and freestanding bassinets (to those sitting in seats on the bulkhead, where there's enough legroom to accommodate them). Make your request when reserving. The annual February/March issue of *Family Travel Times* gives details of the children's services of dozens of airlines ($10; *see above*). "Kids and Teens in Flight" (free from the U.S. Department of Transportation, tel. 202/366–2220) offers tips for children flying alone.

Baby-Sitting An increasing number of hotels are offering day-care and
Services programs for children (*see* Chapter 9), while others actively discourage parents from bringing them. Baby-sitting can usually be arranged through the hotel or guest house upon advance request. The charge is $4–$8 per hour, and sitters expect paid transportation. Check with your hotel for specifics.

Hints for Travelers with Disabilities

The Bermuda Chapter of the **Society for the Advancement of Travel for the Handicapped** (SATH, 347 Fifth Ave., Suite 610, New York, NY 10016, tel. 212/447–7284) publishes the *Access Guide to Bermuda for the Handicapped Traveler*, available for $2. You can also send away for the guide by writing to Kitsan & Company, Ltd. (Box HM 449, Hamilton

HM BX, Bermuda, tel. 809/295–2525, fax 809/295–5682) or through any Bermuda Department of Tourism office.

Public buses in Bermuda are not equipped for wheelchairs; however, the **Bermuda Physically Handicapped Association** has a bus with a hydraulic lift, operated by volunteer drivers. Arrangements for its use must be made in advance by contacting Mr. Willard Fox, Bermuda Physically Handicapped Association, Box HM 08, Hamilton HM AX, tel. 809/292–5025.

Permits must be obtained in advance for importing guide dogs to the island. Application forms are available at all Bermuda Department of Tourism offices. Once approved, the Department of Agriculture, Fisheries, and Parks will send an import permit to the traveler; the permit must accompany the dog at the time of arrival.

Organizations Several organizations provide travel information for people with disabilities, usually for a membership fee, and some publish newsletters and bulletins. Among them are the Information Center for Individuals with Disabilities (Fort Point Pl., 27–43 Wormwood St., Boston, MA 02210, tel. 617/727–5540 or 800/462–5015 in MA between 11 and 4, or leave message; TDD/TTY tel. 617/345–9743); Mobility International USA (Box 3551, Eugene, OR 97403, voice and TDD tel. 503/343–1284), the U.S. branch of an international organization based in Britain (see below) and present in 30 countries; MossRehab Hospital Travel Information Service (1200 W. Tabor Rd., Philadelphia, PA 19141, tel. 215/456–9603, TDD tel. 215/456–9602); the Society for the Advancement of Travel for the Handicapped (SATH, 347 5th Ave., Suite 610, New York, NY 10016, tel. 212/447–7284, fax 212/725–8253); the Travel Industry and Disabled Exchange (TIDE, 5435 Donna Ave., Tarzana, CA 91356, tel. 818/368–5648); and Travelin' Talk (Box 3534, Clarksville, TN 37043, tel. 615/552–6670).

In the Main information sources include the **Royal Association for**
United Kingdom **Disability and Rehabilitation** (RADAR, 25 Mortimer St., London W1N 8AB, tel. 071/637–5400), which publishes travel information for the disabled in Britain, and **Mobility International** (228 Borough High St., London SE1 1JX, tel. 071/403–5688), the headquarters of an international membership organization that serves as a clearinghouse of travel information for people with disabilities.

Travel Agencies **Directions Unlimited** (720 N. Bedford Rd., Bedford Hills,
and Tour NY 10507, tel. 914/241–1700), a travel agency, has exper-
Operators tise in tours and cruises for the disabled. **Evergreen Travel Service** (4114 198th St. SW, Suite 13, Lynnwood, WA 98036, tel. 206/776–1184 or 800/435–2288) operates Wings on Wheels Tours for those in wheelchairs, White Cane Tours for the blind, and tours for the deaf and makes group and independent arrangements for travelers with any disability. **Flying Wheels Travel** (143 W. Bridge St., Box 382,

Owatonna, MN 55060, tel. 800/535–6790; in MN, 800/722–9351), a tour operator and travel agency, arranges international tours, cruises, and independent travel itineraries for people with mobility disabilities. **Nautilus**, at the same address as TIDE (*see above*), packages tours for the disabled internationally.

Publications In addition to the fact sheets, newsletters, and books mentioned above are several free publications available from the Consumer Information Center (Pueblo, CO 81009): "New Horizons for the Air Traveler with a Disability," a U.S. Department of Transportation booklet describing changes resulting from the 1986 Air Carrier Access Act and those still to come from the 1990 Americans with Disabilities Act (include Department 608Y in the address), and the Airport Operators Council's *Access Travel: Airports* (Dept. 5804), which describes facilities and services for the disabled at more than 500 airports worldwide.

Twin Peaks Press (Box 129, Vancouver, WA 98666, tel. 206/694–2462 or 800/637–2256) publishes the *Directory of Travel Agencies for the Disabled* ($19.95), listing more than 370 agencies worldwide; *Travel for the Disabled* ($19.95), listing some 500 access guides and accessible places worldwide; the *Directory of Accessible Van Rentals* ($9.95) for campers and RV travelers worldwide; and *Wheelchair Vagabond* ($14.95), a collection of personal travel tips. Add $2 per book for shipping.

Lodging The most readily accessible hotels are the large resort hotels, such as the Belmont Hotel, Elbow Beach, Marriott's Castle Harbour, the Sonesta Beach, theHamilton Princess and the Southampton Princess.

Those in search of a vacation apartment suitable for the disabled should contact Mrs. Ianthia Wade ("Summer Haven," Box HS 30, Harrington Sound HS BX, tel. 809/293–2099). Mrs. Wade can also assist with sightseeing arrangements.

Hints for Older Travelers

February in Bermuda is Golden Rendezvous Month, with special events for older travelers. Contact the Bermuda Department of Tourism for details.

Organizations The **American Association of Retired Persons** (AARP, 601 E St. NW, Washington, DC 20049, tel. 202/434–2277) provides independent travelers the Purchase Privilege Program, which offers discounts on hotels, car rentals, and sightseeing, and arranges group tours, cruises, and apartment living through AARP Travel Experience from American Express (400 Pinnacle Way, Suite 450, Norcross, GA 30071, tel. 800/927–0111); these can be booked through travel agents, except for the cruises, which must be booked directly (tel. 800/745–4567). AARP membership is open to those 50 and over; annual dues are $8 per person or couple.

Two other membership organizations offer discounts on lodgings, car rentals, and other travel products, along with such nontravel perks as magazines and newsletters. The **National Council of Senior Citizens** (1331 F St. NW, Washington, DC 20004, tel. 202/347–8800) is a nonprofit advocacy group with some 5,000 local clubs across the United States; membership costs $12 per person or couple annually. **Mature Outlook** (6001 N. Clark St., Chicago, IL 60660, tel. 800/336–6330), a Sears Roebuck & Co. subsidiary with 800,000 members, charges $9.95 for an annual membership.

Note: When using any senior-citizen identification card for reduced hotel rates, mention it when booking, not when checking out. At restaurants, show your card before you're seated; discounts may be limited to certain menus, days, or hours. If you are renting a car, ask about promotional rates that might improve on your senior-citizen discount.

Educational Travel **Elderhostel** (75 Federal St., 3rd floor, Boston, MA 02110, tel. 617/426–7788) is a nonprofit organization that has offered inexpensive study programs for people 60 and older since 1975. Programs are held at more than 1,800 educational institutions in the United States, Canada, and 45 other countries; courses cover everything from marine science to Greek myths and cowboy poetry. Participants generally attend lectures in the morning and spend the afternoon sightseeing or on field trips; they live in dorms on the host campuses. Fees for two- to three-week international trips—including room, board, and transportation from the United States—range from $1,800 to $4,500.

Interhostel (University of New Hampshire, 6 Garrison Ave., Durham, NH 03824, tel. 800/733–9753), a slightly younger enterprise than Elderhostel, caters to a slightly younger clientele—that is, 50 and over—and runs programs in some 25 countries. But the idea is similar: Lectures and field trips mix with sightseeing, and participants stay in dormitories at cooperating educational institutions or in modest hotels. Programs are usually two weeks in length and cost $1,500–$2,100, not including airfare from the United States.

Tour Operators **Saga International Holidays** (222 Berkeley St., Boston, MA 02116, tel. 800/343–0273), which specializes in group travel for people over 60, offers a selection of variously priced tours and cruises covering five continents. If you want to take your grandchildren, look into **GrandTravel** (*see* Traveling with Children, *above*).

Further Reading

The well-respected historian William Zuill wrote extensively about the island. Published in 1945 and now somewhat outdated, Zuill's 426-page *Bermuda Journey: A Leisurely Guide Book* provides a fascinating look at the island and its people, with historical notes and anecdotes.

The book is out of print; check with the Bermuda Book Store in Hamilton (tel. 809/295–3698) to see if used copies are available. Zuill's other books include *The Wreck of the Sea Venture*, which details the 1609 wreck of Admiral Sir George Somers's flagship and the subsequent settlement of the island, and *Tom Moore's Bermuda Poems*, a collection of odes by the Irish poet who spent four months on Bermuda in 1804.

W.S. Zuill, the son of the historian, wrote *The Story of Bermuda and Her People*, a recently updated volume tracing the history of the island from the *Sea Venture* wreck to the present. *Bermuda*, by John J. Jackson, contains an abundance of facts on Bermudian business, economics, law, ecology, and history, as well as tourist information. John Weatherill's *Faces of Bermuda* is a marvelous collection of photographs, and those curious about the legendary Bermuda Triangle can read about its history in *The Bermuda Triangle Mystery Solved*, by Larry David Kusche.

For a charming account of growing up in Bermuda during the 1930s and 1940s, refer to *The Back Yard*, by William Zuill's daughter Ann Zuill Williams. *"Rattle and Shake": The Story of the Bermuda Railway*, by David F. Raine, tells the tale of the fabled narrow-gauge railroad in photos and prose. The island is showcased in several coffee-table books of color photographs, such as *Bermuda*, by Scott Stallard, *Bermuda Abstracts*, by Graeme Outerbridge, and *Bermudian Images*, by Bruce Stuart. Among the books for younger audiences are Willoughby Patton's *Sea Venture*, about the adventures of a young boy on the crew of the ill-fated ship, E. M. Rice's *A Child's History of Bermuda*, which tells the story of the island in terms children can readily understand, Dana Cooper's illustrated book, *My Bermuda ABC's*, and Bermudian artist Elizabeth Mulderig's *Tiny the Tree Frog*.

Arriving and Departing

From North America by Plane

Flights are either nonstop, direct, or connecting. A **nonstop** flight requires no change of plane and makes no stops. A **direct** flight stops at least once and can involve a change of plane, although the flight number remains the same; if the first leg is late, the second waits. This is not the case with a **connecting** flight, which involves a different plane and a different flight number.

Airport and Airlines The **Civil Air Terminal** (Kindley Field Rd., St. George's, tel. 809/293–1640, fax 809/293–2417) is on the east end of the island, approximately 9 miles from Hamilton and 17 miles from Somerset.

Airlines with direct flights to Bermuda include **American Airlines** (tel. 809/293–1420 or 800/433–7300) from New York, Boston, and Raleigh/Durham; **Continental** (tel. 809/293–3092 or 800/525–0280) from Newark; **Delta Airlines** (tel. 809/293–2000 or 800/221–1212) from Boston and Atlanta; **Northwest** (tel. 800/225–2525) from Boston and Detroit; **USAir** (tel. 809/293–3072 or 800/428–4322) from Baltimore, Boston, Philadelphia, and New York; and **Air Canada** (tel. 809/293–2121 or 800/776–3000) from Toronto, with connections from all over Canada.

Flying Time From New York, Boston, Raleigh/Durham, and Baltimore, the flight to Bermuda takes about two hours; from Atlanta, 1½ hours; and from Toronto, 2¾ hours.

Cutting Flight Costs The Sunday travel section of most newspapers is a good source of deals. When booking, particularly through an unfamiliar company, call the Better Business Bureau to find out whether any complaints have been registered against the company, pay with a credit card if you can, and consider trip-cancellation and default insurance (*see* Insurance, *above*).

Promotional Airfares All the less expensive fares, called promotional or discount fares, are round-trip and involve restrictions. The exact nature of the restrictions depends on the airline, the route, and the season and on whether travel is domestic or international, but you must usually buy the ticket—commonly called an APEX (advance purchase excursion) when it's for international travel—in advance (seven, 14, or 21 days are usual). You must also respect certain minimum- and maximum-stay requirements (for instance, over a Saturday night or at least seven and no more than 30, 45, or 90 days), and you must be willing to pay penalties for changes. Airlines generally allow some changes for a fee. But the cheaper the fare, the more likely the ticket is to be nonrefundable; it would take a death in the family for the airline to give you any of your money back if you had to cancel. The lowest fares are also subject to availability; because only a certain percentage of the plane's total seats will be sold at that price, they may go quickly.

Consolidators Consolidators or bulk-fare operators—also known as bucket shops—buy blocks of seats on scheduled flights that airlines anticipate they won't be able to sell. They pay wholesale prices, add a markup, and resell the seats to travel agents or directly to the public at prices that still undercut the airline's promotional or discount fares. You pay more than on a charter but ordinarily less than for an APEX ticket, and, even when there is not much of a price difference, the ticket usually comes without the advance-purchase restriction. Moreover, although tickets are marked nonrefundable so you can't turn them in to the airline for a full-fare refund, some consolidators sometimes give you your money back. Carefully read the fine print detailing penalties for changes and cancellations. If you doubt the reliability of a company, call the airline once you've made your booking and confirm that you do, indeed, have a reservation on the flight.

The biggest U.S. consolidator, C.L. Thomson Express, sells only to travel agents. Well-established consolidators selling to the public include **UniTravel** (Box 12485, St. Louis, MO 63132, tel. 314/569–0900 or 800/325–2222); **Council Charter** (205 E. 42nd St., New York, NY 10017, tel. 212/661–0311 or 800/800–8222), a division of the Council on International Educational Exchange and a longtime charter operator now functioning more as a consolidator; and **Travac** (989 6th Ave., New York, NY 10018, tel. 212/563–3303 or 800/872–8800), also a former charterer.

Charter Flights Charters usually have the lowest fares and the most restrictions. Departures are limited and seldom on time, and you can lose all or most of your money if you cancel. (Generally, the closer to departure you cancel, the more you lose, although sometimes you will be charged only a small fee if you supply a substitute passenger.) The charterer, on the other hand, may legally cancel the flight for any reason up to 10 days before departure; within 10 days of departure, the flight may be canceled only if it becomes physically impossible to operate it. The charterer may also revise the itinerary or increase the price after you have bought the ticket, but if the new arrangement constitutes a "major change," you have the right to a refund. Before buying a charter ticket, read the fine print for the company's refund policy and details on major changes. Money for charter flights is usually paid into a bank escrow account, the name of which should be on the contract. If you don't pay by credit card, make your check payable to the escrow account (unless you're dealing with a travel agent, in which case, his or her check should be payable to the escrow account). The Department of Transportation's Consumer Affairs Office (I–25, Washington, DC 20590, tel. 202/366–2220) can answer questions on charters and send you its "Plane Talk: Public Charter Flights" information sheet.

Charter operators may offer flights alone or with ground arrangements that constitute a charter package. Well-established charter operators include **Council Charter** (205 E. 42nd St., New York, NY 10017, tel. 212/661–0311 or 800/800–8222), now largely a consolidator, despite its name, and **Travel Charter** (1120 E. Long Lake Rd., Troy, MI 48098, tel. 313/528–3500 or 800/521–5267), with Midwestern departures. **DER Tours** (Box 1606, Des Plains, IL 60017, tel. 800/782–2424), a charterer and consolidator, sells through travel agents.

Discount Travel Travel clubs offer their members unsold space on airplanes,
Clubs cruise ships, and package tours at nearly the last minute and at well below the original cost. Suppliers thus receive some revenue for their "leftovers," and members get a bargain. Membership generally includes a regular bulletin or

access to a toll-free telephone hot line giving details of available trips departing anywhere from three or four days to several months in the future. Packages tend to be more common than flights alone, so if airfares are your only interest, read the literature before joining. Reductions on hotels are also available. Clubs include **Discount Travel International** (114 Forrest Ave., Suite 203, Narberth, PA 19072, tel. 215/668–7184; $45 annually, single or family), **Moment's Notice** (425 Madison Ave., New York, NY 10017, tel. 212/486–0503; $45 annually, single or family), **Travelers Advantage** (CUC Travel Service, 49 Music Sq. W, Nashville, TN 37203, tel. 800/548–1116; $49 annually, single or family), and **Worldwide Discount Travel Club** (1674 Meridian Ave., Miami Beach, FL 33139, tel. 305/534–2082; $50 annually for family, $40 single).

Enjoying the Flight Unless you're flying from the West Coast or Britain, jet lag won't be a problem. Because the air aloft is dry, drink plenty of beverages while on board; remember that drinking alcohol contributes to jet lag, as do heavy meals. If you're lucky enough to be able to sleep on an aircraft, request a window seat to curl up against; restless passengers ask to be on the aisle. Bulkhead seats, in the front row of each cabin, have more legroom, but since there's no seat ahead, trays attach awkwardly to the arms of your seat, and you must stow all possessions overhead. Bulkhead seats are usually reserved for the disabled, the elderly, and people traveling with babies. PADI recommends that you not scuba dive and fly within a 24-hour period.

Smoking Smoking is banned on all domestic flights of less than six hours' duration; the ban also applies to domestic segments of international flights aboard U.S. and foreign carriers. On U.S. carriers flying to Bermuda, a seat in a no-smoking section must be provided for every passenger who requests one, and the section must be enlarged to accommodate such passengers if necessary as long as they have complied with the airline's deadline for check-in and seat assignment. If smoking bothers you, request a seat far from the smoking section.

Foreign airlines are exempt from these rules but do provide no-smoking sections, and some nations, including Canada as of July 1, 1993, have gone as far as to ban smoking on all domestic flights; other countries may ban smoking on flights of less than a specified duration. The International Civil Aviation Organization has set July 1, 1996, as the date to ban smoking aboard airlines worldwide, but the body has no power to enforce its decisions.

Between the Airport and Hotels *By Taxi* Taxis are readily available at the airport. The approximate fare not including tip to Hamilton is $15; to St. George's, $7; to south-shore hotels, $19; and to the West End, $26. A surcharge of 25¢ is added for each piece of luggage stored in the trunk or on the roof. Between 10 PM and 6 AM, and on Sundays and public holidays, fares are 25% higher. Depending on traffic, the driving time to Hamilton is about 20 minutes, and about 45 minutes to the West End.

By Bus **Bermuda Hosts Ltd.** (tel. 809/293–1334, fax 809/293–1335) offers roundtrip transportation to hotels and guest houses aboard air-conditioned six- and 18-seat vans. Reservations should be made in advance. One-way fares, based on zones: Zone 1, to Grotto Bay Beach Hotel, $5; zone 2, to the Flatts Village area, $7; zone 3, to Cobb's Hill Road, $9; zone 4, to Church Rd, $11; zone 5, westward to Dockyard, $13.

From the United Kingdom by Plane

Only **British Airways** (tel. 071/897–4000) flies direct to Bermuda, with six flights a week from Gatwick. Flying time is approximately seven hours. No charter flights are available, but travel packages offer reduced fares on the British Airways flights. Flying to New York, and then taking a connecting flight to Bermuda, takes longer and costs as much—even with the cheapest fares—as the scheduled British Airways flight direct to Bermuda.

From the United States by Cruise Ship

Bermuda has long been a favorite destination of cruise lines, and, except for a few cruises that continue down to the Caribbean, is usually a ship's only port of call. Most ships make seven-day loops from New York, with four days spent at sea and three days in port; other cruises leave from Baltimore, Philadelphia, Boston, and Charleston. The cruise season in Bermuda runs from March to October. For more information on cruises to Bermuda, *see* Chapter 3, Cruising in Bermuda.

Concerned about overcrowding, the Bermudian government recently limited visits by cruise ships to four per week, none on weekends. The restrictions will probably make it more difficult to find cabins on cruises to Bermuda, and prices are likely to rise. At the same time, however, passengers will be able to enjoy the island without being jostled by other tourists, and many of the island's attractions are relatively empty during the week.

Ships tie up at one of three harbors on Bermuda: Hamilton, St. George's, or the West End. The traditional port is Hamilton, the capital and the most commercial area on the island. If you like to shop, choose a cruise that anchors here. Passengers whose ship ties up at St. George's walk off the vessel into Bermuda's equivalent of Colonial Williamsburg, a charming town of 17th-century buildings, narrow lanes, and small boutiques. West End is the farthest cruise port from Bermuda's main attractions, but is home to the Royal Naval Dockyard, an erstwhile shipyard that's now a developing minivillage with a shopping mall, museums, and crafts stores. (For more information about Bermuda's ports and attractions, *see* Chapter 4, Exploring Bermuda.)

Staying in Bermuda

Important Addresses and Numbers

Tourist Information Visitors Service Bureaus, which provide tourist information and assistance with reservations and ticketing, can be found in Hamilton (Ferry Terminal Bldg., 8 Front St., tel. 809/295–1480 or 809/295–4201; open weekdays 9–4:45), and at the Civil Air Terminal-Airport. (2 Kindley Field Rd., tel. 809/293–0736; open daily 9–5).

Visitors Information Centres, which offer tourist information but no other services, are located at the Royal Naval Dockyard (The Cooperage, tel. 809/234–3824; open Mon.–Sat. 9:30–4:30 and Sun. noon–4), in St. George's (7 King's Sq., next to Town Hall, tel. 809/297–1642; open Mon.–Wed., Fri, and Sat. 10–3; closed Thurs. and Sun), and in Somerset (86 Somerset Rd., near St. James's Church, tel. 809/234–1388; open Apr.–Nov., weekdays 10–4).

You can also contact the Bermuda Department of Tourism (43 Church Street, Hamilton, tel. 809/292–0023, fax 809/292–7537).

Consulates American Consulate General, Crown Hill, 16 Middle Rd., Devonshire, tel. 809/295–1342. Open weekdays 9–noon and 1:30–4.

Neither the Canadian nor the British government has a consulate in Bermuda.

Emergencies Police, fire, or ambulance (tel. 911). Air/Sea Rescue (tel. 809/297–1010). The Government Emergency Broadcast Station is FM 100.1 MHz.

Hospitals The King Edward VII Memorial Hospital (7 Point Finger Rd., outside Hamilton near the Botanical Gardens, tel. 809/236–2345) is open 24 hours.

Doctors and Dentists Contact the hospital or the Government Health Clinic (67 Victoria St., Hamilton, tel. 809/236–0224) for referrals.

Late-Night Pharmacies Hamilton Pharmacy (Church and Parliament Sts., Hamilton, tel. 809/295–7004; open weekdays and Sat. 8 AM–9 PM), Phoenix Centre (3 Reid St., Hamilton, tel. 809/295–0698 or 809/295–3838; open Mon.–Sat. 8–6, Sun. and holidays noon–6:30), and Collector's Hill Apothecary (Collector's Hill, Smith's, tel. 809/236–8664; open Mon.–Sat.).

Travel Agencies The American Express agent is L. P. Gutteridge Ltd. (L. P. Gutteridge Bldg., Bermudiana Rd., Hamilton, tel. 809/295–4545, fax 809/295–8637). Thomas Cook is represented by Butterfield Travel Ltd. (75 Front St., Hamilton, tel. 809/292–1510, fax 809/292–1243).

Telephones

Local Calls Pay phones, identical to those found in the United States, are found on the streets of Hamilton, St. George's, and Somerset, as well as at ferry landings, some bus stops, and public beaches. Deposit 20¢ (U.S. or Bermudian) in the meter as soon as your party answers. Most hotels charge 20¢–$1 for local calls.

International Calls Direct dialing is possible from anywhere on the island. Most hotels impose a surcharge for long-distance calls, even those made collect. Many of the small guest houses and apartments have no central switchboard; if you have a phone in your room, it's a private line from which you can make only collect, credit-card, or local calls. Some of the small hotels have a telephone room or kiosk where you can make long-distance calls. Specially marked **AT&T USADirect** phones can be found at the airport, the cruise-ship dock in Hamilton, and at King's Square and Ordnance Island in St. George's. International calls can also be made from the **main post office** (Church and Parliament Sts., Hamilton, tel. 809/295–5151) and from the **Cable & Wireless Office** (20 Church St., opposite City Hall, Hamilton, tel. 809/297–7000), with public telephone, telex, cable, and fax facilities available Monday–Saturday 9–5.

To call the United States, Canada, and most Caribbean countries, dial 1 (or 0 if you need an operator's assistance), plus the area code and the number. For all other countries, dial 011 (or 01 for an operator), the country code, the area code, and the number. Using an operator for an overseas call is more expensive than dialing direct. For calls to the United States, rates are highest 10 AM–7 PM, and discounted from 7 PM to 11 PM; the lowest rates are from 11 PM to 7 AM. Calls to Alaska and Hawaii are not discounted. Calls to Canada are cheapest from 9 PM to 7 AM, and to the United Kingdom from 6 PM to 7 AM.

AT&T and **MCI** have direct calling programs in Bermuda. AT&T's **USADirect** service, which charges $1.27 for the first minute, 85¢ for each additional minute, allows you to call collect or charge calls to your AT&T calling card. To make your call, call 800/872–2881. For additional information call 412/553–7458, ext. 314 (collect from outside the U.S.) or 800/874–4000. MCI charges $1.26 for the first minute, 86¢ for each additional minute, and works the same as AT&T; dial 800/623–0484 to get an MCI operator. For information call 800/950–5555, or 800/623–0700 from Bermuda.

Operators and Information For directory assistance, dial 411. For information about international calls, dial 01.

Mail

Postal Rates Airmail letters and postcards to the United States and Canada require 60¢ postage per half ounce, and 75¢ per half ounce to the United Kingdom.

Receiving Mail If you have no address in Bermuda, you can have mail sent care of General Delivery (General Post Office, Hamilton HM GD, Bermuda).

Tipping

A service charge of 10% (or an equivalent per diem amount), which covers everything from baggage handling to maid service, is added to your hotel bill. Most restaurants tack on a 15% service charge; if not, a 15% tip is customary (more for exceptional service). Porters at the airport expect about a dollar, while taxi drivers usually receive 15% of the fare.

Opening and Closing Times

Banks Branches of the **Bank of Bermuda** are open Monday–Thursday 9:30–3, Friday 9:30–4:30. The airport branch is open Monday–Thursday 11–4, Friday 11–4:30. All other banks on the island operate Monday–Thursday 9:30–3, Friday 9:30–3 and 4:30–5:30.

Museums Hours vary greatly, but generally museums are open weekdays and Saturday from 9 or 9:30 until 4:30 or 5; some museums close on Wednesday or Saturday. Check with the museum or the Visitors Information Centre for exact hours.

Stores Most stores are open weekdays and Saturday from around 9 until 5 or 5:30. Some Hamilton stores keep evening and Sunday hours when cruise ships are in port.

Convention and Business Services

Its proximity to Eastern U.S. cities and its diverse range of attractions have made Bermuda a popular convention and conference center. An increasing number of hotels and resorts offer comprehensive meeting facilities and help with customs procedures for business and convention materials. The **Bermuda Chamber of Commerce** (tel. 809/295–4201, fax 809/292–5779) helps organizers plan a variety of activities for group participants and/or spouses, including lectures, shopping tours, fashion shows, and sightseeing excursions. In 1988, Bermuda and the United States signed a tax treaty, giving business meetings in Bermuda the same tax privileges as those held in the United States. For more information about convention facilities and services in Bermuda, *Bermuda: A Meeting and Incentive Travel Planner's Guide*, is available from the Bermuda Department of Tourism. Listed below are some of the business services available on the island.

Dry Cleaners Full-service hotels and cottage colonies have laundry and dry-cleaning services, but guest houses and housekeeping apartments do not. **Hamilton Valcleners Ltd.** (Bermudiana Rd., Hamilton, tel. 809/292–3063) and **Paget Dry Cleaners Ltd.** (Lovers La., Paget, tel. 809/236–5142) provide free pick-up and delivery, and express service on request.

Flowers and Gift Baskets FTD florists on the island include **The Flower Shop** (14 Reid St., Hamilton, tel. 809/295–2903, fax 809/295–9599); **House of Flowers** (Washington Mall, Hamilton, tel. 809/292–4750, fax 809/292–6927); and **Designer Flowers** (Windsor Pl., Queen St., Hamilton, tel. 809/295–4380; Market Place Plaza, Heron Bay, tel. 809/238–1490). House of Flowers also has fruit baskets and gift baskets.

Formal Wear Formal wear for men and women, can be rented at **Karl's Guys 'n Dolls** (Church St., Hamilton, tel. 809/292–5948).

Group Tours Group tours of the island are available through **Bermuda Hosts Ltd.** (Box CR 46, Hamilton Parish, CR BX,tel. 809/ 293–1334, fax 809/293–1335); **Bee–Line Transport Ltd.** (Box HM 2270, Hamilton HM JX, tel. 809/293–0303, fax 809/293–8015); **L. P. Gutteridge Hospitality Management** (Box HM 1024, Hamilton HM DX, tel. 809/295–4545, fax 809/295–4199); **ButterfieldTravel** (Box HM 656, Hamilton HM CX, tel. 809/292–1520, fax 809/292–1243); and **Penboss Destination Management–Meyer Tours** (Box HM 510, Hamilton HM CX, tel. 809/295–9733 or 800/468–3310, fax 809/ 292–4823).

The **Bermuda National Trust** (tel. 809/236–6483, fax 809/ 236–0617) offers a variety of events for groups, including private house and garden tours, a champagne reception at the Verdmont house, walking tours, and slide shows and lectures.

Group Transportation From March to November, **Bermuda Hosts Ltd.** (tel. 809/ 293–1334, fax 809/293–1335) and **Bee–Line Transport** (tel. 809/293–0303, fax 809/293–8015) provide group transport from the airport in minibuses and motorcoaches. From December through February, only taxis are available. Taxi companies offering group service include **Bermuda Taxi Operators Company Ltd.** (tel. 809/292–4175), **Trott Travel Ltd.** (tel. 809/295–0041), and **B.I.U. Taxi Co-op Transportation** (tel. 809/292–4476).

Messenger Services **International Bonded Couriers** (Mechanics Bldg., Hamilton, tel. 809/295–2467) offer radio-dispatched 90-minute pick-up and delivery of packages island-wide. Two-day international deliveries are available through **Federal Express** (Par-la-Ville Rd., Hamilton, tel. 809/295–3854, and Washington Mall, Hamilton), **DHL Worldwide Express** (Express Centre, 22 Washington Mall, tel. 809/295–3300), and

UPS (Atlantic House, Par-la-Ville Rd., Hamilton, tel. 809/292–6760).

Photocopying **The Copy Shop** (The Walkway, Reid St., Hamilton, tel. 809/292–5355; open Mon.–Sat. 8:30–5, Sat. 8:30–1).

Secretarial Secretarial services on the island include **Business Services**
Services **of Bermuda** (tel. 809/295–5175), **Cranleigh Limited** (tel. 809/292–3458), and **ExecuTemps** (tel. 809/295–8608, fax 809/292–7783).

Video and **Electronic Services** (tel. 809/295–3885) rents audiovisual
Film Services equipment and operators. **Panatel VDS Ltd.** (tel. 809/292–1600, fax 809/295–8982) is a full-service film and video production house. **Jenn-Star Productions** (tel. 809/238–0818, fax 809/238–0977) videotapes special functions, conventions, and seminars.

Computer and **Bermuda Business Machines Ltd.** (tel. 809/295–4672, fax
Fax Machine 809/292–6181) rents personal computers, photocopiers, mi-
Rentals crofilm, microfiche, and fax machines.

Getting Around Bermuda

Despite its small size, Bermuda does pose some transport problems. Rental cars are not allowed, so visitors must travel by bus, taxi, ferry, moped, bike, or on foot. More than 1,200 miles of narrow, winding roads and a strictly enforced 20-mph speed limit (15 mph in town) make moving around the island a time-consuming process. Traveling the length of this long, skinny island takes particularly long: The trip from St. George's to Hamilton takes an hour by bus, and the onward journey to the West End takes another hour, although an express bus from Hamilton to the West End takes only 30 minutes. Hiring a taxi can cut down the amount of time you spend on the road, but the cost may discourage you. Fortunately, Hamilton, St. George's, and Somerset are all manageable on foot. Anyone who plans to do a lot of traveling around the island should pick up a copy of the *Bermuda Islands Guide,* an atlas of every road, alley, lane, and landmark on the island. Available at the Bermuda Book Store (Queen and Front Sts., Hamilton, tel. 809/295–3698), it is well worth the $4.95 price tag.

By Bus Bermuda's modern pink-and-blue buses travel the island from east to west. Hamilton buses arrive and depart from the **Central Bus Terminal** (Washington and Church Sts., Hamilton, tel. 809/292–3854), a small kiosk that is open daily 7:30–5. Finding a bus stop outside Hamilton can be difficult; some are easily identifiable stone shelters, but others are marked only by striped poles by the road. These poles can be short or tall, green and white, or black and white; the net effect can be confusing. Remember to wait on the proper side of the road—driving in Bermuda is on the left. Exact change is necessary when boarding a bus; the fare depends on your destination. Bermuda is divided into 14

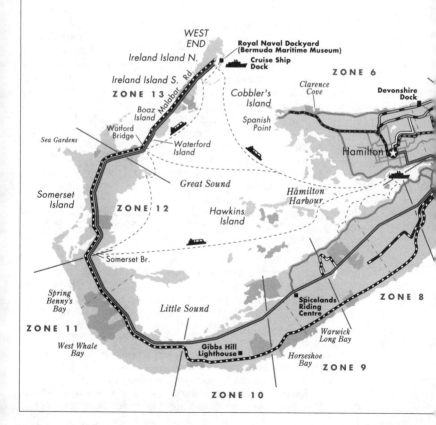

ATLANTIC OCEAN

WEST
END
Ireland Island N.

Royal Naval Dockyard
(Bermuda Maritime Museum)
Cruise Ship
Dock

ZONE 6

Clarence
Cove

Devonshire
Dock

Ireland Island S.
ZONE 13

Cobbler's
Island

Malabar Rd.

Boaz
Island

Spanish
Point

Watford
Bridge

Waterford
Island

Sea Gardens

Hamilton

Great Sound

ZONE 12

Somerset
Island

Hamilton
Harbour

Hawkins
Island

Somerset Br.

ZONE 8

Spring
Benny's
Bay

Little Sound

Spicelands
Riding
Centre

ZONE 11

Warwick
Long Bay

West Whale
Bay

Gibbs Hill
Lighthouse

Horseshoe
Bay ZONE 9

ZONE 10

ZONE 1

Tobacco Bay
Fort St. Catherine
St. Catherine Beach

Town of St. George
St. George's Island

Cruise Ship Dock

St. George's Harbour

St. David's Lighthouse

Bermuda Airport

St. David's Island

ZONE 2

Grotto Bay

Bermuda Perfumery

Blue Hole
Bermuda Pottery
Crystal Caves

ZONE 14

Castle Harbour

ZONE 3

Church Bay

Leamington Caves

Harrington Sound

Railway Museum
Aquarium, Museum, and Zoo

John Smith's Bay

N

ZONE 4

| 0 | | 2 miles |
| 0 | | 3 km |

ZONE 5

ZONE 7

BUS ROUTES		
	1	Hamilton–Castle Harbour/St. George's
	2	Hamilton–Ord Road
	3	Hamilton–Grotto Bay
	4	Hamilton–Spanish Point
	5	Hamilton–Pond Hill
	6	St. George's–St. David's
	7	Hamilton–Sonesta
		Hamilton–Somerset/Dockyard
	8	Hamilton–Somerset
		Hamilton–Dockyard
	8c	Hamilton–Cedar Hill
	9	Hamilton–Prospect
	10	Hamilton–St. George's
	11	Hamilton–St. George's
		Zone Division

KEY
⛴ Cruise Ship
⛴ Ferry

bus zones, each about 2 miles in length. Within the first three zones, adults pay $1.50 (coins, tickets, or tokens only; no dollar bills). For greater distances, the fare is $3. Children 3–12 pay 65¢ for all zones. If you plan to do much bus travel, it makes sense to buy a booklet of 15 14-zone tickets for $18 (or 15 three-zone tickets for $10). Ticket booklets and packets of discounted tokens are available at the Hamilton bus terminal and at post offices. Three- and seven-day passes ($17.50 and $27.50, respectively) are available at the bus terminal and the visitor's center in Hamilton. Buses run about every 15 minutes, except on Sunday when they usually come every hour. Bus schedules, which also contain ferry timetables, are available at the bus terminal in Hamilton and at many of the hotels. Bermudian bus drivers are sometimes rude, but they do answer questions about fares and destinations; upon request, they will also tell you when you've reached your stop.

In addition to the public buses to and from Hamilton, private minibuses serve the eastern and western ends of the island. In the West End, **Sandys Taxi Service** (tel. 809/234–2344) operates a minibus service hourly between Somerset Bridge and Dockyard. The fare depends upon the destination, although you won't have to pay more than $3 (half price for senior citizens). Minibuses, which you can flag down on the road or summon by phone, drop passengers wherever they want to go. The service operates daily 7:20–7.

St. George's Transportation (tel. 809/297–8199) has a similar minibus service around St. Geroge's and St. David's in the east. The minimum fare is $1.35 for adults, 85¢ for senior citizens, and 75¢ for children. Buses are available in King's Square in St. George's, or they can be flagged down from the roadside. The service operates March–November, daily 7 AM–10 PM, December–February, daily 7–7.

By Ferry Quick and enjoyable, ferries sail every day from the **Ferry Terminal** (tel. 809/295–4506) in Hamilton, with routes to Paget, Warwick, and across the Great Sound to Somerset in the West End. On weekdays, most ferries run until 11 PM, although the last ferry from Hamilton to Somerset leaves at 6 PM; on Sunday, ferry service is limited and ends around 7 PM. A one-way fare to Paget or Warwick is $1.50, $3 to Somerset; children 3–13 pay 50¢. Bicycles can be brought aboard free, but passengers must pay $3 extra to take a motor scooter to Somerset; scooters are not allowed on the smaller Paget and Warwick ferries. The friendly and helpful ferry operators will answer questions about routes and schedules, and they'll even help get your bike aboard. Schedules, posted at each landing, are available at the Ferry Terminal, Central Bus Terminal, and most hotels.

By Taxi Taxis are the fastest and easiest way around the island— and also the costliest. Taxis charge $4 for the first mile, and $1.40 for each subsequent mile. A half-hour trip costs about

$20, including tip. Between 10 PM and 6 AM, or on Sunday and public holidays, a 25% surcharge is added to the fare. There is a 25¢ charge for each piece of luggage stored in the trunk or on the roof. For radio-dispatched taxis, contact **Radio Cabs Bermuda** (tel. 809/295–4141) and **Bermuda Taxi Operators** (tel. 809/292–5600).

By Moped and Scooter Mopeds, or motor-assisted vehicles as Bermudians call them, offer visitors the most flexibility for moving about the island. Bermudians routinely use the words "moped" and "scooter" interchangeably, even though a scooter is actually a type of moped. The difference between the two is horsepower and passenger capacity. Mopeds have 3-horsepower engines and scooters 6-horsepower. Unless you request otherwise, what generally happens is that those riding with a passenger get a 6-h.p. scooter, and solo riders are given a 3-h.p. moped. Riding a moped, however, is not without hazards—especially for first-time riders. The roads are narrow, winding, and full of blind curves, and accidents occur frequently. The best ways to avoid mishaps are to obey the 20-mph speed limit, remember to stay on the left-hand side of the road, especially at traffic circles, and avoid riding in the rain and at night. It also helps to keep a sharp eye out for other moped riders, many of whom seem to adopt an alarming disregard for local traffic regulations—and their own and everyone else's safety—and display a singular lack of skill at maneuvering their vehicles. Don't assume that others on the road know what they're doing. Helmets are required by law. Single- or double-seat mopeds and scooters can be rented from cycle liveries by the hour, the day, or the week. The liveries will show first-time riders how to operate the vehicles. Rates vary, but single-seat mopeds cost about $21 per day, or $74 per week (plus a mandatory $12 repair waiver). The fee includes helmet, lock, key, third-party insurance, breakdown service, pick-up and delivery, and a tank of gas. A $20–$50 deposit is required for the lock, key, and helmet, and you must be at least 16 to rent. Recommended liveries are **Oleander Cycles** (Valley Rd., Paget, tel. 809/236–5235, and Gorham Rd., Hamilton, tel. 809/295–0919), **Eve's Cycle Livery** (Middle Rd., Paget, tel. 809/236–6247), **Devil's Hole Cycles** (Harrington Sound Rd., Smith's, tel. 809/293–1280), and **St. George's Cycles** (Water St., St. George's, tel. 809/297–1463). Major hotels have their own cycle liveries, and all hotels and guest houses will make rental arrangements. Gas stations are open daily 7–7, and a few stay open until 11 PM. Gas for cycles is about $1.15 per liter.

By Bicycle Push bikes, as Bermudians call bicycles, are a pleasant way to travel around the island, if you don't mind hilly terrain (*see* Chapter 7, Sports and Fitness). Bikes can be rented at **Eve's Cycle Livery** (Middle Rd., Paget, tel. 809/236–6247), **St. George's Cycles** (Water St., St. George's, tel. 809/297–1463), and **Georgiana Cycles** (Cambridge Rd., Somerset, tel. 809/234–2404). Rentals cost $10–$15 for the first day and $5 for each subsequent day.

By Limousine A limousine isn't the cheapest way to tour the island, but it is the most luxurious. With 24 hours notice, **London Taxi Limousine Service** (tel. 809/292–3691, fax 809/295–8606) will provide a London-type cab, replete with liveried chauffeur, to drive you around for $70 per hour; corporate rates are available.

Guided Tours

Orientation **Butterfield Travel Ltd.** (tel. 809/292–1510), the local Gray
Tours Line representative, runs custom-designed tours for groups and individuals. Among their offerings are a glass-bottom boat trip ($25 per person), a three-hour taxi tour around Harrington Sound ($30), and a five-hour island cruise with stops at Dockyard and St. George's ($50).

L. P. Gutteridge Ltd. (tel. 809/295–4545) specializes in group tours, but individual packages can also be arranged.

Taxi Tours A blue flag on the hood of a cab indicates that the driver is a qualified tour guide. These cabs can be difficult to find, but most of their drivers are friendly, entertaining, and well-informed about the island and its history. Ask your hotel to arrange a tour with a knowledgeable driver. Cabs are four- or six-seaters, and the legal rate for island tours is $20 per hour, with a three-hour minimum. A 25% surcharge is added between 10 PM and 6 AM, and on Sunday and public holidays.

Bus and **Bermuda Hosts Ltd.** (tel. 809/293–1334, fax 809/293–1335)
Minibus Tours offers three- and five-hour narrated tours of the East End and of the West End in six- or 18-seat air-conditioned vans. The three-hour East End tour visits the Bermuda Aquarium & Zoo, Harrington Sound, Crystal Caves, and the North Shore; the five-hour tour includes those sights as well as St. George's, a stop for shopping and lunch (extra charge), and either the Glass Blowing Studio or the Perfume Factory. West End tours take in South Shore Road, Somerset Village, and Dockyard, with the five-hour tour adding a lunchstop (extra charge). Prices include admissions to museums and attractions. Tour prices are based on the number of passengers, so families or groups will get a better price than invididuals. For the three-hour tour, one person pays $108, while six people sharing the van pay $28.50 each.

St. George's Transportation (tel. 809/297–8199) runs minibus tours of St. George's and St. David's, leaving from King's Square in St. George's. A one-hour tour costs $12 per person, and the two-hour tour is $17.50.

Carriage Tours The few horse-drawn carriages on the island are a romantic way to see the sights. The raconteurs at the reins dispense a wealth of local lore and information and misinformation.

Regardless of the veracity of their tales, you'll enjoy the telling. Carriages can be hired on Front Street in Hamilton; for tours of the West End and Dockyard, contact **Bermuda Carriages** (tel. 809/238–2640). Rates for a one-horse carriage are $15 for a half hour, and $10 for each additional half hour. A two-horse carriage is $20 for the first half hour, and $15 for each half hour thereafter.

Special-Interest Tours
Open Houses and Garden Tours
For six weeks each spring, several Bermudian homes and gardens are open for public tours. Most of the homes date from the 17th century, and all have lovely lawns and gardens. Arranged by the **Garden Club of Bermuda** (tel. 809/295–1301), tours visit three different houses each Wednesday between 2 and 5. Admission is $8.

Free guided tours of the **Botanical Gardens** leave at 10:30 AM from the Visitors Information Centre just inside the Berry Hill Road entrance. These 90-minute tours are conducted April–October on Tuesday, Wednesday, and Friday, and November–March on Tuesday and Friday.

Boat Trips
A host of boats offers sightseeing, snorkeling, and swimming excursions. Major attractions include the Sea Gardens, with their splendid underwater scenes, and the coral-wrapped wreck of HMS *Vixen*, both of which lie off the West End. Many of the boats operate only during high season, so call in advance for schedules.

Bermuda Island Cruises (tel. 809/292–8652) operates the 120-passenger *Reef Explorer*, which leaves Albuoy's Point in Hamilton on Tuesday, Wednesday, Friday, and Saturday night for a "Pirate Party Cruise" ($60 adults, $30 children under 12). The boat travels along the reefs, stopping at Hawkins Island for dinner, dancing, and a show featuring limbo dancers and calypso music. Two-hour glass-bottom-boat tours of the Sea Gardens ($25 adults, $12.50 children) leave twice daily from the Ferry Terminal in Hamilton. The "Starlight Reef & Wreck Cruise" ($30) leaves from Hamilton on Tuesday and from the Waterlot Inn, Southampton, on Thursday; cruises leave at 10 PM and return at midnight. A six-hour cruise departing from Albuoy's Point in Hamilton on Monday, Wednesday, and Friday at 10:30 AM stops at Dockyard and St. George's ($50 adults, $25 children), with a rum swizzle party on the return leg.

Pitman's Snorkeling (tel. 809/234–0700) offers combined sightseeing/snorkeling excursions aboard the glass-bottom *Fathom*. The $38, four-hour outing, which includes snorkeling instruction and gear, departs twice daily (May–October) from the Somerset Bridge Hotel dock and cruises on the calm side of Bermuda's fringe reefs.

Submarine *Enterprise* (tel. 809/234–3547) takes passengers on submarine dives off the West End in a 44-passenger air-conditioned submarine with large viewing ports. This trip is definitely not for the claustrophobic. Dives take in the

1878 wreck of the *Lartington*, now home to schools of tropical fish. The two-hour excursion ($70 adults, $35 children under 12) includes travel from Dockyard to the submarine and back. Weather conditions must be ideal; call ahead to find out if the submarine will be operating. The *Enterprise* does not operate in January and February. Dive updates are available from the Visitor Service Broadcasting Radio, 1160 AM.

Bermuda Water Tours (tel. 809/295-3727) operates the 65-foot *Ovation*, which departs from Hamilton twice daily except Sunday on a combined snorkeling and glass-bottom sightseeing trip ($35), and Tuesday through Saturday at 6:30 PM for a barbecue dinner cruise that includes live calypso music and an open bar ($55).

Jessie James Cruises (tel. 809/236-4804 or 809/234-7725) offers several motor-yacht cruises from Albuoy's Point in Hamilton. A Saturday four-and-a-half to five-hour $39 snorkelling/lunch cruise to Somerset Village includes lunch at the Loyalty Inn. A Saturday snorkeling/dinner cruise (4½ hours, $45) departs in the late afternoon for snorkeling in the Sea Gardens and a barbecue buffet with complimentary rum swizzles. A champagne cruise (two hours, $25), offered on Wednesdays, tools around Hamilton Harbor. Sunday through Friday a two-hour moonlight cruise ($25) heads through the Great Sound toward Dockyard, and includes complimentary rum swizzles.

Salt Kettle Boat Rentals Ltd. (tel. 809/236-4863) offers sailing parties for $30 per person. The three-hour trips depart Salt Kettle Monday-Saturday twice daily, and include a stop for swimming and snorkeling, complimentary rum swizzles, soft drinks, and snorkeling gear.

Butterfield Travel Ltd., Bermuda Hosts Ltd., and **L. P. Gutteridge Ltd.** (*see* Orientation Tours, *above*) also arrange boat trips.

Walking Tours   The Bermuda Department of Tourism publishes brochures for self-guided tours of Hamilton, St. George's, the West End, and the Railway Trail. **Heritage Walks,** a cooperative venture between the Bermuda National Trust and the Bermuda Government, are several brochures designed to help visitors explore the parishes on foot. Each "Walks in Bermuda" brochure contains a map and description of sights along the way. The Bermuda Nature Guide, issued by the Bermuda Department of Tourism, has details about the island's flora, fauna, and pink coral sand. Available free at all Visitors Information Centres and at hotels and guest houses, these brochures also contain detailed directions for walkers and cyclists, and historical notes and anecdotes.

From November 15 to March 31, the **Bermuda National Trust** (tel. 809/236-6483) conducts one-hour walking tours of Hamilton, St. George's, and Somerset. The tours of Hamilton and St. George's take in the towns' large number of 17th- and 18th-century buildings, while the Somerset tour focuses more on the island's flora. Hamilton tours begin from the Visitors Information Centre in the Ferry Terminal on Front Street every Monday at 10 AM; tours of St. George's are conducted on Wednesday and Saturday, starting at 10:30 AM in King's Square; the Somerset walk departs from the Country Squire Restaurant on Thursday at 10 AM.

Other free guided walks during the low season include a 2-mile walk through woodlands and scenic areas, leaving from the Clock Tower Building at Dockyard at 11:30 AM; and a tour around Dockyard, departing from the Craft Market on Sunday at 2 PM.

2 Portraits of Bermuda

Bermuda at a Glance: A Chronology

1503 Juan de Bermudez discovers the islands while searching for the New World. The islands are eventually named after him.

1603 Diego Ramirez, a Spanish captain, spends several weeks on Bermuda making ship repairs.

1609 An English fleet of nine ships, under the command of Admiral Sir George Somers, sets sail for Jamestown, Virginia, with supplies for the starving colony. Struck by a hurricane, the fleet is scattered, and the admiral's ship, the Sea Venture, runs aground on the reefs of Bermuda. The colonization of Bermuda begins.

1610 After building two ships, *Deliverance* and *Patience*, from the island's cedar trees, the survivors depart for Jamestown, leaving behind a small party of men. Admiral Sir George Somers returns to Bermuda a few weeks later but dies soon afterward. He requests that his heart be buried on the island.

1612 Asserting ownership of the islands, the Virginia Company sends 60 settlers to Bermuda under the command of Richard Moore, the colony's first governor. The Virginia Company sells its rights to the islands to the newly formed Bermuda Company for £2,000.

1616 The islands are surveyed and divided into shares (25 acres) and tribes (50 shares per tribe). The tribes, or parishes, are named after investors in the Bermuda Company. The first slaves are brought to Bermuda to dive for pearls.

1620 The Bermuda Parliament meets for the first time, in St. Peter's Church in St. George's, making it the third oldest parliament in the world after Iceland and Great Britain.

1684 The Crown takes over control of the colony from the Bermuda Company. Sir Robert Robinson is appointed the Crown's first Governor.

1775 The American Continental Congress announces a trade embargo against all colonies remaining loyal to the Crown. Dependent on America for food, Bermuda negotiates to give the rebellious colonies salt if they will lift the embargo. The colonies refuse, but state that they will end sanctions in exchange for gunpowder. Without the knowledge of Governor George Bruere, a group of Bermudians breaks into the magazine at St. George's and steals the island's supply of gunpowder. The gunpowder is delivered to the Americans, who lift the embargo.

1780 The "Great Hurricane" hits Bermuda, driving ships ashore and leveling houses and trees.

1784 Bermuda's first newspaper, *The Bermuda Gazette & Weekly Advertiser*, is started by Joseph Stockdale in St. George's.

1804 Irish poet Thomas Moore arrives in Bermuda for a four-month stint as registrar of the admiralty court. His affair with the married Hester Tucker was the inspiration for his steamy love poems to her (the "Nea" in his odes), which have attained legendary status in Bermuda.

1810 The Royal Navy begins work on Dockyard, a new naval base on Ireland Island.

1812 In response to American raids on York (now Toronto) during the War of 1812, the British fleet attacks Washington, DC, from its base in Bermuda.

1815 Hamilton becomes the new capital of Bermuda, superseding St. George's.

1834 Slavery is abolished.

1846 The first lighthouse in the colony, the 133-foot Gibb's Hill Lighthouse, is built at the western end of the island in an effort to reduce the number of shipwrecks in the area.

1861 Bermuda enters a period of enormous prosperity with the outbreak of the American Civil War. Sympathetic to the South, Bermudians take up the lucrative and dangerous task of running the Union blockade of southern ports. Sailing in small, fast ships, Bermudians ferry munitions and supplies to the Confederates and return with bales of cotton bound for London.

1883 Princess Louise, daughter of Queen Victoria, visits Bermuda. In honor of her visit, the new Pembroke Hotel changes its name to The Princess.

1901 Afrikaner prisoners from the Boer War are incarcerated in Bermuda. By the end of the war, approximately 4,000 prisoners are housed on the islands.

1915 A 120-man contingent of the Bermuda Volunteer Rifle Corps (B.V.R.C.) departs for service in France during World War I. In action at the battles of the Somme, Arras, and the Third Battle of Ypres, the unit loses more than 30% of its men. In 1916, the Bermuda Militia Artillery also heads for France.

1931 Constructed at a cost of £1 million, the Bermuda Railway opens years behind schedule. Maintenance problems during World War II cripple train service, and the whole system is sold to British Guiana in 1948.

1937 Imperial Airways begins the first scheduled air service to Bermuda from Port Washington in the United States.

1940 During World War II, mail bound for Europe from the Americas is off-loaded in Bermuda and taken to the basement of The Princess hotel, where it is opened by British civil servants trying to locate German spies. Several spies in the United States are unmasked. As part of the Lend-Lease Act between Prime Minister Churchill and President Roosevelt, the United States is awarded a 99-year lease for a military base on St. David's Island. Construction of the base begins in 1941.

1944 Women landowners are given the vote.

1946 For the first time, automobiles are permitted by law on Bermuda.

1951 The Royal Navy withdraws from Dockyard and closes the base.

1953 Winston Churchill, Dwight D. Eisenhower, and Prime Minister Joseph Laniel of France meet on Bermuda for the "Big Three Conference."

1959 NASA opens a space tracking station on Coopers Island, which is part of the American base.

1971 Edward Richards becomes Bermuda's first black government leader (a title later changed to premier).

1973 Governor Sir Richard Sharples and his aide, Captain Hugh Sayers, are shot dead. In 1976, Erskine "Buck" Burrows is convicted of the murder, as well as several other murders and armed robberies. He is hanged in 1977.

1979 Gina Swainson, Miss Bermuda, wins the Miss World Contest. An official half holiday is announced and Gina Swainson postage stamps are released in 1980.

1987 Hurricane Emily hits Bermuda, injuring more than 70 people and causing millions of dollars in damage.

1990 President Bush and Prime Minister Thatcher meet on Bermuda.

Bermuda's Hidden Landscapes

By William G. Scheller

William G. Scheller is a contributing editor to National Geographic Traveler. *His articles have also appeared in the* Washington Post Magazine, Islands, *and numerous other periodicals.*

At the pub on the square in St. George's, Bermuda, there is a sign on the second-floor veranda that everyone ignores. "Do not feed the birds," it says, but the clientele keeps handing out crumbs to the sparrows that dart through the open railings.

I sat on that veranda on a sultry October afternoon, finishing a pint of Watney's and looking out over King's Square. I had just enjoyed my first cup of Bermuda fish chowder, which the Pub, like most local restaurants, lets you fine-tune with cruets of dark rum and a fiery concoction called sherry peppers.

At the next table an English toddler was singing a song about a little duck. The 18th-century square below was quiet, partly because it had just rained and partly because at the moment there was no cruise ship anchored at St. George's. I crumbled a few morsels from the bun of my fish sandwich, tossed them to the sparrows, and made up my mind on another Watney's. After all, I wasn't playing golf that afternoon.

Not playing golf? The Bermuda Islands, conventional wisdom has it, are a place where you live on the links. But I was after a different place—a traveler's Bermuda, if I could find it.

On an archipelago roughly 22 miles long and seldom more than a mile wide, traveling can be a difficult order—unless you severely limit your pace. Fortunately, automobiles are out of the question. Visitors can't rent them (even residents weren't allowed to own cars until 1946), and the only option for exploring Bermuda on four wheels is to engage a taxi driven by an accredited guide. But why risk seeing the whole place in a day? If you move at a speed faster than a walk, you miss details like the sign I saw on a small, shuttered yellow building: "Dot & Andy's Restaurant. Operated by Barbara and Donna."

Until recently, walking in Bermuda has meant edging gingerly along the nearly nonexistent shoulders of narrow lanes, ready to press yourself into the hibiscus hedges when a car comes by. A few years ago, though, some enterprising Bermudians got the idea of turning the right-of-way of the abandoned Bermuda Railway into an island-length hiking trail. (The entire railway, down to the spikes, was sold to British Guiana, now Guyana, in 1948).

My first choice, as a rail enthusiast, would have been to have the narrow-gauge locomotive and cars still rattling along the tracks. But being able to walk the route, or part of it, is clearly the next best thing. My problem was that I chose a section that skirted a residential district along Bailey's Bay, near the northeastern end of the main island. Here the old roadbed was frequently severed by sharp inlets of the sea, and the trestles that had once bridged them had long since gone to South America. I'd walk a hundred yards or so and have to go back to the road, often finding no signs to tell me when I could pick up the trail again. (Farther west on the islands, the old route is less frequently broken.) On one side was the ocean, on the other a series of relentlessly suburban backyards—there are no raffish little shacks here, like the ones you find on other islands. Finally, after I had inadvertently wandered into my fourth backyard, it began to rain. It was the kind of rain that makes you so wet in the first couple of minutes that there's no sense in hurrying out of it. I walked to a bus shelter, and admitted defeat . . . and some success, having got into a situation in which I could hardly be mistaken for a tourist, even in Bermuda.

It was in the bus shelter that I met a young American, who was waiting out the storm with his two toddlers. He was a civilian worker at the U.S. naval air station, a submarine-watching facility now largely dedicated to operating the islands' commercial airport. His most telling comment had to do with his younger child, who had been born in Hamilton: "She's a real Bermuda Onion."

He knew, of course, that genuine Bermudian citizenship requires at least one native parent, or jumping through more bureaucratic hoops than most people would care to deal with, but the fact that he liked thinking of his little girl as a Bermudian meant that he wasn't just serving a remunerative sentence in a faraway place. To a wet traveler like me, the message was that there was a community here, and foreigners could become part of it.

The rain that ended my railway trail walk was part of the tail end of Hurricane Nana, which had threatened to strike the island in full force before being pushed off track by a continental cold front. "We don't have hurricanes in Bermuda," a hotel bartender had told me with a wink, obviously remembering 1987's Emily, with her 116-mph winds, 50 injuries, and $35 million damage.

"No," I replied. "I live in Vermont, and we don't have snow."

Nana was a hurricane that missed, although she faded and veered away with great theatrical effect. By nine that evening the rain returned, sheeting sideways against the windows of the hotel restaurant while tall palms thrashed in wild abandon. From the hotel bar the storm was a terrific backdrop—the room was all Key Largo atmosphere heightened by the adrenal tingle that comes with a sudden pres-

sure drop. It didn't last long. Within an hour, all that remained of Nana in Bermuda was a random gusting among
the palm tops, and it was fine outside for a walk down to the
bay.

The next day I reverted to the vehicle of choice for covering
ground in Bermuda. Motorized or "auxiliary" cycles, and
the more modern motor scooters—none for rent with engines larger than 50cc, but powerful enough for islands with
a 20-mph speed limit—have become a virtual postcard cli-
ché in Bermuda, and to strap on your de rigueur white helmet is to feel as if you've somehow become part of the
landscape.

A lot of visitors are afraid the scooters can too easily
help them accomplish just that, but the bikes aren't
all that dangerous, once you learn the controls and
remember to stay on the left, British style. There is, however, a common motorbike injury the locals call "road rash,"
a nasty abrasion of whatever appendage happens to meet
with the road, or with one of Bermuda's limestone walls,
during a badly executed turn.

What I most wanted the bike for was exploring the Bermuda hinterlands. I had already visited St. George's, the islands' oldest settlement and former capital, with its narrow
meandering streets, lovely State House (built in 1620), and
cedar-beamed, 18th-century church of St. Peter. I had been
particularly intrigued with a local attraction called the
Confederate Museum, headquarters of blockade-running
operations during the U.S. Civil War. (What really caught
my interest there was the attitude of the black docent,
"proud," as she put it, of a building that housed the branch
office of a desperate effort to keep her ancestors in chains.
In Bermudian race relations, bygones are bygones to a remarkable degree.)

Towns are best explored on foot, even though it did get to be
great fun to breeze into the capital for dinner after dark and
have maître d's take my helmet. The bike, though, would let
me discover the countryside, with its quiet lanes and
tended meadows and fragments of old estates. One of those
estates—Verdmont, in Smith's Parish, now a Bermuda National Trust property—lay at the end of a delightfully con-
voluted route I had devised, one that was designed to take
me buzzing along as many back roads as possible.

It was on St. Mark's Road, rounding Collector's Hill, that
the essence of this miniature landscape suddenly came
clear: I was looking, I realized, at a near-perfect combination of Martha's Vineyard and the Cotswolds. On the Vineyard account was the gently rolling countryside with the
sea not far away, as on a New England seacoast farm; the
Cotswolds element was provided by a little jewel of a limestone Gothic church, by narrow byways with names like Pi-
geon Berry Lane, and by the faultless juxtaposition of

every stand of trees, half-acre of greensward, and carefully clipped hedgerow.

As it turned out, I wasn't the first to get this feeling about the place: I saw later that two of the local streets were named Nantucket Lane (close enough) and Cotswold Lane. And why not? The Cotswold Hills, Bermuda, and the Massachusetts islands are all essentially English places, the latter two offering their settlers an Englishness of landscape even before any art was applied to it. And that art, in all three locales, was the particular English genius for conjuring tremendous diversity within the most compact of areas. Consummately ordered yet always romantically picturesque, the English landscape aesthetic depends on constant variety and small surprises, and never upon great vistas.

The result is a sense of much in little, of no space wasted; the effect in Bermuda is to shrink the visitor into the islands' scale, rather than to leave him feeling like a scooter-mounted giant in a hibiscus garden.

There was another aspect of Bermuda to consider, one that counters the islands' persona as a serene, ocean-borne fragment of English countryside. This is its past history as fortress Bermuda, a 21-square-mile dreadnought permanently anchored in the Atlantic. Fort St. Catherine, at the colony's extreme northeastern tip, is now decommissioned and restored to reveal its vast warren of tunnels, built to feed shells to guns commanding the northern and eastern approaches to the islands. St. David's Island, too, has its battery, a rusting line of World War II–era shore artillery where feral housecats pad about the empty magazines.

From the 17th to the 20th century, dozens of promontories and harbor entrances throughout Bermuda bristled with guns, reflecting Britain's confrontations with forces that ranged from imperial Spain to the newly independent United States to the U-boats of the Third Reich. And no single installation loomed so mightily as the Royal Navy Dockyard, at the barb of Bermuda's fishhook-shaped western end.

From 1810 to 1950 the dockyard was the "Gibraltar of the West," providing a heavily fortified anchorage for British warships and a citadel of massive limestone support structures. Approaching by ferry from Hamilton, I immediately was struck by the orderliness and permanence of it all, by the twin towers of the main building with clock faces showing the time and the hour of the next high tide, and by the ubiquitous initials VR—"Victoria Regina," shorthand for one of history's most remarkable imperial achievements. The dockyard looks as if it were built to last a thousand years, and it may, though now it houses a cluster of museums, craft galleries, restaurants, and boutiques. Like the rest of Bermuda's defenses, the dockyard was never tested by a serious attack; its bristles were too formidable a challenge.

Time and again in Bermuda, one encounters the opposing tidal pull of British and American influences. This, after all, is a place where they still refer to the panorama of harbor islands as seen from the top of Gibb's Hill as the "Queen's View," because Elizabeth II admired it in 1953. But this British colony also conducts its financial affairs in dollars, not sterling, and nearly 90% of its visitors are American.

There is a continuing Bermudian tradition that many residents link with the long British military presence, and that is a certain formality of dress. I was reminded of it one day in downtown Hamilton, when I saw a white-haired gentleman wearing a blue blazer, a white shirt, and a rep silk tie, along with pink Bermuda shorts, white knee socks, and pink tassels on his garters. The shorts themselves are a throwback to the military, and got their start as a local trademark when Bermuda tailors began refining officers' baggy khaki shorts for civilian wear. They are now ubiquitous as Bermudian business attire, but the most striking thing about them is not the fact that they expose gentlemen's knees but that they are integrated into a very correct, very formal men's civilian uniform. I never once saw a businessman's collar and tie loosened on a hot day in Bermuda—a sure sign that the stiff upper lip can outlast even the presence of the Royal Navy.

I thought about where I might find the quintessence of Bermudian formality and local tradition, and concluded that the place to look was probably afternoon tea at the venerable Hamilton Princess hotel. I was staying elsewhere, and thought it might be appropriate to call the Princess first to see if outsiders were welcome. "Are you serving tea at four?" I asked the English-accented woman who answered the telephone.

"Yes."

"Is it all right to come if you're not registered at the hotel?"

"Are you registered at the hotel?"

"No. That's why I'm asking."

"I'll switch you to dining services."

"Hello?" (Another Englishwoman's voice.)

"Hello, I'm wondering if I can come to tea if I'm not registered at the hotel."

"What is your name, sir?" I gave her the name and spelling. At this point, I was tempted to add "Viscount."

"I don't have you listed as a guest."

"I know that. I'm calling to ask if it's all right to come to tea if I'm not a guest."

"No, sir."

Now we were deep in Monty Python territory, and I had the John Cleese part. Clearly, there was nothing to do but get dressed, scoot into Hamilton, and crash tea at the Princess. But when I sauntered into the hotel with my best ersatz viscount air, all I found was a small antechamber to an empty function room where a dozen people in tennis clothes stood around a samovar and a tray of marble pound cake slices. I poured a cup, drank it, and was gone in five minutes. Crashing tea at the Princess had been about as difficult, and as exciting, as crashing lunch at my late grandfather's diner in New Jersey.

Hamilton is a tidy, cheerful little city, but as the days drew down I returned more and more to the countryside, particularly to the back roads where small farms survive. Bermuda was once a midocean market garden, in the days before the United States restricted imports, and property values skyrocketed beyond the reach of farmers; now, an occasional neat patch of red earth still produces root crops, broccoli, cabbage, and squash. I even saw a truck loaded with onions go by—a reminder of a Bermuda before golf.

America's Rebel Colonies and Bermuda: Getting a Bang for Their Buckwheat

By William Zuill

A native Bermudian and a member of the Bermuda House of Assembly, William Zuill is the author of several historical works about the island. This excerpt about the role of Bermuda in the American War of Independence is taken from his book, Bermuda Journey. *William Zuill died in July 1989.*

When the War of American Independence began, Bermudians at first felt little personal concern. There was some sympathy for the colonists; quarrels between arbitrary executive power and people, which in America had now led to real trouble, had also been part of Bermuda's history, and besides this there were ties of blood and friendship to make for a common understanding. But for all that, Bermudians, while expressing discreet sympathy, were chiefly concerned for their ships and carrying trade, and realizing their helpless position, they believed their wisest course lay in continued loyalty to the Crown. The wisdom of this policy was suddenly brought into question when the Continental Congress placed an embargo on all trade with Britain and the loyal colonies, for as nearly all essential food supplies came from the Continent, the island faced starvation unless the decree was relaxed. Thus there was a swift realization that Bermuda's fate was deeply involved in the war.

The drama now began to unfold and soon developed into a struggle between the governor, George Bruere, and the dominant Bermuda clique led by the Tuckers of the West End. Bruere's chief characteristic was unswerving, unquestioning loyalty, and the fact that two of his sons were fighting with the royalist forces in America—one of them was killed at Bunker Hill—made the ambiguous behavior of Bermudians intolerable to him, both as a father and as an Englishman.

Of the Tuckers, the most prominent member of the family at this time was Colonel Henry, of the Grove, Southampton. His eldest son, Henry, colonial treasure and councillor, had married the governor's daughter, Frances Bruere, and lived at St. George's. There were also two sons in America, Thomas Tudor, a doctor settled in Charleston, and St. George, the youngest, a lawyer in Virginia. The two boys in America, caught up in the events around them and far removed from the delicacies of the Bermuda situation, openly took the side of the colonists.

Up to the time of the outbreak of the war there had been warm friendship between the Tuckers and the Brueres, a relationship made closer by the marriage of Henry Tucker to Frances Bruere. But when it became known in Bermuda that the Tuckers abroad were backing the Americans, Bruere publicly denounced them as rebels and broke off relations with every member of the family except his son-in-law. But Colonel Henry was more concerned with the situation in Bermuda than he was with the rights and wrongs of the conflict itself, and he believed that unless someone acted, the island was facing serious disaster. So, privately, through his sons in America, he began to sound out some of the delegates to the Continental Congress as to whether the embargo would be relaxed in exchange for salt. This move, never in any way official, had the backing of a powerful group, and before long it was decided to send the colonel with two or three others to Philadelphia to see what could be arranged. Meanwhile another but less powerful faction took form and likewise held meetings, the object of which was to oppose in every way these overtures to rebels.

Colonel Henry and his colleagues reached Philadelphia in July 1775 and on the 11th delivered their appeal to Congress. Though larded with unctuous flattery, the address met a stony reception, but a hint was thrown out that although salt was not wanted, any vessel bringing arms or powder would find herself free from the embargo. The fact that there was a useful store of powder at St. George's was by now common knowledge in America, for the Tucker boys had told their friends about it and the information had reached General Washington. Thus, before long, the question of seizing this powder for the Americans was in the forefront of the discussions.

Colonel Henry was in a tight corner. Never for an instant feeling that his own loyalty was in question, he had believed himself fully justified in coming to Philadelphia to offer salt in exchange for food. But these new suggestions which were now being put to him went far beyond anything he had contemplated, and he was dismayed at the ugly situation that confronted him. It is evident that the forces at work were too strong for him. The desperate situation in Bermuda, verging on starvation, could only be relieved by supplies from America, and an adamant Congress held the whip hand. After some agonizing heart-searching, he gave in and agreed with Benjamin Franklin to trade the powder at St. George's for an exemption of Bermuda ships from the embargo.

Colonel Henry returned home at once, arriving on July 25. His son St. George, coming from Virginia, arrived about the same time, while two other ships from America, sent especially to fetch the powder, were already on their way.

On August 14, 1775, there was secret but feverish activity among the conspirators as whaleboats from various parts of the island assembled at Somerset. As soon as it was dark, the party, under the command, it is believed, of son-in-law Henry and a Captain Morgan, set off for St. George's. St. George, lately from Virginia and sure to be suspect, spent the night at St. George's, possibly at the home of his brother Henry, and at midnight was seen ostentatiously walking up and down the Parade with Chief Justice Burch, thus establishing a water tight alibi. Meanwhile the landing party, leaving the boats at Tobacco Bay on the north side of St. George's, reached the unguarded magazine. The door was quickly forced, and before long, kegs of powder were rolling over the grass of the Governor's Park toward the bay, where they were speedily stowed in the boats. The work went on steadily until the first streaks of dawn drove the party from the scene. By that time 100 barrels of powder were on the way to guns that would discharge the powder against the king's men.

When Bruere heard the news he was frantic. A vessel which he rightly believed had the stolen powder on board was still in sight from Retreat Hill, and he determined to give chase. Rushing into town, the distraught man issued a hysterical proclamation:

POWDER STEAL

Advt

Save your Country from Ruin, which
may hereafter happen. The Powder
stole out of the Magazine late last
night cannot be carried far as the
wind is so light.

A GREAT REWARD

will be given to any person that can
make a proper discovery before the
Magistrates.

News of the outrage and copies of the proclamation were hurried through the colony as fast as rider could travel. The legislature was summoned to meet the following day. Many members of the Assembly doubtless knew a good deal, but officially all was dark and the legislature did its duty by voting a reward and sending a wordy message expressing its abhorrence of the crime.

But no practical help was forthcoming, and after several days of helpless frustration Bruere determined to send a vessel to Boston to inform Admiral Howe what had happened. At first no vessels were to be had anywhere in the island; then, when one was found, the owner was threatened with sabotage, so he withdrew his offer. Another vessel was found, but there was no crew, and for three whole weeks, in an island teeming with mariners, no one could be found to go to sea. At last, on September 3, the governor's ship put to sea, but not without a final incident, for she was boarded offshore by a group of men who searched the captain and crew for letters. These had been prudently hidden away in the ballast with the governor's slave, who remained undiscovered. The captain hotly denied having any confidential papers, so the disappointed boarders beat him up and then left.

In due course the ship reached Boston, and Admiral Howe at once sent the *Scorpion* to Bermuda to help Bruere keep order. Thereafter for several years His Majesty's ships kept a watchful eye on the activities of Bermudians, and in 1778 these were replaced by a garrison. It has always seemed extraordinary that no rumor of this bargain with the Americans reached Bruere before the actual robbery took place. It is even more amazing that within a stone's throw of Government House such a desperate undertaking could have continued steadily throughout the night without discovery.

The loss of the powder coincided with the disappearance of a French officer, a prisoner on parole. At the time it was thought that he had been in league with the Americans and had made his escape with them. But 100 years later when the foundation for the Unfinished Church was being excavated, the skeleton of a man dressed in French uniform was disclosed. It is now believed that he must have come on the scene while the robbery was in progress and, in the dark, been mistaken for a British officer. Before he could utter a sound he must have been killed outright by these desperate men and quickly buried on the governor's doorstep.

Following in the Tracks of the Bermuda Railway

By Ben Davidson

A former travel editor for Sunset Travel magazine, Ben Davidson specializes in travel writing and photography.

Bermuda is lovely, but a walk along its narrow roads can involve close encounters with countless madcap moped drivers and a stream of cars. A more serene way to sample Bermuda's lush terrain, stunning seascapes, and colorful colonies of island homes is to follow the route of the railroad that once crossed this isolated archipelago. The Bermuda Railway Trail goes along the old train right-of-way for 18 miles, winding through three of the several interconnected islands that make up Bermuda.

Opened in 1931, the railway provided smooth-running transportation between the quiet village of Somerset at the west end and the former colonial capital of St. George's to the east. But by 1948 it had fallen a victim to excessive military use during World War II, soaring maintenance costs, and the automobile. The railroad was closed down, and all its rolling stock was sold to Guyana (then called British Guiana). In 1984, Bermuda's 375th anniversary, the government dedicated the lands of the old railway for public use and began to clear, pave, and add signs to sections of its route.

The trail's most enchanting aspect is that it reveals a parade of island views hidden from the public for nearly 30 years, scenes similar to what the first colonists must have found here in the early 1600s. In a few places the trail joins the main roads, but mostly it follows a tranquil, car-free route from parish to parish, past quiet bays, limestone cliffs, small farms, and groves of cedar, allspice, mangrove, and fiddlewood trees. Short jaunts on side trails and intersecting tribe roads (paths that were built in the early 1600s as boundaries between the parishes, or "tribes") bring you to historic forts and a lofty lighthouse, coral-tinted beaches, parks, and preserves.

I explored the Railway Trail on foot, moped, and horseback, using an 18-page guide available free at the Visitors Service Bureau in Hamilton. (You can also find the guide at some of the big hotels.) The booklet contains historical photos, a brief history of the railroad, maps, and descriptions of seven sections of trail, which range from 1¾ to 3¾ miles.

Sporting a pair of proper Bermuda shorts, I revved up my rented moped and headed out to the Somerset Bus Terminal, one of eight former railroad stations and the westernmost end of the trail. From there I followed the paved path to Springfield—an 18th-century plantation house used by the Springfield Library. A leisurely stroll in the adjoining five-acre Springfield & Gilbert Nature Reserve took me through thick forests of fiddlewood. I also saw stands of Bermuda cedars that once blanketed the island but were nearly wiped out by blight in the 1940s.

Back on the trail I spotted oleander, hibiscus, bougainvillea, and poinsettia bursting through the greenery at every turn. In backyards I could see bananas, grapefruit, oranges, lemons, and limes growing in profusion, thanks to Bermuda's consistent year-round subtropical climate.

I parked the moped at the trailhead to Fort Scaur—a 19th-century fortress built by the Duke of Wellington, conqueror of Napoleon at Waterloo—and strolled up to its mighty walls and deep moat. Through a dark passage I reached the grassy grounds with their massive gun mounts and bunkers. A telescope atop the fort's walls provided close-up views of the Great Sound and Ely's Harbor, once a smuggler's haven. A caretaker showed me around the fort, one of the three largest in Bermuda.

On my moped again, I motored past Skroggins Bay to the Lantana Colony Club, a group of beachside cottages. I stopped to sip a Dark and Stormy—a classic Bermudian rum drink—and to enjoy the view of the sail-filled Great Sound. My post-swizzle destination: Somerset Bridge. Only 32 inches wide, this tiny bridge was built in 1620 and looks more like a plank in the road than the world's smallest drawbridge—its opening is just wide enough for a sailboat's mast to pass through.

I ended my first Railway Trail ride at the ferry terminal near the bridge, where I boarded the next ferry back to Hamilton. Had I continued, the trail would have taken me through what was once the agricultural heartland of Bermuda. The colony's 20 square miles of gently rolling landscape, graced by rich volcanic soil and a mild climate, once yielded crops of sweet, succulent Bermuda onions, potatoes, and other produce. But tourism has become bigger business here, and today only some 500 acres are devoted to vegetable crops.

Just west of Sandys Parish the trail runs for some 3¾ miles through Warwick Parish. The path, now dirt, overlooks Little Sound and Southampton, where fishing boats are moored. Here the Railway Trail begins to intersect many of Bermuda's tribe roads, which make interesting diversions. Tribe Road No. 2 brings you to the Gibb's Hill Lighthouse, built around 1846. This 133-foot structure is one of the few lighthouses in the world made of cast iron. You pay $2 for the dubious privilege of climbing 185 steps to the lens house, where you're rewarded with far-reaching views of the island and Great Sound. The 1,500-watt electric lamp can be seen as far away as 40 miles.

Spicelands, a riding center in Warwick, schedules early-morning rides along sections of the Railway Trail and South

Shore beaches. I joined a ride to follow part of the trail where it cuts deep into the rolling limestone terrain—so deep that at one point we passed through the 450-foot Paget Tunnel, whose walls are lined with roots of rubber trees.

We rode through woodlands and fields, past stands of Surinam cherry trees and houses equipped with domed water tanks and stepped, pyramid-shaped roofs designed to catch rainwater. As we trotted through the cool darkness beneath a dense canopy of trees it was hard to imagine a time when noisy rolling stock rattled along the same route, carrying some of the 14 million passengers who rode the railway while it was in operation. Finally, a tribe road led us through tropical vegetation to the clean, coral-pink beaches of Bermuda's beautiful South Shore.

East of Hamilton, the Railway Trail follows the North Shore, beginning in Palmetto Park in the lush, hilly parish of Devonshire. It hugs the coastline past Palmetto House (across-shaped, 18th-century mansion belonging to the Bermuda National Trust) and thick stands of Bermuda cedar to Penhurst Park, where there are walking trails, agricultural plots, and good swimming beaches.

Farther east the trail hits a wilder stretch of coast. The Shelley Bay Park and Nature Reserve along here has native mangroves and one of the few beaches on the North Shore. After a short walk on North Shore Road, the trail picks up again at Bailey's Bay and follows the coast to Coney Island. The park here has an old lime kiln and a former horse-ferry landing.

The remaining sections of the trail are in St. George's. Start at the old Terminal Building (now called Tiger Bay Gardens) and stroll through this historic town. The trail passes by Mullet Bay and Rocky Hill Parks, then heads to Lover's Lake Nature Reserve, where nesting longtails can be seen amid the mangroves. The end of the trail is at Ferry Point Park, directly across from Coney Island. In the park there's a historic fort and a cemetery.

Evenings are perhaps the most enchanting time to walk along the Railway Trail. As the light grows dim, the moist air fills with songs from tiny tree frogs hidden in hedges of oleander and hibiscus. The sound sets a tranquil, tropical mood that, for nearly a half century, has been undisturbed by the piercing whistle and clickety-clack of Bermuda's bygone railroad.

3 Cruising in Bermuda

Choosing Your Cruise

Cruise Information

Magazines **Cruises & Tours** profiles new ships and covers ports and itineraries; $11.80 per year for four issues (Vacation Publishers, 1502 Augusta St., Suite 415, Houston, TX 77057, tel. 713/974–6903).

Cruise Travel Magazine has photos and features on ships and ports of call. $9.97 per year for six issues (Box 342, Mt. Morris, IL 61054, tel. 815/734–4151 or 800/877–5983).

Newsletters *Cruise Digest Reports* has detailed ship reports, evaluations and ratings, and cruise industry news; $35 per year for six issues (1521 Alton Rd., Suite 350, Miami Beach, FL 33139, tel. 305/374–2224).

The Millegram is a newsletter with information on new ships, shipbuilding contracts, and changes in itineraries; $10 per year for four issues (Bill Miller Cruises Everywhere, Box 1463, Secaucus, NJ 07096, tel. 201/348–9390).

Ocean & Cruise News is a newsletter that profiles a different ship each month (World Ocean & Cruise Liner Society, Box 92, Stamford, CT 06901).

Types of Ships

The bigger the ship, the more it can offer: a greater number of activities, public rooms, dining options; a broader range of entertainment; and, of course, more passengers—a boon if you're gregarious, a burden if you're not. Rates on large ships can be slightly lower; the newer megaships are significantly less expensive per passenger to operate. Some ships, though, are too unwieldy to dock in smaller ports, and passengers may be shuttled to shore in a tender (a small boat).

Smaller cruise ships offer intimacy; the crew may be more informal, the level of activity less intense. Small ships can often slip into tiny, shallow harbors and dock right at quayside. Small ships come in two versions: simple excursion vessels and ultra luxurious ships. The excursion vessels usually don't have such amenities as pools, theaters, casinos, or libraries, and cabins are almost always closetlike. Small luxury ships, which usually carry up to 200 passengers, have all the big-ship amenities, all-outside suites, and an exacting level of personalized service.

In considering size, don't forget to factor in other variables. Below, individual ship reviews show the passenger/crew ratio (or service ratio), which indicates how many passengers each crew member must serve. A service ratio of 2:1 indicates that there's a crew member for every two passengers. All things being equal, choose the ship with the lower service ratio.

Space ratio, which indicates the relative size of cabins and public areas, is also very important. Divide a ship's gross tonnage by its passenger capacity to find this. A 25,000-ton vessel carrying 1,000 passengers will have a 25:1 space ratio. By industry standards, a ratio of 45:1 or above is considered spacious. Vessels with ratios under 25:1 can feel a bit like floating cans of sardines.

Also study carefully a ships on-board facilities. Is there a pool? How many entertainment lounges and movie theaters? How well equipped is the library or the health club? Facilities vary greatly.

Mainstream Ships These ships carry between 700 and 2,000 passengers and are similar to self-contained, all-inclusive resorts. You'll find pools, spas and saunas, movie theaters, exercise rooms, Las Vegas–style entertainment, a casino, and shore excursions, not to mention plenty of planned group activities.

The per diem is the daily rate, per passenger, when two persons share a cabin. Differences in ships, cabin categories, itineraries, and discounts, however, can skew that figure.

Within the mainstream cruise ship category, there are several subcategories: standard, premium, and luxury. The per diem listed with each one is based on a standard outside cabin in peak season—this being any ship's middle-of-the-road accommodation. Inside cabins have lower fares; fancy suites, with verandas or VCRs, cost more.

Luxury Here you'll savor the finest cuisine afloat, dining at single seatings and by special order, and unusually large cabins. Most cabins are outside; some have verandas. These ships have high service and space ratios and extremely personalized service. Passengers are experienced and sophisticated cruisers. Evenings are dressy, with some formal occasions. You'll find fewer families and more seniors. **Per diem: $300–$800.**

Premium Most ships fall into this category. They are run by highly experienced cruise lines, and you can expect competent, consistently professional service and entertainment and above-average itineraries. Waiters are apt to be of one nationality, adding a distinctive flair to the dining room. Hours and room service selection are better, the menu choice and quality of food higher, than those of the standard class. Featured dishes may be prepared tableside, and you're often able, with advance notice, to place special orders. Evenings are dressier, and the ambience similar to that of a good restaurant. There are usually a couple of formal nights. **Per diem: $260–$590.**

Standard Menus are probably not extensive, and the food good but not extraordinary. Dress is more casual. Some of these ships are older, refitted vessels lacking modern amenities and state-of-the-art facilities. Others are gleaming new 60,000-ton megaships, carrying more than 2,000 passengers, that have been patterned after all-inclusive resorts where everything, from staff members to cabins to public spaces, seem rather impersonal. **Per diem: $200–$410.**

Cost

For one all-inclusive price (plus tips, shopping, bar bills, and other incidentals), you can have what many have called the trip of a lifetime. The axiom "the more you pay, the more you get" doesn't always hold true: Most mainstream ships are one-class vessels on which the passenger in the cheapest inside cabin eats the same food, sees the same shows, and shares the same amenities as one paying more than $1,000 per day for the top suite. (A notable exception is the *Queen Elizabeth 2*, where your dining-room assignment is based on your per diem.) To some, a larger cabin—used principally for sleeping, showering, and changing clothes is not worth the extra money. Where price does make a difference is in the choice of ship.

A handy way to compare costs is to look at the per diem cost—the price of a cruise on a daily basis for each passenger, when two people occupy one cabin. In other words, if a seven-day cruise costs $700 per person, then the per diem for each person is $100. To select a cruise you can afford, consider the following elements.

Pre- and post-cruise arrangements: If you plan to arrive a day or two early at the port of embarkation, or linger a few days for sightseeing afterward, estimate the cost of your hotel, meals, car rental, sightseeing, and other expenditures. Cruise lines sell packages for pre- and post-cruise stays that can include hotel accommodations, transportation, tours, and extras such as car rentals, and some meals. These packages can cost less than similar stays you arrange on your own, but comparison shopping may reveal that you can do better on your own.

Airfare: Airfare and transfers are often included in the basic cruise fare; however, the cruise line chooses your airline and flight. Lines give an air transportation credit of $200–$400 for passengers who make their own arrangements. You may find a better airfare or more convenient routing, or use frequent-flyer miles.

Pretrip incidentals: These may include trip or flight insurance, the cost of boarding your pets, airport or port parking, departure tax, visas, long-distance calls home, clothing, film or videotape, and other miscellaneous expenses.

Shore excursions/expenses: Estimate an average of $70–$140 per passenger on a seven-day cruise.

Amusement and gambling allowance: Losses at bingo, in the casino, or in other forms of gambling, plus the cost of video games, can set you back a bundle. Of course, this is an entirely avoidable expense, but if you plan to bet, plan to lose. You must be over 18 to gamble on a cruise ship.

Shopping: Include what you expect to spend both for inexpensive souvenirs and major duty-free purchases.

On-board incidentals: According to the Cruise Lines International Association (CLIA), the typical tip total works out to $7–$11 per passenger per day. Daily on-board expenditures, including bar tabs, wine with meals, laundry, beauty parlor services, and gift shop purchases, average about $22.50 per person.

Accommodations

Where you sleep matters only if you enjoy extra creature comforts and are willing to pay for them; on most of today's one-class cruise ships no particular status or stigma is attached to your choice of cabin. Having said that, there's certainly an advantage to selecting the best cabin within your budget personally, rather than allowing your travel agent or cruise line representative to book you into the next available accommodation. Also, the earlier you book, the better the selection.

Cabin Size The term "stateroom," used on some ships, is usually interchangeable with cabin. Price is directly proportional to size and location.

Suites are the roomiest and best-equipped accommodations, although even on the same ship they may differ in size, facilities, and prices. Most have a sitting area with a sofa and chairs; some have two bathrooms, occasionally with a whirlpool bathtub. The most expensive suites may be priced without regard to the number of passengers occupying them.

Furnishings Almost all modern cabins are equipped with individually controlled air-conditioning and a private bathroom—usually closet-size, with a toilet, small shower, and washbasin. More expensive cabins, especially on newer ships, may have a bathtub. Most cabins also have limited closet space, a small desk or dresser, a reading light, and, on many ships, a phone and TV, sometimes even a VCR.

Depending upon the ship and category, a cabin may have beds or berths. The beds may be twins, either side-by-side or at right angles. On many new ships, twin beds convert into a double. Lower-price cabins and cabins on smaller or older ships may have upper and lower bunks, or berths, especially when three or four people share the same accommodation. To provide more living space in the daytime, the room stewards fold the berths into the wall and frequently convert single beds into couches. More and more ships are reconfiguring their cabins to offer double beds; if that is what you want, get an assurance in writing that you have been assigned a cabin with a double bed.

Sharing Most cabins are designed for two people. If more than two people share a cabin, a substantial discount to the third or fourth person is usually offered. An additional discount is often offered for children sharing a cabin with their parents. When no single cabins are available, passengers traveling on their own must pay a single supplement, which usually ranges from 125% to 200% of the double-occupancy per person rate. On request, however, many cruise lines will match up two strangers of the same sex in a cabin at the double-occupancy rate.

Location On all ships, regardless of size or design, the bow (front) and stern (back) bounce up and down on the waves far more than amidships (middle). Similarly, the closer your deck is to the true center of the ship—about halfway between the bottom of the hull and the highest deck—the less you will feel the ship's movement. Some cruise lines charge more for cabins amidships; most charge more for the higher decks.

Outside cabins have portholes or windows (which cannot be opened); on the upper decks, the view from outside cabins may be partially obstructed by lifeboats or look out onto a public deck. Because outside cabins are more desirable, many newer upscale and luxury ships are configured with outside cabins only. On a few ships more expensive outside cabins have a private veranda that opens onto the sea.

Inside cabins on older vessels are often smaller and oddly shaped in order to fit around the ship's particular configuration. On newer ships, the floor plans of inside cabins are virtually identical to those of outside cabins. If sleeping in windowless inside cabins doesn't make you feel claustrophobic, it's a great way to save money.

Cruise brochures show the ship's layout deck by deck and the approximate location and shape of every cabin and suite. Study the map to make sure the cabin you pick is not near the noise of public rooms or the ship's engine, and to make sure that you are near stairs or an elevator. If detailed layouts of typical cabins are printed, you can determine what kind of beds the cabin has, if it has a window or a porthole, and what furnishings are provided. Be aware that configurations within each category can differ.

Booking Your Cruise

Most cruise ships sail at or near capacity, especially during high season, so consider making reservations as much as two years in advance. On the other hand, you may be able to save hundreds of dollars by booking close to the sailing date, especially if you go through a cruise broker or a discounter.

Getting the Best Cruise for Your Dollar

It used to be an article of faith that one travel agent would give you cruise rates identical to those offered by any other. In fact, until airline deregulation in 1978, it was illegal for travel agents to discount the set price, for airline tickets. And by custom, most other bookings—from cruise ships to hotels to car rentals—were also sold at the same price, regardless of the agency. The rare discount or rebate was kept discreetly under the table. In recent years, however, this practice among travel agencies has gradually declined—and cruise travelers benefit.

Like everything in retail, each cruise has a *list* price. However, the actual selling price can vary tremendously: These days, if you ask any 10 passengers on almost any given ship what they're paying per diem, they'll give you 10 sharply different answers. Discounts on the same accommodation can range from 5% on a single fare to 50% on a second fare in a cabin. Approach deep discounts with skepticism. Fewer than a dozen cabins may be offered at the discounted price, they may be inside cabins, and the fare may not include air transportation or transfer.

Though a single, sure-fire path to whopping savings may not exist, you can maximize your chances in several ways:

Full-Service Travel Agents Consider booking with a full-service travel agent. He or she can make your arrangements and deal directly with airlines, cruise companies, car-rental agencies, hotels, and resorts. You won't be charged a service fee—agents make money on commissions from the cruise lines and other suppliers—and you'll eliminate such expenses as long-distance phone calls and postage. Some good agents throw in complimentary flight bags and champagne.

However, don't rely solely on your agent when selecting your cruise. Since most travel agencies book everything from cruises to business flights to theme-park vacations, your local agent may not possess a full knowledge of the cruise industry. Agents may have sailed on some of the ships and seen some ports, but most have acquired their knowledge of competing cruise lines from the same booklets and brochures available to the public. Because agents work on commission, there is some potential conflict of interest. Fortunately, reputable agents remain relatively unbiased.

Cruise-Only Travel Agencies "Cruise-only" travel agencies constitute one of the fastest growing segments of the travel industry, and most major towns or cities have at least one or two. Their knowledgeable employees may have sailed on many of these ships themselves. But that's only one of their strengths. Working in conjunction with specific cruise lines, cruise-only agencies obtain significant discounts by agreeing to sell large blocs of tickets. To make their quotas, they pass along savings to their clients. The discount you get depends on agency, cruise line, season, the ship's popularity, and current demand.

Cruise Travel Clubs Some cruise-only agencies are run as private clubs, and for an annual fee of $25 to $50 offer members a newsletter, flight bags or other free gifts, special benefits to repeat clients, and sometimes, if the agency negotiates a group charter with the cruise line, better rates.

Haggling Shopping around may or may not get you a better deal. A number of cruise-only travel agencies discount every cruise they sell—one agency may sell at fixed prices, while another may charge whatever supply and demand will allow. Even when an agent quotes a particular price, go ahead and ask for a further discount. You have absolutely nothing to lose. If you don't ask for the lowest price, you're probably not going to get it. On the other hand, this ploy is best used by experienced cruisers who know what they're looking for. Beginners may find it's worth paying a little more for the sound advice an experienced agent may offer.

Last-Minute Booking When cruise companies have cancellations or unsold cabins, they use cruise-only agencies and cruise specialists to recoup revenue. The closer it is to the sailing date, the bigger the savings. Typically, discounts range from 25% to more than 60%. To obtain the best discount, you can't book very far in advance (usually only from two weeks to a month) and you have to be flexible—ideally prepared to leave on as little as 24 hours' notice. You might end up spending your vacation at home, or you might luck into the travel bargain of a lifetime.

A caveat: Cabin choice is limited, air transportation may not be included, and you may not get the meal seating you prefer. Also, think about why those cabins haven't been sold. Do you want to sail for less on the leftovers, or pay more to sail on a ship that is consistently full because it is consistently good?

Early Booking Several cruise lines have recently begun offering discounts to customers who book early. In addition to the discount, an early booking gives you a better choice of cabin and sailing date. Some lines guarantee that passengers who book early will receive any lower rate that the line subsequently posts on that particular cruise. Some lines offer an additional discount for paying the full fare in advance.

Swindlers Always be on the lookout for a scam. Though reputable agencies far outnumber crooks, a handful of marketeers use deceptive and unethical tactics. The best way to avoid being fleeced is to deal with an agency that has been in business for at least five years. If you have any doubts about its credibility, consult your local Better Business Bureau or consumer protection agency before you mail in any deposits. Be wary of bait-and-switch tactics: If you are told that an advertised bargain cruise is sold out, *do not* be persuaded to book a more expensive substitute. Also, if you are told that your cruise reservation was canceled due to overbooking and that you must pay extra for a confirmed rescheduled sailing, demand a full refund. Finally, if ever you fail to receive a voucher or ticket on the promised date, place an inquiry immediately.

Choosing the Right Agency or Club How do you find an honest, competent travel agent? Word of mouth is always a safe bet—get recommendations from friends, family, and colleagues, especially those who have cruised before. Or look in the Yellow Pages for agents identified as members of "CLIA" (Cruise Lines International Association) or "ASTA" (American Society of Travel Agents). In theory, there's little difference between the level of service you'll receive from a tiny mom-and-pop agency and a national chain. In practice, however, larger, well-established agencies are more likely to employ experienced cruisers, and smaller agencies may give you more personal attention. Check around and weigh your options carefully. Then phone for an appointment to interview a few prospects. Choose the agent who takes a personal interest in finding the right cruise line for you.

Major cruise publications such as *Cruise Travel Magazine* also list agencies that handle cruises. Here are a few of the better ones:

Ambassador Tours, Inc. (165 Post St., 2nd floor, San Francisco, CA 94108, tel. 415/981–5678 or 800/989–9000).
Cruise Fairs of America (2029 Century Park E, Los Angeles, CA 90067, tel. 310/556–2925 or 800/456–4386).
Cruise Headquarters (4225 Executive Sq. #1200, La Jolla, CA 92037, tel. 619/453–1201 in CA or 800/424–6111).
Cruise Holidays International (9665 Chesapeake Dr., Suite 401, San Diego, CA 92123, tel. 619/279–4780 or 800/866–7245).
The Cruise Line, Inc. (4770 Biscayne Blvd., Penthouse 1, Miami, FL 33137, tel. 800/777–0707).
Cruise Pro (99 Long Ct., Suite 200, Thousand Oaks, CA 91360, tel. 800/222–7447, 800/258–7447 in CA, or 800/433–8747 in Canada).
Cruise Quarters of America (1241 E. Dyer Rd., Suite 110, Santa Ana, CA 92705, tel. 714/549–3445 or 800/648–2444).

Crui$e Value (c/o Golden Bear Travel, 16 Digital Dr., Suite 100, Box 6115, Novato, CA 94948, tel. 415/382–8900 in CA or 800/551–1000).

CruiseMasters (3415 Sepulveda Blvd., Suite 645, Los Angeles, CA 90034, tel. 800/242–9444 or 800/242–9000 in CA).

Cruises of Distinction (460 Bloomfield Ave., Montclair, NJ 07042, tel. 201/744–1331 or 800/634–3445).

Don Ton Cruise Tours (3151 Airway Ave., E–1, Costa Mesa, CA 92626, tel. 800/688–4785).

Kelly Cruises (2001 Midwest Rd., Suite 108, Oak Park, IL 60521, tel. 800/837–7447 or 708/932–8300 in IL).

Landry and Kling East, Inc. Cruise Specialists (1390 S. Dixie Hwy., Suite 1207, Coral Gables, FL 33148, tel. 800/223–2026).

MVP Cruise Club (917 N. Broadway, North Massapequa, NY 11758, tel. 800/253–4242 or 516/541–7782 in NY; $30 annual membership).

South Florida Cruises (5352 N.W. 53rd Ave., Fort Lauderdale, FL 33309, tel. 305/739–7447 or 800/327–7447).

Time to Travel (582 Market St., San Francisco, CA 94104, tel. 415/421–3333 or 800/524–3300).

The Travel Company (El Camino Real, Suite 250, Dept. CT, Atherton, CA 94027, tel. 415/367–6000 or 800/367–6090).

Trips 'n Travel (9592 Harding Ave., Surfside, FL 33154, tel. 800/331–2745 or 305/864–2222 in FL).

Vacations at Sea (4919 Canal St., New Orleans, LA 70119, tel. 800/274–1572 or 504/482–1572 in LA).

White Travel Service, Inc. (127 Park Rd., West Hartford, CT 06119, tel. 203/233–2648 or 800/547–4790).

Videotapes

Most travel agencies have a library of travel tapes, including some on specific cruise ships; usually you can also borrow, rent, or buy tapes directly from the cruise line. As you view the tape, keep in mind that the cruise company made this tape to show its ship to the best advantage. Still, you will get a visual idea of the size and shape of the cabins, dining room, swimming pool, and public rooms; the kinds of attractions, amenities, and entertainment on board; and the ports and islands at which you'll stop.

You can also obtain VHS or Beta videos about many cruises and cruise ships from **Vacations on Video** (1309 E. Northern St., Phoenix, AZ 85020, tel. 602/483–1551; about $20 per tape). **Vacations Ashore & All the Ships at Sea** (173 Minuteman Causeway, Cocoa Beach, FL 32931, tel. 407/868–2131; $90 per year or $25 per issue), a bimonthly video magazine, reviews five ships per issue.

Cruise Brochures

Although a brochure is as promotional as a videotape, it can provide valuable information about a ship and what it has to offer. Make sure the brochures you select are the most recently published versions: Schedules, itineraries, and prices change constantly. Study the maps of the decks and cabin layouts, and be sure to read the fine print to find out just what you'll be getting for your money. Check out the details on fly/cruise programs; optional pre- and post-cruise packages; the ship's credit card and check-cashing policy; embarkation and debarkation procedures; and legal matters of payment, cancellation, insurance, and liability.

Payment

Deposit Most cruises must be reserved with a refundable deposit of $200–$500 per person, depending upon how expensive the cruise is; the balance is to be paid one to two months before you sail. Don't let a travel agent pressure you into paying a larger deposit or paying the balance earlier. If the cruise is less than a month away, however, it may be legitimate for the agency to require you to pay the entire amount immediately.

If possible, pay your deposit and balance via credit card. This gives you some recourse if you need to cancel, and you can ask the credit card company to intercede on your behalf in case of problems. Don't forget to get a receipt.

Handing money over to your travel agent constitutes a contract, so before you pay your deposit, study the cruise brochure to find out the provisions of the cruise contract. What is the payment schedule and cancellation policy? Will there be any additional charges before you can board your ship, such as transfers, port fees, local taxes, or baggage charges? If your air connection requires you to spend an evening in a hotel near the port before or after the cruise, is there an extra cost?

Cancellation If you cancel your reservation 45–60 days prior to your scheduled cruise (the grace period varies from line to line), you may receive your entire deposit or payment back. You will forfeit some or even all of your deposit if you cancel any closer to cruise time. In rare cases, however, if your reason for canceling is unavoidable, the cruise line may decide, at its discretion, to waive some or all of the forfeiture. An average cancellation charge would be $100 one month before sailing, $100 plus 50% of the ticket price 15–30 days before sailing, and $100 plus 75% of the ticket price between 14 days and 24 hours before sailing. If you simply fail to show up when the ship sails, you will lose the entire amount you've paid. Many travel agents also assess a small cancellation fee. Check their policy.

Insurance Cruise lines sell cancellation insurance for about $50 per ticket (the amount varies according to the line, the number of days in the cruise, and the price you paid for the ticket). Such insurance protects you against cancellation fees; it may also reimburse you, on a deductible basis, if your luggage is lost or damaged. Note, however, that there are usually some restrictions. For instance, the trip cancellation policy may insure that you receive a full refund *only* if you cancel and notify the cruise line no less than 72 hours in advance. Some travel agencies and cruise clubs give customers free trip insurance; be sure to ask when booking your cruise.

Before You Go

Tickets, Vouchers, and Other Travel Documents

Some cruise companies will give you your cruise ticket and transfer vouchers (which will get you from the airport to the ship and vice versa) at the time you make the final payment to your travel agent. Depending upon the airline, and whether or not you have purchased a fly/cruise package, you may receive your plane tickets or charter flight vouchers at the same time; you may also receive vouchers for any shore excursions, although most cruise lines prefer to hand those over when you board your ship. There are some cruise companies that mail tickets, either to you or your travel agent, only after they have received payment in full. Should your travel documents not arrive when promised, contact your travel agent or call the cruise line directly on its toll-free line. Occasionally tickets are delivered directly to the ship for those who book late.

Once you board your ship you may be asked to turn over your passport for group immigration clearance or to turn over your return plane ticket so the ship's staff may reconfirm your flight home. Otherwise, be sure to keep all travel documents in a safe place, such as a shipboard safe-deposit box.

Cruise Ships

Celebrity Cruises

MV Horizon
Specifications

Type of ship: Upscale mainstream
Type of cruise: Traditional
Size: Large (46,811 tons)
Number of cabins: 677
Outside cabins: 84%

Passengers: 1,354
Crew: 642 (international)
Officers: Greek
Passenger/crew ratio: 2.1 to 1
Year built: 1990

Chart Symbols. The following symbols are used in the charts in this chapter. D: *Double bed;* K: *King-size bed;* Q: *Queen-size bed;* T: *Twin bed;* U/L: *Upper and lower berths;* ●: *All cabins have this facility;* ○: *No cabins have this facility;* ◑: *Some cabins have this facility*

Cruise Facilities

Ship	Cruise Line	Principle Cruising Regions	Size (in tons)	Type of Ship	Type of Cruise	Per Diem Rates	Length of Cruise	Number of Passengers	Passenger/Crew Ratio	Sanitation Rating*	Disabled Access	Special Dietary Options	Gymnasium	Walking/Jogging Circuit	Swimming Pool	Whirlpool	Sauna/Massage	Deck Sports	Casino	Disco	Cinema/Theater	Library	Boutiques/Gift Shops	Video Arcade	Child Care
Dreamward	Norwegian	Caribbean & Bermuda	41,000	Mainstream	Traditional	$182-$427	7-day	1246		89	●	●	●	●	2	●	●	●	●	●	●	●	●	●	●
Horizon	Celebrity Cruises	Caribbean & Bermuda	46,811	Upscale mainstream	Traditional	$171-$439	7-day	1354		90	●	●	●	●	2	3	●	●	●	●	○	●	●	●	●
Meridian	Celebrity Cruises	Caribbean & Bermuda	30,440	Upscale mainstream	Traditional	$160-$410	7,10,11-day	1106		89	◐	●	●	●	2	3	●	●	●	●	●	●	●	●	●
Queen Elizabeth 2	Cunard Line	Worldwide	67,139	Luxury/Up. mainstream	Traditional	$202-$455	4.5-day	1864		88	◐	●	●	●	4	4	●	●	●	●	●	●	●	●	●
Song of America	Royal Caribbean Cruise Line	Caribbean & Bermuda	37,584	Mainstream	Traditional/Party	$177-$435	10,11-day	1402		86	○	●	●	●	2	○	●	●	●	●	●	○	●	○	◐

*Sanitation ratings are provided by the Vessel Sanitation Program, Center for Environmental Health and Injury Control. Ships are rated on water, food preparation and holding, potential contamination of food, and general cleanliness, storage, and repair. A score of 86 or higher indicates an acceptable level of sanitation. According to the center, "a low score does not necessarily imply an imminent outbreak of gastrointestinal disease." Chart ratings come from the center's May 8,1992 report.

Itinerary **Early fall:** Seven-night cruises leave New York Saturdays for Bermuda, with two nights each at Hamilton and St. George's. **Late fall-winter:** Seven-night loops leave San Juan Saturdays, calling at Martinique, Barbados, St. Lucia, Antigua, and St. Thomas/St. John. **Spring-summer. Same as fall.**

Port tax: $87 per passenger.

Overview As with many huge modern cruise ships, the exterior looks ungainly—primarily because of the long rows of large windows and portholes along the side, squared-off stern, and boxy smokestack (which, like all Celebrity ships, is marked with a large, distinctive X). However, the interior is surprisingly gracious, airy, and comfortable. Because there is no central architectural focus (such as an atrium), the *Horizon* seems more intimate than other 1,300-passenger ships. The design makes the most of natural light through strategically placed oversize windows. The nine passenger decks sport a generous number of bars, entertainment lounges, and ample deck space. Wide corridors, broad staircases, seven elevators, and well-placed signs make it a relatively easy ship on which to get around. Decor is contemporary and attractive, the art work pleasant rather than memorable.

Cabins and Rates

	Beds	Phone	TV	Sitting Area	Fridge	Tub	Per Diem
Deluxe Suites	D	●	●	●	○	●	$367–$439
Deluxe Cabins	D or T/K	●	●	●	○	○	$296–$310
Outside	D or T/K	●	●	○	○	○	$240–$293
Inside	D or T/K	●	●	○	○	○	$171–$239

Cabins are modern and quite roomy. Suites come with butler service. A number of upper priced cabins have tubs with whirlpool jets. The view from many outside cabins on Bermuda Deck is partially obstructed by lifeboats.

Outlet voltage: 110 AC.

Single supplement: 150% of double-occupancy rate.

Discounts: a third or fourth passenger in a cabin is $121. Children 2–12 traveling with two full-paying adults pay $56 per day. Children under 2 travel free. Airfare is not included in the rates.

Sports and Fitness **Health club:** Bright and sunny upper-deck spa with sauna, massage, weight machines, stationary bicycles, rowing machine, treadmill, separate mirrored aerobics area, massage, facial/body treatments.

Walking/jogging: Marina Deck (5 laps=1 mile).
Other sports: Exercise classes, putting green, shuffleboard, snorkeling, trapshooting, ping-pong, three whirlpools, two pools.

Facilities **Public rooms:** Eight bars, three showrooms, disco, teen room/juice bar, casino, restaurant, library/reading room, card room, video arcade.
Shops: Gift shops, specialty boutique, perfume shop, cigarette/liquor store, and photo shop.
Health care: On-board hospital staffed by doctor and nurse. Limited dispensary for prescriptions. Refrigerated insulin storage provided.
Child care: Playroom, teen room on sun deck, preteen and teen youth programs supervised by counselors, baby-sitting arranged with crew member.
Services: Photographer, valet laundry, barber/beauty shop.
Other: Safe-deposit boxes.

Access for Four cabins with 39½-inch doorways are wheelchair-
the Disabled accessible. Public elevators are 35½ inches wide. Certain areas may not be wide enough for wheelchairs. The captain cannot guarantee that wheelchair-bound passengers will be accommodated at every port. Disabled passengers are asked to provide their own small collapsible wheelchairs and to travel with an able-bodied passenger.

SS Meridian *Type of ship:* Upscale
Specifications mainstream
Type of cruise: Traditional
Size: Large (30,440 tons)
Number of cabins: 553
Outside cabins: 54%

Passengers: 1,106
Crew: 580 (international)
Officers: Greek
Passenger/crew ratio: 1.7 to 1
Year built: 1967 (Rebuilt 1990)

Itinerary **Fall:** Seven-day loops leave New York (or, occasionally, Baltimore, Boston, Charleston, Philadelphia, or Fort Lauderdale) for Somerset, Bermuda. **Winter:** Out of San Juan, 10-day cruises call at Aruba, Caracas/La Guaira, Grenada, Barbados, St. Lucia, Martinique, St. Maarten/St. Martin, and St. Thomas/St. John; and 11-day cruises call at Montego Bay (Jamaica), Aruba, Caracas/La Guaira, Grenada, Barbados, Martinique, Virgin Gorda, and Tortola (British Virgin Islands), and St. Thomas/St. John. **Spring–summer:** Same as fall.

Port tax: $90 per passenger.

Overview Originally the *Galileo*, this former transatlantic liner was stretched and totally refurbished before reemerging as the *Meridian*. It now possesses a relaxed, personable charm— it's like staying in someone's home. The beige tile that borders the pool is pretty and unpretentious, and the Zodiac Club's simple terra-cotta theme is quite cozy. Most of the public rooms are located on the same deck, allowing easy access from one to the other.

Cabins and Rates

	Beds	Phone	TV	Sitting Area	Fridge	Tub	Per Diem
Presidential Suite	T	●	●	●	○	●	$395–$410
Starlight Suite	T	●	●	●	○	●	$370–$385
Deluxe Suite	T	●	●	●	○	●	$335–$350
Deluxe Cabin	T or D	●	○	●	○	○	$275–$305
Outside	T or D	●	○	○	○	○	$235–$285
Inside	T, D, or U/L	●	○	○	○	○	$160–$247

Bathtubs in the Presidential, Starlight, and Deluxe suites have whirlpool jets. The outside cabins on the Horizon deck have picture windows. Many outside cabins on the Atlantic Deck have an obstructed or partially obstructed view.

Outlet Voltage: 110/220 AC

Single supplement: 150% of double-occupancy rate.

Discounts: A third or fourth passenger in a cabin pays $56 per diem. Children 2–12 sharing a cabin with two full-paying adults pay $35–$99 per diem. Children under 2 travel free. Airfare is not included in the rates.

Sports and Fitness **Health club:** Stationary bicycles, weight machines, treadmill, rowing machines, sauna, massage.
Walking/jogging: Jogging track on Captain Deck (8 laps = 1 mile).
Other sports: Exercise classes, putting green and driving range, shuffleboard, snorkeling, trapshooting, ping-pong, pool, children's pool, three outdoor whirlpools.

Facilities **Public rooms:** Seven bars, four entertainment lounges (including main showroom), card room/library, casino, chapel/synagogue, cinema, dining room, disco, Lido, video arcade.
Shops: Boutique, perfumerie, drug store, photo shop, beauty salon/barber shop.
Health care: A doctor is on call.
Child care: Playroom with large windows, patio, and wading pool; youth programs with counselors when needed; baby-sitting arranged privately with crew member.
Services: Photographer, valet laundry, barber/beauty shop.
Other: Safe-deposit boxes.

Access for the Disabled Two cabins have wheelchair access. Celebrity requires that passengers in wheelchairs travel with an able-bodied adult who will take full responsibility for them in case of an emergency.

For More   Celebrity Cruises (5200 Blue Lagoon Dr., Miami, FL
Information   33126, tel. 800/437–3111).

Cunard Line Limited

RMS Queen   *Type of ship:* Luxury/   *Passengers:* 1,864
Elizabeth 2   upscale mainstream   *Crew:* 1,025 (international)
Specifications   *Type of cruise:* Traditional   *Officers:* British
               Size: Megaship/liner   *Passenger/crew ratio:* 1.8 to 1
               (67,139 tons)   (varies according to cabin
               Number of cabins: 957   price)
               Outside cabins: 70%   *Year built:* 1969

Itinerary   **Year-round:** Several five-day transatlantic crossings run be-
              tween New York and Southampton, England. Several loop
              cruises leave New York for the Caribbean, calling at St.
              Maarten/St. Martin, Barbados, Martinique, and St. Thom-
              as/St. John. A 100-day circumnavigation of the globe leaves
              New York, calling at 33 ports on six continents, including
              Fort Lauderdale, several Caribbean islands, the east and
              west coasts of South America, Acapulco, Los Angeles, sev-
              eral Hawaiian ports, Auckland, the Australian coast, Bali,
              Singapore, Bangkok, Hong Kong, other Far East ports,
              along the Panama Canal, Southampton (U.K.), and various
              Mediterranean ports. Several 11- and 13-day Panama Canal
              Transits leave New York, calling at Fort Lauderdale, St.
              Thomas/St. John, Cartagena (Colombia), Acapulco, and
              Los Angeles. Several seven-day cruises sail from New York
              to Bermuda. Several four-day cruises sail along the North-
              eastern U.S. and Canadian coast, calling at Bar Harbor,
              Halifax, and Martha's Vineyard. Itineraries change, often
              with little notice, from month to month; it's best to check
              with Cunard for the latest information on the *QE2*'s itine-
              raries.

              Port tax: $135–$155 per passenger.

Overview   Built in 1969 as the last of the true ocean liners, the *QE2* is
             designed as both a two-class crossing ship and a one-class
             cruise ship. Even when cruising, however, passengers are
             assigned (according to their per diem) to one of four restau-
             rants, each offering a different level of quality and service.
             Outside the cabin and restaurants, however, all passengers
             enjoy the same level of facilities and amenities.

             The ship has undergone numerous refits, including one that
             transformed it into a military carrier during the Falklands
             War. Taking the *QE2*'s unique historical and social position
             to heart, Cunard continues to invest its flagship with the
             best, the most, and the largest of whatever can fit into this
             floating city. An $8 million refurbishment completed in De-
             cember 1992 saw the redecoration of public rooms and the
             addition of an art gallery and one of the most comprehen-
             sive spas on land or sea.

             Big as it is—13 stories high, three football fields long—the
             QE2 possesses a grace that eludes new megaships. With its

high ceilings, wood paneling, and expensive furnishings, the interior of the *QE2* looks less like a ship than it does a grand hotel. The ship features a magnificent shopping arcade with stores like Harrods and Gucci. In addition, you'll find a spa, an American Express office, a florist, a nursery staffed with professional nannies, and a large, well-equipped computer center. Passengers on the transatlantic run have use of a 30-car garage and a even dog kennel. If you look closely, you will see signs of its age. Still, everything that a passenger could want is on board somewhere. Some passengers may find it too large, others too proud, but amid the wealth of space, service, and options, the *QE2* remains a beautiful ship, filled with pizzazz and excitement, that still reserves a few private corners to remind you of its essentially British dignity.

The quality of the restaurant to which you are assigned depends on the price of your cabin. The gourmet Queen's Grill and Princess Grill are elegant, single-seating restaurants that are reserved for occupants of the suites and the luxury and ultra-deluxe cabins. In these two restaurants passengers can order anything they want. Both grills are consistently awarded four stars by international food critics—and with good reason, since they serve the finest food afloat. The larger, single-seating Columbia Restaurant is for the occupants of the deluxe and higher-priced outside cabins, and while the cuisine is beautifully prepared and served, it isn't quite up to the standards of the Queen's Grill or Princess Grill. All others are served in two seatings in the Mauritania Restaurant. Were it on any other ship, the Mauritania Restaurant would be rated very highly, but it suffers by comparison with the *QE2*'s other restaurants. In addition, on transatlantic crossings there is a special early dinner for children so parents may dine on their own. Spa meals are available, but other dietary requests should be made at least three weeks before sailing. Two formal evenings are held each week, though dinners in the Queen's Room and the Princess Grill are never casual. Unsupervised kosher meals are available only in the Columbia Restaurant. The ship's wine cellar stocks more than 20,000 bottles of wine.

The Lido serves early morning coffee and pastries, a buffet breakfast and lunch, plus hamburgers and hot dogs. Health-conscious passengers can take their breakfast, and sometimes their lunch, from a spa buffet. An International Food Bazaar is dished up occasionally in the Mauritania Restaurant. Other food service includes midmorning bouillon, a traditional British high tea, and a midnight buffet.

Cabins and Rates

	Beds	Phone	TV	Sitting Area	Fridge	Tub	Per Diem*
Suite *Queen's Grill*	Q or T/D	●	●	●	●	●	$2,422–$4,155 (per) suite
Luxury *Queen's Grill*	Q or T	●	●	●	●	●	$554–$1,334
Ultra Deluxe *Queen's/ Princess*	T	●	●	●	●	●	$387–$769
Deluxe *Columbia Restaurant*	T	●	●	○	○	●	$325–$527
Outside *Columbia Mauritania*	T	●	●	○	○	◐	$258–$505
Inside *Mauritania Restaurant*	T or U/L	●	●	○	○	○	$202–$370

The wide range of daily rates reflects differences between cabins in the lower-priced categories as well as differences between itineraries.

Suites accommodate up to four passengers, at no extra charge per passenger, making them more economical for a family of four than two luxury cabins. Penthouse Suites, with verandas and whirlpools, are the largest, most luxurious accommodations afloat; first-class cabins (all with VCRs) compare with those of any luxury ship. Luxury cabins, except No. 8184, have private verandas. Lifeboats partially obstruct the view from some cabins on the Sports Deck, and Boat Deck cabins look onto a public promenade.

Outlet voltage: 110 AC.

Single supplement: 175%–200% of double-occupancy rate; several single cabins are available at $179–$726 a day.

Discounts: A third or fourth passenger in a cabin pays half the minimum fare in the cabin's restaurant grade. Various discounts exist for combining consecutive itineraries, booking and paying early on the World Cruise, and arranging your own airfare.

Sports and Fitness **Health club:** Thalassotherapy pool, inhalation room, French hydrotherapy bath treatment, computerized nutritional and lifestyle evaluation, aerobics and exercise classes, weight machines, Lifecycles, Rowers, Stairmasters, treadmills, sauna, whirlpools, hydrocalisthenics, massage.
Walking/jogging: Jogging track (3.5 laps = 1 mile).
Other sports: Putting green and golf driving range, paddle

tennis, table tennis, shuffleboard, tetherball, trapshooting, volleyball, two outdoor and two indoor swimming pools, four whirlpools, private whirlpools in suites.

Facilities **Public rooms:** Six bars, five entertainment lounges, card room, casino, chapel/synagogue, cinema, Epson computer center, disco, executive boardroom, library/reading room, Lido, piano bar, video-game room.

Shops: Arcade with men's formal rental shop, Harrods, designer boutiques (Gucci, Christian Dior, Louis Vuitton), florist, beauty center, barber shop.

Health care: Extensive hospital fully staffed by doctors and nurses.

Child care: Playroom, teen center, baby-sitting, wading pool, youth programs run by counselors.

Services: Full-service laundry, dry-cleaning, valet service, laundromat, ironing room, photographer, film-developing service.

Other: American Express foreign exchange and cash center, garage, kennel, safe-deposit boxes, Alcoholics Anonymous.

Access for the Disabled A few cabins have wide doors, low threshold ledges, and specially equipped bathrooms. However, wheelchairs may not be carried aboard tenders, so passengers who use wheelchairs may not have access to every port.

For More Information Cunard Line Limited (555 Fifth Ave., New York, NY 10017, tel. 800/221–4770).

Norwegian Cruise Line

MS Dreamward
Specifications

Type of ship: Mainstream	*Passengers:* 1,246
Type of cruise: Traditional	*Crew:* 482 (international)
Size: Large (41,000 tons)	*Officers:* Norwegian
Number of cabins: 623	*Passenger/crew ratio:* 2.5 to 1
Outside cabins: 85%	*Year built:* 1992

Itinerary **Fall–spring:** Alternating seven-day loops out of Ft. Lauderdale call at Grand Cayman, Cozumel/Playa del Carmen (Mexico), and a private island; or at Nassau, San Juan, and St. Thomas/St. John. **Summer:** Seven-day loops out of New York call at St. George's and Hamilton (Bermuda).

Port tax: $82 per passenger.

Overview In December 1992 NCL introduced the *Dreamward* a sleek ship that utilizes terracing extensively (both forward and aft) to provide unobstructed panoramic views from two dining rooms, the Sun Deck pool, and the show lounge. On this ship, NCL has tossed out the mega-dining room–concept in favor of four smaller formal dining rooms each with a more intimate ambience. The largest, the Terrace, seats only 282 on several levels and has windows on three sides. A variety of special menus and theme meals are available in the various dining rooms; all have children's menus. Dinner has two seatings, but breakfast and lunch are open, so you can try the other restaurants. Hamburgers and hot dogs are served at the casual Sports Bar & Grill. The *Dreamward* offers the usual festive shows, but with a twist: A proscenium stage in the Stardust Lounge allows the production of elaborate full-length Broadway-style shows. After the show, the Stardust Lounge metamorphoses into a late-night lounge and disco. Two-deck-high Casino Royale offers roulette, craps, blackjack, and slot machines. In keeping with NCL's "Athlete's Fleet" approach, the *Dreamward* has a series of sports cruises with players on board from championship teams—including football, golf, tennis, hockey, basketball, baseball, and volleyball. The Sports Bar & Grill transmits live ESPN and NFL broadcasts on multiple screens. There's plenty of space for relaxing on the five-tier Sun Deck, and the especially broad Promenade Deck is good for walking and jogging.

Cabins and Rates		Beds	Phone	TV	Sitting Area	Fridge	Tub	Per Diem
Grand Deluxe Suite	T/Q	●	●	●	●	●		$406–$427
Suite	T/Q	●	●	●	●	○		$313–$335
Outside	T/Q	●	●	●	○	○		$246–$313
Inside	T/Q	●	●	○	○	○		$182–$232

The *Dreamward* has an unusually high percentage of outside cabins, most with picture windows. Some cabins on the Norway deck have obstructed views. The suites have floor-to-ceiling windows, and some have private balconies. Special suite amenities include daily fruit baskets, champagne and trays of hors d'oeuvres, and concierge service. Adjoining suites are available on the Norway, International, and Star decks. Outside cabins have couches that convert into beds. Deluxe suites can accommodate up to four people, and adjoining U-shape suites work well for families of up to six.

Outlet voltage: 110 AC.

Single supplement: 150%–200% of double-occupancy rate.

Other discounts: A third or fourth passenger in a cabin (including children) pays $99 per diem. You get up to $300 off for arranging your own airfare.

Sports and Fitness **Health club:** Lifecycles, Lifesteps, exercise equipment, Jacuzzis, a variety of massage treatments.
Walking/jogging: Jogging track on Promenade Deck.
Other sports: Basketball court, exercise course, two pools, golf range.

Facilities **Public rooms:** Four restaurants, six bars, entertainment lounge/theater, nightclub, casino, ice cream parlor (at extra cost), library, video-game room, conference center.
Shops: Gift shops and boutiques, beauty salon/barber.
Health care: Doctor on call.
Child care: Supervised children's playroom with organized kids' program.
Other: Safe-deposit boxes.

Access for the disabled All decks and activities are wheelchair-accessible, except the Sky Deck and public lavatories. Travel with an able-bodied companion is required. Six specially-equipped cabins are accessible to wheelchairs, others for hearing-impaired passengers.

For More Information Norwegian Cruise Line (95 Merrick Way, Coral Gables, FL 33134, tel. 800/327–7030).

Royal Caribbean Cruise Line

MS Song of America *Specifications*

Type of ship: Mainstream	*Passengers:* 1,402
Type of cruise: Traditional/party	*Crew:* 535 (international)
	Officers: Norwegian
Size: Large (37,584 tons)	*Passenger/crew ratio:* 2.6 to 1
Number of cabins: 701	*Year built:* 1982
Outside cabins: 57%	

Itinerary **Fall:** Ten-day loops out of New York call at St. George's and Hamilton (Bermuda). **Winter–spring:** Ten- and 11-day cruises between San Juan and Miami call at St. Thomas/St. John, St. Maarten/St. Martin, St. Lucia, Tobago, Guadaloupe, Dominica, St. Croix, and CocoCay (Bahamas). **Summer:** Same as fall.

Port tax: $92 per passenger.

Overview The *Song of America* is unusually handsome. Despite its size, it looks more like a yacht than a cruise ship, though its width gives it space and stability that a yacht could never manage. Plentiful chrome, mirrors, and overhead lights give the ship a flashier look than other RCCL vessels, but the overall effect is clean, crisp, and airy. As on its sister ships, public rooms on the *Song of America* are patterned after famous musical comedies, including the Guys and Dolls Night Club.

Cabins and Rates

	Beds	Phone	TV	Sitting Area	Fridge	Tub	Per Diem
Owner's Suite	D or T	●	●	●	●	●	$413–$435
Suite	T	●	●	●	●	●	$370–$392
Deluxe Outside	T	●	●	○	○	○	$285–$306

Standard Outside	T or T/D	●	●	○	○	○	$249–$270
Inside	T or T/D	●	●	○	○	○	$177–$256

Cabins are above the waterline, but suites on the Promenade Deck look onto a public area.

Outlet voltage: 110/220 AC.

Single supplement: 150% of double-occupancy rate; however, less expensive singles are available if you are willing to wait for your cabin assignment until embarkation time.

Discounts: A third or fourth passenger in a cabin pays $99 per diem. Senior citizen discounts are offered on specific sailings. You get a discount for arranging your own airfare, and for early booking—the earlier you book, the lower your cabin rate (excluding inside cabins and suites).

Sports and Fitness **Health club:** Rowing machines, treadmills, stationary bikes, massage, men's and women's saunas.
Walking/jogging: Unobstructed circuits on Sun Deck and Promenade Deck.
Other sports: Aerobics, golf putting, table tennis, ring toss, snorkeling lessons, shuffleboard, skeet shooting, two pools.

Facilities **Public rooms:** Six bars, four entertainment lounges, card room, casino, cinema, disco, Lido, piano bar.
Shops: Gift shop, drugstore, beauty salon/barber.
Health care: Doctor on call.
Child care: Youth programs with counselors during holidays and in summer, baby-sitting arranged privately with crew member.
Services: Full-service laundry, dry-cleaning, photographer, film processing.
Other: Safe-deposit boxes.

Access for the Disabled Wheelchair access is limited. Doorways have lips, and public bathrooms are not specially equipped. Disabled passengers must bring a portable wheelchair and be escorted by an able-bodied companion. Tenders are easy to board; if seas are rough, crew members will carry disabled passengers and their wheelchairs on board.

For More Information Royal Caribbean Cruise Line (1050 Caribbean Way, Miami, FL 33132, tel. 800/327–6700).

4 Exploring Bermuda

By Honey Naylor

The major contributor to Fodor's New Orleans *and* Caribbean, *Honey Naylor has worked on various other Fodor's guides. Her featured articles have appeared in* Travel & Leisure, USA Today, New Orleans Magazine, Travel-Holiday, *and other national publications.*

Bermuda is nothing if not colorful. The streets are lined with hedges of hibiscus and oleander, and rolling green hills are shaded by tall palms and casuarina trees. The limestone buildings are painted in pretty pastels (pink and white seem to be most popular), and their gleaming white roofs are steeply pitched to channel the rain upon which Bermudians depend—the island has no freshwater lakes or streams. In addition, many houses have quaint butteries, miniature cottages that were once used as ice houses. House numbers are a relatively new phenomenon on the island, although most houses have names, such as Tranquillity, Struggle, and Last Penny. Another architectural feature indigenous to Bermuda is moon gates. These freestanding stone arches can be found in gardens all over the island, and Bermudians favor them as backdrops for wedding pictures.

For exploring purposes, we've divided Bermuda into four separate tours. The first tour is of Hamilton, the island's capital. Hamilton is of primary interest for its harbor, its shops—housed in small pastel-colored buildings—and the government buildings, where visitors can watch sessions of Parliament. In addition, the town is the major departure point for sightseeing boats, ferries, and the pink-and-blue buses that ramble all over the island. Don't confuse Hamilton town with the parish of the same name—Hamilton town is in Pembroke Parish. The second tour is of the Town of St. George on the eastern end of the island, near the site of Bermuda's first settlement. History mavens will find much of interest in St. George's, which boasts several noteworthy 17th-century buildings. The third tour explores the West End, the site of the sleepy hamlet of Somerset and the Royal Naval Dockyard, a former British naval shipyard that is home to the Maritime Museum and a developing tourist center. The West End is in Sandys Parish, which can be pronounced either "Sandies" or "Sands."

The fourth tour is a rambling journey through the island's other parishes that is best done by moped, bicycle, or taxi. The parishes date back to 1616, when Bermuda was first surveyed and the island was divided into eight tribes or parishes, each named for an investor in the Bermuda Company, an offshoot of the Virginia Company, which controlled the island until 1684. The parishes are Sandys, Southampton, Warwick, Paget, Smith's, Hamilton, Pembroke, and Devonshire. St. George's, which was considered public land in the early days, is the ninth parish and includes the Town of St. George. Bermudians customarily identify sites on the island by the parish in which they are located: "It's in Pembroke," a resident will say, or "It's in Warwick." The main roads connecting the parishes are self-explanatory: North Shore Road, Middle Road, South Road, and Harbour Road. Almost all traffic traversing the island's 20-mile length uses these roads, although some 1,200 smaller roads crisscross the island. Visitors will see several "tribe roads" that date back to the initial survey of the island; many of these are now no more than country lanes, and some are dead ends. As you travel around the island you'll see small brown-and-white signs pointing to the Railway Trail. Built along the route of Bermuda's old railway line, the trail is now a peaceful route reserved for pedestrians and cyclists (*see* Off the Beaten Track, *below*).

Tour 1: Hamilton

Numbers in the margin correspond to points of interest on the Tour 1: Hamilton map.

Historically, Bermudians were seafarers, and the government relied for revenues on the duties paid on ships' cargoes. Ships were required by law to anchor in the harbor at St. George's to declare their goods, but most captains preferred to anchor closer to their homes, and the law was largely ignored. To combat the loss of revenues, legislation was passed in 1790 to establish a second port and customs house at Crow Lane Harbour (now Hamilton Harbour). Largely because of Hamilton's excellent harbor and central location, the seat of government was moved from St. George's to Hamilton on January 1, 1815. Today, the capital is home to about a quarter of the island's 58,460 residents.

❶ Your first stop should be the **Visitors Service Bureau** in the Ferry Terminal Building, where the friendly staff can provide you with maps and brochures. Step out of the bureau onto the capital's main avenue, **Front Street.** Running alongside the harbor, Front Street bustles with small cars, mopeds, bicycles, buses, pedestrians, and the occasional horse-drawn carriage. It's fun to imagine what the street must have looked like prior to the arrival of automobiles in 1946. From 1931 to 1946, railroad tracks ran along Front Street, carrying "Old Rattle and Shake," as the Bermuda Railway was called. Today, Front Street is lined with colorful little buildings, many with balconies and arcades that house shops and boutiques selling everything from imported woolens to perfumes and cosmetics. This is the main shopping area on the island, and shoppers will probably want to spend plenty of time—and money—here (*see* Chapter 5, Shopping).

The docks behind the Ferry Terminal are the departure points for ferries making the short trip to Paget and Warwick parishes, or the longer trip across the Great Sound to the West End. Next to the terminal are the slips for glass-bottom boats and other sightseeing vessels that take passengers on excursions to the Sea Gardens, St. George's, and Dockyard. Beyond these is **No. 1 Shed,** the pink passenger-ship terminal (two other terminals are situated farther east on Front Street). During high season, a cruise ship is usually moored in the harbor—all but the largest ships, such as the *QE2,* can sail right into Hamilton Harbour. During the

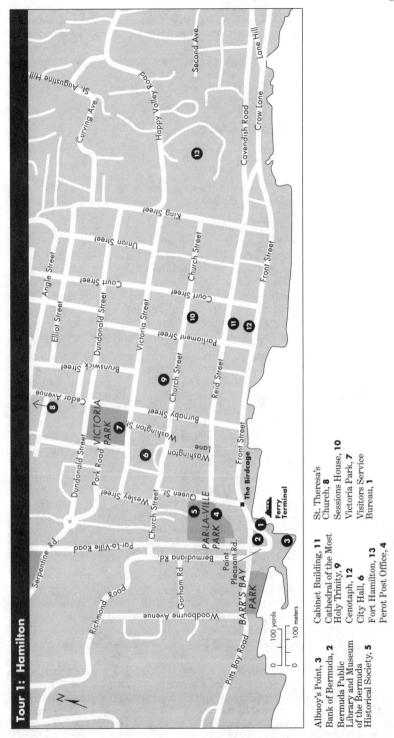

Tour 1: Hamilton

Second Ave.
Lane Hill
Crow Lane
St. Augustine Hill
Curving Ave.
Happy Valley Road
Cavendish Road
13
King Street
Union Street
Court Street
Angle Street
Court Street
Church Street
Front Street
Elliot Street
Dundonald Street
Victoria Street
Parliament Street
10
11
12
Brunswick Street
Church Street
9
Reid Street
Cedar Avenue
8
Burnaby Street
VICTORIA PARK
7
Washington St.
Washington Lane
Dundonald Street
Park Road
6
Front Street
Serpentine Rd.
Wesley Street
Church Street
Queen St.
PAR-LA-VILLE PARK
5
4
The Birdcage
Richmond Road
Par-la-Ville Road
Bermudiana Rd.
Point Pleasant Rd.
2
1
3
Gorham Rd.
BARR'S BAY PARK
Ferry Terminal
Woodbourne Avenue
Pitts Bay Road

0   100 yards
0   100 meters

N

Albuoy's Point, **3**
Bank of Bermuda, **2**
Bermuda Public
Library and Museum
of the Bermuda
Historical Society, **5**

Cabinet Building, **11**
Cathedral of the Most
Holy Trinity, **9**
Cenotaph, **12**
City Hall, **6**
Fort Hamilton, **13**
Perot Post Office, **4**

St. Theresa's
Church, **8**
Sessions House, **10**
Victoria Park, **7**
Visitors Service
Bureau, **1**

low season (mid-November–March 31), No. 1 Shed is the site of regularly scheduled afternoon teas, fashion shows, and performances by the Gombey Dancers (*see* Chapter 10, The Arts and Nightlife).

The oddly shaped traffic box at Heyl's Corner, at the intersection of Front and Queen streets, is known as the **"Birdcage,"** from which the police (locally known as "bobbies" as in Great Britain) sometimes direct traffic. Named for its designer, Michael "Dickey" Bird, the traffic box has been a Hamilton landmark for more than 20 years. The corner itself is named for J. B. Heyl, a Southerner who came to Bermuda in the 19th century and opened an apothecary shop on Queen Street.

Visitors interested in coins should cross Point Pleasant Road and go up to the mezzanine of the **Bank of Bermuda.** British and Spanish coins, many of them ancient, are displayed in glass cases. The collection includes some pieces of "hog money," Bermuda's first currency, which was issued by the Bermuda Company in 1615. Hog money, the oldest of all British colonial coins, is stamped on one side with a replica of the *Sea Venture* and on the other with an unattractive wild hog ringed with the words "Somer Ilands." Pigs, which had survived a shipwreck or been released by Spanish sailors, were the only inhabitants encountered by Sir George Somers and his crew when they foundered on Bermuda's shores in 1609. *Admission free. Open Mon.– Thurs. 9:30–3, Fri. 9:30–4:30.*

Following Point Pleasant Road toward the water, you'll come to **Albuoy's Point,** a pleasant waterfront park with benches, trees, and a splendid view of the activity in the harbor. Nearby is the **Royal Bermuda Yacht Club,** which was built in the 1930s. The idea for the yacht club was conceived in 1844 beneath the Calabash Tree at Walsingham, and Prince Albert gave permission for the club to use the word "Royal" in 1845. Today, royalty, international yachting celebrities, and the local elite hobnob at the posh club, which sponsors the Newport–Bermuda Yacht Race.

Barr's Bay Park to the west also affords a good view of the Yacht Club and the harbor. Opposite the Bermudiana Hotel on Front Street, steps and a ramp lead from the street to the park's vast expanse of green grass, its benches, and scenic vistas.

If you plan to do a lot of exploring, visit the **Bermuda Book-Store,** on Front and Queen streets, to buy a copy of the *Bermuda Islands Guide* ($4.95). The paperback atlas contains every lane, tribe road, alley, and landmark on the island. The bookstore, a marvelous Dickensian place with creaky wood floors, is filled with books about the island.

From the bookstore, continue along Queen Street to the **Perot Post Office,** a white two-story edifice that dates back to around 1842. Still a post office, this shuttered building is where Bermuda's first postage stamps originated. The island's first postmaster was William Bennet Perot. Appointed in 1821, Perot used to meet arriving steamers to collect the mail, stash it in his beaver hat, and then stroll around Hamilton to deliver it. Customers wishing to post a letter paid Perot, who hand-stamped each letter. Obviously, the postmaster had to be at his station to do this, which annoyed Perot, who preferred pottering around in the garden. Local historians credit Perot's friend, the pharmacist J. B. Heyl, for the idea for Bermuda's first book of stamps. Heyl suggested that Perot make a whole sheet of postmarks, write "Wm B. Perot" on each postmark, and sell the sheet for a shilling. People could then tear off a postmark, paste it on a letter, and post it—without having to extricate Mr. Perot from the garden shrubbery. The extremely rare Perot stamps, some of which are in the Queen's Royal Stamp Collection, are now coveted by collectors. In 1986, one of them sold at auction in Chicago for $135,000. *Queen St., tel. 809/295-5151. Admission free. Open weekdays 9-5.*

Time Out The garden where Perot liked to pass his time is now **Par-la-Ville Park,** a pleasant spot that occupies almost an entire block. The Queen Street entrance (there's another on Par-la-Ville Road) is next to the post office. Paths wind through the luxuriant gardens, and the park benches are ideal for picnicking or a short rest. At noon you may have trouble finding a place to sit, because this is a favorite lunch spot of Hamilton office workers. One block along Queen Street is a Kentucky Fried Chicken franchise (open daily 11-10).

Next to the post office is a giant rubber tree from British Guiana (now Guyana) that was planted by Perot. On a visit to Bermuda, Mark Twain lamented that the rubber tree didn't bear fruit in the form of hot-water bottles and rubber overshoes. The tree is in the front yard of the Georgian house where Mr. Perot and his family lived. Now the **⑤ Bermuda Public Library** and **Museum of the Bermuda Historical Society,** the house is a wonderful find for history buffs. The library, which was founded in 1839, moved to its present quarters in the 1940s. One early librarian was an eccentric gentleman with the Pickwickian name of Florentius Frith, who rode in from the country on horseback and struck terror into the heart of anyone who interrupted his chess games to check out a book. The reference section of the library has virtually every book ever written about Bermuda, as well as a collection on microfilm of Bermudian newspapers dating back to 1787. The collection of rare books contains a 1624 edition of John Smith's *Generall Historie of Virginia, New England and the Somers Isles*. In the museum's entrance hall are portraits of Sir George Somers and his wife, painted about 1605; portraits of Postmaster Perot and his wife can be seen in the back room. Notice Admiral Sir George Somers's lodestone (circa 1600), used for magnetizing compass needles, and a Bermuda map from 1622 that shows the division of the island into 25-acre shares by the original Bermuda Company. The museum also contains an eclectic collection of old English coins and Confederate money; Bermuda silver; Oriental porcelains; portraits of the major investors in the Bermuda Company; and pictures of horse-and-buggy Bermuda juxtaposed with modern-day scenes. There are several cedar pieces, including two Queen Anne chairs from about 1740; a handsome grandfather clock; a Waterford chandelier; handmade palmetto hats; and a sedan chair from around 1770 that is beginning to show its age. Ask to see the letter from George Washington, written "to the inhabitants of Bermuda" in 1775, asking for gunpowder. *13 Queen St. Library: tel. 809/295–2905. Admission free. Open weekdays 9:30–6, Sat. 9:30–5. Museum: tel. 809/295–2487. Donation: $2. Open Mon.–Sat. 9:30–12:30 and 1:30–5:30.*

Time Out **Fourways Pastry Shop** (Reid St., at the entrance to Washington Mall) and the **Gourmet Store** (Windsor Place Mall, across Queen St. from the library), both operated by Fourways Inn, are great places to relax over diet-destroying pastries.

Continue up Queen Street, or cut through Washington Mall, to Church Street. Set back from the street behind a lawn, fountains, and a lily pond is **City Hall.** Built in 1960, the large white structure is topped by a weather vane shaped like the *Sea Venture.* Massive cedar doors open into a large lobby that boasts huge chandeliers, high ceilings, and a portrait gallery. The regal portrait of Queen Elizabeth II was painted by Curtis Hooper and unveiled on April 29, 1987, by the Duke of Gloucester. Oil paintings of all Bermuda's mayors hang here as well. Behind tall cedar doors on the right is the Benbow Collection of stamps. The City Hall Theatre is often the venue for musical, dance, and theatrical performances. A handsome cedar staircase leads to the second floor exhibition galleries (*see* below). *Church St., tel. 809/292–1234. Admission free. Open weekdays 9:30–5.*

The East Exhibition Room on the second floor of City Hall houses the **Bermuda National Gallery,** the island's only climate-controlled gallery. Opened in 1992, the gallery displays European paintings from the early 16th century to the 19th century, including works by Thomas Gainsborough, Sir Joshua Reynolds, and George Romney; 20th-century lithographs, sculptures, acrylics, and oils; and an extensive collection showcasing Bermudian artists. *East Wing, City Hall, Church St., Hamilton, tel. 809/295–9428. Admission: $3 adults, children under 16 free. Open Mon.–Sat. 10–4, Sun. 12:30–4. Closed holidays.*

Changing exhibits are displayed in the Bermuda Society of Arts Gallery. The annual Autumn Members' Show is an exhibition of watercolors, oils, and sculpture. *West Wing, City Hall, Church St., Hamilton, tel. 809/292–3824. Admission free. Open weekdays 10–4, Sat. 9–noon. Closed holidays.*

7 Behind City Hall on Victoria Street, **Victoria Park** has a sunken garden, trees, and a Victorian bandstand, where concerts are sometimes held in the summer. The 4-acre park, built in 1887 in honor of Queen Victoria's Golden Jubilee, opened with great fanfare in 1890. The park is perfectly safe when filled with people, but it isn't a good place to wander alone—some fairly seedy-looking characters hang out here.

Cedar Avenue forms the eastern border of Victoria Park.
8 Follow it north for two blocks to **St. Theresa's Church,** a Roman Catholic church built in 1927 in Spanish Mission style. St. Theresa's serves as head of the island's six Roman Catholic churches. During a visit in 1968, Pope Paul VI presented Bermuda's Roman Catholic diocese with a gold and silver chalice that is housed in this church. *Cedar Ave. and Elliot St., tel. 809/292–0607. Open daily 8–7.*

Return to Victoria Street and walk down Washington Street, a one-block boulevard that is the site of the **Central Bus Terminal.** Pink-and-blue buses depart from here to all points on the island. Stop at the kiosk on the median to pick up bus and ferry schedules, and to buy discounted bus tokens for future use.

Time Out   Executives, secretaries, shoppers, and store owners flock to The Spot for breakfast, plate lunches, burgers, sandwiches, and coffee. In business for more than 40 years, this simple little restaurant serves full meals for about $8 and sandwiches for about $3. *6 Burnaby St., tel. 809/292–6293. Open Mon., Tues., Thurs.–Sat. 6:30–8. Closed Wed. and Sun.*

One of the island's most impressive structures is the
9 **Cathedral of the Most Holy Trinity,** the seat of the Anglican Church of Bermuda. The cathedral is the second church to have been built on this site: Twelve years after its completion in 1872, Trinity Church was burned to the ground by an arsonist who torched several houses of worship on the island. Work began on the present church the following year, and it was consecrated in 1911. Designed in Early English style with Gothic flourishes, the church is constructed of Bermuda limestone and materials imported from Scotland, Nova Scotia, France, Ireland, and Indiana. The tower rises to a height of 143 feet, and the clerestory in the nave is supported by piers of polished Scottish granite. The four smaller columns in each aisle were added after a hurricane shook the cathedral—and its architect—during construction. The altar in the Lady Chapel is of Italian marble, and above

it is a copy of Andrea del Sarto's *Madonna and Child*. In the south transept, the Warrior Chapel was dedicated in 1977 to honor those who serve in the armed forces of the Crown, and to commemorate those who died in service to their country. The Great Warrior Window is a memorial to 85 Bermudian men who died in World War I; the flags represent military units of Bermuda and England. The choir stalls and bishop's throne are of carved English oak, and the pulpit is a replica of the one in St. Giles Cathedral, Edinburgh. On a wall near the lectern, the Canterbury Cross, set in stone taken from the walls of Canterbury Cathedral, is a copy of one made in Kent in the 8th century. The stained-glass windows are lovely; note especially the Angel Window on the east wall of the north transept, which was made by local artist Vivienne Gilmore Gardner. *Church St., tel. 809/292-4033. Open daily 8-7.*

The eye-catching Italianate edifice on the next block is ❿ **Sessions House,** home of the House of Assembly (the lower house of Parliament) and the Supreme Court. The original two-story structure was built in 1817; the Florentine towers and colonnade, decorated with red terra-cotta, were added in 1887 to commemorate Queen Victoria's Golden Jubilee. The Victoria Jubilee Clock Tower made its striking debut at midnight, December 31, 1893. Bermuda's Parliament, which is the world's third oldest after Iceland's and England's, met for the first time in 1620 in St. Peter's Church in St. George's. It later moved to the State House, where deliberations were held for almost 200 years until the capital was moved to Hamilton. In its present location, the House of Assembly meets on the second floor, where business is conducted in a style befitting such a venerable body. The Sergeant-at-Arms precedes the Speaker into the chamber, bearing a silver-gilt mace. Introduced in 1921, the mace is fashioned after a James I mace in the Tower of London. The Speaker, in wig and flowing black robe, solemnly calls the meeting to order with a cedar gavel made from an old belfry tree that has been growing in St. Peter's churchyard since before 1620. The proceedings are no less ceremonious and colorful in the Supreme Court on the lower floor, where judges in red robes and full wigs hear the arguments of barristers in black robes and wigs. Visitors are welcome to watch the proceedings in the Assembly and the Supreme Court, but you must call to find out when sessions are scheduled. *Parliament St., between Reid and Church Sts., tel. 809/292-7408. Admission free. Open weekdays 9-5. Closed holidays.*

The next street over from Reid Street is Court Street. Although Court Street is safe during daylight hours, it is not advisable to wander around here at night. Bermuda doesn't have much of a drug problem, but what traffic there is centers on Court and Victoria streets after dark.

The Senate, which is the upper house of Parliament, sits in the **Cabinet Building,** a dignified two-story structure surrounded by trees and gardens. Amid great ceremony, the official opening of Parliament takes place in the Senate Chamber in late October or early November. His Excellency the Governor, dressed in a plumed hat and full regalia, arrives on the grounds in a landau drawn by magnificent black horses and accompanied by a military escort. A senior police officer, carrying the Black Rod made by the Crown jewelers, summons the elected representatives to convene. The governor makes his Throne Speech from in front of a tiny cedar throne crudely carved with the words "Cap Josias Forstore Govornour of the Sumer Islands Anodo 1642" (Josias Foster was governor in 1642). The portraits above the dais are of King George III and Queen Charlotte. The chamber is open to visitors, but come on a Wednesday if you want to watch the Senate in action; call first to find out about scheduling. *Front St., tel. 809/292–5501. Admission free. Open weekdays 9–5. Closed holidays.*

In front of the Cabinet Building, the **Cenotaph** is a memorial to the war dead; on Remembrance Day (November 11), the governor and other dignitaries lay wreaths at the base of the monument. The Cenotaph is a smaller version of the famous one in Whitehall, London. The cornerstone was laid in 1920 by the Prince of Wales, who as King Edward VIII abdicated to wed Mrs. Simpson.

On the eastern outskirts of Hamilton is **Fort Hamilton,** an imposing old fortress, complete with a moat, 18-ton guns, and underground passageways that were cut through solid rock by Royal Engineers in the 1870s. If you've done enough walking, consider taking a taxi or moped there, because it's quite far. Head east on East Reid Street, turn left on King Street, and then right onto Happy Valley Road. The restored fort is one of several built by order of the Duke of Wellington. Outdated even before its completion, the fort never fired a shot in anger. Today, it affords splendid views of the capital and the harbor. Accompanied by drummers and dancers, the kilted Bermuda Isles Pipe Band performs a stirring skirling ceremony on the green every Monday at noon during the low season. Afterward the fort's "Tea Shoppe" is open for light refreshments. *Happy Valley Rd., Pembroke, no phone. Admission free. Open weekdays 9:30–5.*

Tour 2: The Town of St. George

Numbers in the margin correspond to points of interest on the Tour 2: The Town of St. George map.

The settlement of Bermuda began on the eastern end of the island in 1609, when the *Sea Venture* was wrecked off the coast. Despite its small size, St. George's encompasses much of historical interest, and visitors should plan to spend a full day poking around in the houses and museums. Much of the fun of St. George's is exploring the little alleys and walled lanes that wind through the town. The tour of the town is easily managed on foot.

⑭ **King's Square** is the hub of St. George's, although it is comparatively new. For 200 years after St. George's was settled, the square was a marshy part of the harbor—the area

⑮ was filled in only in the last century. Stop at the **Visitors Information Centre** for maps, brochures, and advice. A combination ticket for $6 buys admission to Tucker House and the Confederate Museum (and to Verdmont in Smith's Parish), which are all operated by the Bermuda National Trust.

Prominently displayed in King's Square is a cedar replica of the stocks and pillory originally used to punish criminals. Today, they serve as props for tourist photos and for the street theater staged here on Wednesdays during the low season. If you decide to take the walking tour (*see* Guided Tours in Chapter 1, Essential Information), you will be greeted in the square by the mayor of St. George's. The town crier, who has a voice to wake the dead (his voice is in the *Guinness Book of World Records*), is on hand in full colonial costume. After the official welcome, the crier bellows a few pronouncements and places any perceived malefactors in the stocks.

⑯ Stroll across the bridge to **Ordnance Island** and the splendid Desmond Fountain statue of Sir George Somers, titled *Land Ho!* The **ducking stool** on the island is a replica of the one used to dunk gossips, nagging wives, and suspected witches in the water. Demonstrations are sometimes given, although volunteers say that getting dunked is no fun, even in fun.

Also on the island is the ***Deliverance II,*** a replica of the *Deliverance* built by the survivors of the wreck. After their shipwreck in 1609, Somers and his crew built two ships, the *Deliverance* and the *Patience,* to carry them to Jamestown, Virginia. Below deck, life-size mannequins in period costume are used to depict the realities of ocean travel in the 17th century—it's not the *QE2. Ordnance Island, no phone. Admission: $2.50 adults, 50¢ children under 12. Open daily 10–4. Closed Good Friday, Easter, and Christmas.*

⑰ The waterside **White Horse Tavern** is a popular restaurant today, but it was the Davenport home for much of the 19th century. After his arrival in St. George's in about 1815, John Davenport opened a small dry-goods store on the square. He was able to wangle a profitable contract to supply beef to the garrison, and gold and silver began to pour in. There were no banks on Bermuda, but Davenport wasn't the trusting sort anyway. He stashed the money in a keg that he kept beneath his bed. When the keg was full, he

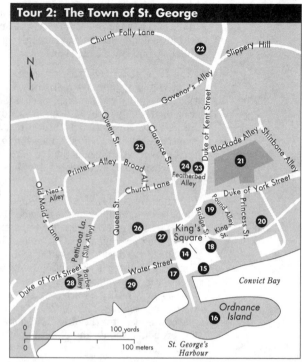

Tour 2: The Town of St. George

took it down to the cellar and put another one under his bed. By the time he was an old man, Davenport would spend hours each day gloating over the kegs that now filled his cellar. After his death, it was discovered that the old miser had amassed a fortune in gold and silver worth £75,000.

18 Across the square is **Town Hall,** a two-story building that houses administrative offices. Constructed in 1808 and subsequently restored, the hall is paneled and furnished with cedar, and there's a delightful collection of photographs of former mayors. Many years ago Town Hall was the scene of a memorable con. A gentleman calling himself Professor Trott appeared in town and announced a spectacular production of *Ali Baba and the Forty Thieves.* A great crowd collected at Town Hall for the play, and thievery was duly performed: Having lured the residents away from their homes, the wily "professor" made off with an iron safe. The *Bermuda Journey,* a worthwhile audiovisual presentation, is shown in the second-floor theater. *King's Sq. Admission to Town Hall free. Open Mon.–Sat. 9–4. Closed holidays.* Bermuda Journey, *tel. 809/297–1642. Admission: $2.50 adults, $1.75 children under 12, $2 senior citizens. Open May–Nov., weekdays 10–3; call for Dec.–Apr. hrs. Closed holidays.*

Time Out **Pub on the Square** (King's Sq., tel. 809/297–1522) is exactly what its name implies. The balcony overlooking the square is a great place to knock back a beer, have a burger, and watch the action below.

🄳 On your left as you walk up King Street is **Bridge House,** so named for a bridge that once crossed a small creek here. Built around 1700, the house is a fine example of Bermudian architecture, has two verandas, and was the home of several governors. Now an art gallery and souvenir shop, the house is furnished with 18th- and 19th-century pieces. *King St., tel. 809/297–8211. Admission free. Open Mon.–Sat. 10–5 (also Sun. 11–3 in June–Aug.). Closed Christmas, Boxing Day, Easter, mid-Jan.–mid-Feb., depending on demand.*

🄴 At the top of King Street, the **Old State House** is the oldest stone house in Bermuda. Constructed in 1620 in what Governor Nathaniel Butler believed was the Italian style, the limestone building used a mixture of turtle oil and lime as mortar and set the style for future Bermudian buildings. Upon completion, it became home to the Parliament, which had been meeting in St. Peter's Church; dances and social gatherings were also held there. After the capital was moved to Hamilton, the old State House was rented to Lodge St. George's No. 200 of the Grand Lodge of Scotland. The annual rent charged by the city was one peppercorn, the payment of which is still made upon a velvet pillow amid much pomp and circumstance. The Peppercorn Ceremony takes place each April. *Princess St., no phone. Admission free. Open Wed. 10–4.*

Proceeding down Princess Street, you'll pass the place where a hotheaded tailor named Joseph Gwynn gunned down one Henry Folger in 1826. Enraged after his son had been sentenced to jail, Gwynn went out one night looking for the magistrate who had punished his son. Apparently blind with rage, he mistook Folger for the magistrate and shot him dead. A few months later, Gwynn was hanged near the very spot where the murder took place.

🄵 Nearby is **Somers Garden,** a pleasant tree-shrouded park where the heart of Sir George Somers is said to be buried. After sailing to Jamestown and back in 1610, Somers fell ill and died. According to local lore, Somers told his nephew Matthew Somers that he wanted his heart buried in Bermuda, where it belonged. Matthew, who never seemed to pay much attention to his uncle's wishes, sailed for England soon afterward, sneaking Somers's body aboard in a cedar chest to avoid alarming the superstitious seamen. (Somers's body is buried near his birthplace in Dorset.) When the tomb where Somers's heart was supposedly interred was opened many years later, only a few bones, a pebble, and some bottle fragments were found—no one knows if Matthew Somers ever carried out his uncle's wishes. Nevertheless, ceremonies were held at the empty grave upon the 1920 visit of the Prince of Wales, during which the prince christened the park Somers Garden. *Bordered by Shinbone Alley, Blockade Alley, Duke of Kent and Duke of York Sts., no phone. Admission free. Open daily 7:30–4:30.*

Time Out Off the tourist beat, **Clyde's Cafe** (Duke of York St. at Somers Garden, tel. 809/297–0158) is popular with locals as a lunch spot. Nothing fancy is served here—just plate lunches, sandwiches, and burgers—but the prices aren't fancy, either.

Walk through Somers Garden and up the steps to Blockade ㉒ Alley. On the hill ahead is the **Unfinished Church.** Considering how much attention and affection are lavished on St. Peter's these days, it's hard to believe that residents in the 19th century wanted to replace the old church with a new one. Work began on this church in 1874, but construction was halted when a schism developed in the church. Money for construction was later diverted to rebuild Trinity Church in Hamilton when it burned down; work on the new church in St. George's was abandoned by the turn of the century. In 1992 the Bermuda National Trust obtained a 50-year lease on the church, and is repairing and stabilizing the structure.

At the corner of Featherbed Alley and Duke of Kent Street ㉓ is **St. George's Historical Society Museum.** A typical Bermudian structure from the early 1700s, the house is furnished much the same as when it was a private home. One of Bermuda's oldest pieces is a table believed to have been used as the High Court bench in the State House. The house is also filled with documents (including a doctor's bill from 1790), old letters, and displays of pewter, china, and rare books; there's even a whale-blubber cutter. A torpedo raft is one of the relics from the American Civil War. Constructed of heavy timber with projecting arms to hold torpedoes, the raft was part of a Union plan to blow up the submarine barricade in Charleston harbor. After breaking loose from its towing ship during a gale, the raft drifted for six years before washing ashore in Dolly's Bayon St. David's Island. When the captain of the towing ship later visited Bermuda, he recognized the raft and explained its purpose to the puzzled Bermudians. On the south wall of the house is an iron grate that is said to have come from the cell where Bermuda's first Methodist missionary, the Reverend John Stephenson, was confined for preaching to slaves. The persistent missionary continued to preach from his cell to a crowd that collected outside. Local artist Carole Holding has her studio and craft's shop in the former slave quarters of the house. *Featherbed Alley, tel. 809/297–0423. Admission: $1 adults, 50¢ children 6–16, children under 6 free. Open weekdays 10–4. Closed holidays. Holding Studio, tel.*

809/297–1883. Admission free. Open Mon.–Sat. 10–4. Closed holidays.

24 Around the corner, the **Featherbed Alley Printery** is as quaint as its name. Inside the cottage is a working printing press of the kind invented by Johann Gutenberg in the 1450s. *Featherbed Alley, tel. 809/297–0009. Admission free. Open Mon.–Sat. 10–4. Closed holidays and Wed. 11–2.*

Cross Clarence Street to Church Lane, and then turn right **25** on Broad Alley to reach the **Old Rectory,** now a private residence but owned by the Bermuda National Trust. Built around 1705 by a reformed pirate, it's a charming little house with Dutch doors, shutters, chimneys, and a welcoming-arms staircase. For many years it was the home of Alexander Richardson, the "Little Bishop," who was rector of St. Peter's from 1755 to 1805, except for a five-year stint on St. Eustatius. Richardson's diary is filled with anecdotes about 18th-century St. George's. *Broad Alley, tel. 809/297–0879. Admission free (donations appreciated). Open Wed. noon–5. Closed holidays.*

Straight ahead (if "straight" is applicable among these twisted alleys) is **Printer's Alley,** where Bermuda's first newspaper was published. On January 17, 1784, less than a year after his arrival on the island, Joseph Stockdale printed the first copy of the *Bermuda Gazette.* The paper was published weekly for 20 years until Stockdale's death in 1805. The house where Stockdale worked is now a private home.

Nea's Alley is a short street connecting Printer's Alley with Old Maid's Lane. The 19th-century Irish poet Tom Moore lived on this street, then known as Cumberland Lane, during his four-month tenure as registrar of the admiralty court. Moore, who was endowed with considerable charm, had an impact on the island that endures to this day. He was invited to stay in the home of Admiral Mitchell, the neighbor of Mr. William Tucker and his wife, Hester—the "Nea" to whom Moore pours out his heart in several poems. Moore is thought to have first seen her in Cumberland Lane, which he describes in one of his odes as "the lime-covered alley that leads to thy home." However discreet Nea and Moore may have been about their affair, his odes to her were on the steamy side—much to the dismay of her husband. Although it was rather like locking the barn door after the horse has bolted, William Tucker refused to allow his former friend into his house again. Some Bermudians speculate that Nea was very much in love with Tom, but that he considered her merely a pleasant divertissement. He returned to Ireland after his assignment, and Nea died in 1817 at the age of 31. Bermudians are much enamored of the short-lived romance between Hester and Moore, and visitors are likely to hear a good deal about it.

㉖ Return to Church Lane and enter the churchyard of **St. Peter's Church.** The tombstones in Bermuda's oldest churchyard tell some interesting tales, indeed—this is the resting place of governors, doctors, simple folk, and pirates. East of the church is the grave of Hester, or "Nea," marked "Mr. William Tucker's Family Vault." One of the best-known monuments stands over the grave of Richard Sutherland Dale, who died in 1815 at age 20. An American navy midshipman, Dale was mortally wounded during a sea battle with the British in the War of 1812. The monument was erected by his parents as a tribute to the St. Georgians whose "tender sympathy prompted the kindest attentions to their son while living and honoured him when dead." In an enclosure to the west of the church is the slaves' graveyard. The ancient cedar tree, which dates back to before 1620, is the old belfry tree. St. Peter's is the oldest Anglican church in the Western Hemisphere, constructed in 1620. It was not the first church to stand on this site, however; it replaced a 1612 structure of posts and palmetto leaves that was destroyed in a storm. The present church was extended in 1713, and the galleries on either side were added in 1833. The oldest part of the church is the area around the 17th-century triple-tier pulpit. The dark-red cedar altar is the oldest piece of woodwork in the colony, carved under the supervision of Richard Moore, a shipwright and the first governor. The font, brought to the island by the early settlers, is about 500 years old, and the late-18th-century bishop's throne is believed to have been salvaged from a wreck. Among the treasures displayed in the vestry are a 1697 William of Orange communion set and a Charles I chalice, sent from England by the Bermuda Company in 1625. Commemorative plaques hang on the walls, and some of the names are wonderfully Pickwickian: One large memorial is to Governor Allured Popple. If you enter through the back door, be sure to look at the front of the church when you leave. *Duke of York St., tel. 809/297–8359. Donations appreciated. Open daily.*

㉗ Across the street, the **Confederate Museum** has a colorful history. Built in 1700 by Governor Samuel Day, the building served for 150 years as the Globe Hotel. During the American Civil War, the house was occupied by Major Norman Walker, who came to Bermuda as a Confederate agent. St. George's—which had suffered a depression after the capital moved to Hamilton in 1815—sided with the South for economic reasons, and the town became a hotbed of blockade-running activity. The first woman to run the blockade was Major Walker's pregnant wife, who risked capture by the North to join him in Bermuda. She was determined to have their baby born on Confederate soil, however, beneath the Stars and Bars. In the room where she gave birth, therefore, the four-poster bed was draped with the Confederate flag, and it's said that Confederate soil was spread beneath the bed. A wall map, designed by Desmond

Fountain, shows the blockade-running routes from Bermuda to Southern ports. Also on display are a model of a blockade-runner, a replica of the Great Seal of the Confederacy, and an antique Victorian Seal Press, which makes reproductions of the Great Seal as souvenirs for visitors. *Duke of York St., tel. 809/297–1423. Donation: $3. Open Apr.–Oct., Mon.–Sat. 9:30–4:30; Nov.–Mar., Mon.–Sat. 10–4. Closed holidays.*

Continuing down Duke of York Street, you come to **Barber Alley,** named for Joseph Hayne Rainey, a former slave from South Carolina. Rainey's father had bought him his freedom, so when the Civil War broke out, Rainey and his French wife fled to Bermuda. Living in the kitchen of the Tucker House, Rainey became a barber and his wife made fashionable clothes. After the Civil War, they returned to South Carolina, where he went into politics. Elected to the House of Representatives in 1870, Rainey was the first African-American to serve in the United States Congress.

Petticoat Lane, which is also called Silk Alley, received its name in 1834 after the emancipation of Bermudian slaves. Legend has it that two freed slaves, who had always wanted petticoats like those worn by their mistresses, strolled down the lane on Emancipation Sunday amid much rustling of petticoat skirts.

Antiques aficionados will find much of interest in the **Tucker House,** one of the showplaces of the Bermuda National Trust. Built of native limestone in 1711, the house sat above green hills that sloped down to the waterside (the area is now all built up). Henry Tucker, president of the Governor's Council, lived in the house with his family from 1775 to 1800. His grandson donated most of the furnishings, which date from the mid-18th and early 19th centuries. Much of it is cedar, but there are some handsome mahogany pieces as well: The mahogany dining table was crafted from a tree grown in Cuba, and an English mahogany breakfront holds a collection of Tucker-family silver engraved with the family's coat of arms. Notice the tiny wig rooms off the dining room, where ladies and gentlemen went to fix their wigs after dinner. A short flight of stairs leads down to the kitchen, where Joseph Rainey lived and ran his barber shop. There is a small bookstore in the cellar. The Tucker name has been important in Bermuda since the island's beginnings (Henry Tucker's son St. George built the Tucker House in Williamsburg, Virginia), and a number of interesting family portraits hang in the house. Henry Tucker's father and brother were both involved in the famed "Gunpowder Plot" of 1775. The Continental Congress had imposed a ban on exports to all British colonies not taking part in the revolt against England. Bermuda depended upon the American colonies for grain, so a delegation of Bermudians traveled to Philadelphia offering salt in exchange for the resumption of grain shipments. Congress rejected the salt but agreed to lift the ban if Bermuda sent gunpowder instead. A group of Bermudians, including the two Tuckers, then sneaked into the island's arsenal, stole the gunpowder, and shipped it to Boston. The ban was soon lifted. *Water St., tel. 809/297–0545. Donation: $3. Open Apr.–Oct., Mon.–Sat. 9:30–4:30; Nov.–Mar., Mon.–Sat. 10–4. Closed holidays.*

With the arrival of cars on Bermuda in 1946, horse-drawn carriages were put out to pasture, so to speak. Across the street from the Tucker House, the **Carriage Museum** offers a fascinating look at some of the island's old carriages. Yes, there's a surrey with a fringe on top as well as isinglass curtains that roll down. Among the other displays are a dignified Brougham; a six-passenger enclosed Opera Bus; and a small two-wheeler for children, called the Little Red Dog Cart. The carriages are labeled, but it's fun to hear the curator, Mr. Frith, describe them. *Water St., tel. 809/297–1367. Admission free (donations appreciated). Open weekdays 10–5 (and occasionally Sat.). Closed holidays.*

Somers Wharf, where the Carriage Museum is located, is part of a multimillion-dollar waterfront restoration that includes several shops and the pleasant Carriage House Restaurant. St.George's passenger-ship terminal is in this area.

Tour 3: The West End

Numbers in the margin correspond to points of interest on the Tour 3: The West End map.

In contrast to Hamilton and St. George's, the West End is a rather bucolic part of Bermuda. With the notable exception of Dockyard, many of the attractions here are natural rather than manmade: nature reserves, wooded areas, and beautiful harbors and bays. In the waters off Daniel's Head, the Sea Gardens are regularly visited by glass-bottom boats from Hamilton: With its bow jutting out of the water, the coral-wrapped wreck of HMS *Vixen* is a major attraction. The ship was deliberately sunk by the British to block the channel and protect Dockyard from attack. The West End is part of Sandys Parish, named after Sir Edwin Sandys, an investor in the Bermuda Company. Local lore contends that Sir George Somers took a keen interest in this region, and in the early days it was known as "Somers's seate"—hence the name of Somerset Village. Today, Somerset is a sleepy little hamlet with a few shops and not much else. The West End's big attraction is Dockyard, a bastion of the British Royal Navy for 150 years. You should plan to spend at least a day exploring this area.

If you take the ferry to Somerset, look closely at the ferry schedule: The trip can take anywhere from a half hour to more than an hour, depending on which ferry you take. However, there are worse ways to while away an hour than churning across Bermuda's Great Sound. Take your bicycle or moped aboard the ferry, too, because you will need wheels in the West End. Bus service is available for those without their own transport.

The Somerset ferry stops at Somerset Bridge, Cavello Bay, Watford Bridge, and Dockyard. This tour begins at **⑩ Dockyard** on Ireland Island, a sprawling complex housing several notable attractions. After the American Revolution, Britain found itself with neither an anchorage nor a major ship-repair yard in the western Atlantic. When Napoleon started to make threatening noises in Europe and British ships became increasingly vulnerable to pirate attack, Britain began construction of a major stronghold in Bermuda in 1809. The work was done by slaves and English convicts toiling under appalling conditions—thousands of workers died before the project was completed. This was a functioning shipyard for nearly 150 years; it was closed in 1951, but the Royal Navy still maintains a small presence here. With the opening of the Maritime Museum (*see below*) in 1975, the decision was made to transform the entire naval port into a tourist attraction. Dockyard is currently under development as a minivillage, and Bermudians are enormously proud of the entire project. The area includes a shopping arcade and visitor center in the handsome, century-old Clocktower Building, a cruise-ship terminal, a marina and deepwater berth, and the submarine *Enterprise*. The erstwhile shipyard continues to blossom, having undergone extensive landscaping to replace its vast stretches of concrete with shrubs, trees, and grassy lawns. New additions include an extension of the shopping mall, a restaurant, and a nightclub. Also planned are scuba-diving facilities and a snorkel park, and horse-drawn carriage tours. You can reach Dockyard in a half hour from Hamilton via an express bus that leaves the capital every 15 minutes. Hold on to your hair when you're strolling around Dockyard—it's very windy, particularly along the water.

Opened by Queen Elizabeth II in 1975, the sprawling 6-acre **⑪ Maritime Museum** is housed in the huge fortress built to defend Dockyard. Entry to the museum is over a moat. The exhibition rooms are in old magazines and munitions warehouses arranged around the parade grounds. Several exhibits pertain to the *Sea Venture* and the early history of the island. Treasures and relics from some of the approximately 300 ships wrecked on the island's reefs are exhibited, as are maps, diving gear, ship models, uniforms, and costumes. Sailors will particularly enjoy the Bermuda dinghies (14-foot sailboats which can carry as much as 1,000 feet of canvas) on display in the Boat Loft. The museum's newest exhibit—the *Age of Discovery*, which traces the wrecks of ancient vessels—was opened in October, 1992, and officiated over by Columbus descendant Diega Colon. Visitors can also explore the ramparts, although this walk is only for dedicated (and hardy) fortress buffs. Currently

undergoing renovation, the 19th-century Commissioner's
House is an elaborate cast-iron affair set high on a bluff. It
is the world's oldest cast-iron residence. Home to Dockyard
commissioners from 1827 to 1837, and later a barracks, the
house was formally commissioned a "ship"—the HMS *Malabar*—in 1919. Fundraisers for the $2.5 million restoration
hope to complete work on the house by 1994. *Dockyard, tel.
809/234-1418. Admission: $6 adults, $2 senior citizens and
children under 12. Open daily 10–5. Closed Christmas.*

Across the street from the Maritime Museum is the Old
Cooperage, or barrel-maker's shop. Dating back to 1831,
❷ the reconstructed building houses the **Neptune Cinema,**
which shows first-run films, the popular **Frog & Onion** pub-
restaurant, and the **Craft Market.**

The Craft Market displays the works of local artists. Jaded
tourists, for whom "craft" usually means tacky souvenirs,
are in for a pleasant surprise. There are some delightful
items on sale here, including stained glass and miniature
cedar furniture (*see* Chapter 5, Shopping). *Dockyard, tel.
809/234-3208. Admission free. Open daily 11–4. Closed
Christmas, Boxing Day, New Year's Day, Good Friday.*

Since its opening by Princess Margaret in 1984, the
❸ **Bermuda Arts Centre** has been a showcase for local artists
and artisans, and an excellent place to see Bermudian work

(*see* Chapter 5, Shopping). Exhibits, which cover such subjects as underwater photography, change monthly. *Dockyard, tel. 809/234–2809. Admission free. Open Tues.–Sat. 10–4, Sun. noon–5. Closed Mon., Christmas, Boxing Day, New Year's Day, and Good Friday.*

Take the main road out of Dockyard along Ireland Island South. Turn left on Craddock Road and cycle down to

㉞ Lagoon Park. Hidden in the mangroves are a lovely lagoon, footpaths, wild birds, and places to picnic. Next to the park, **The Crawl** is a picturesque inlet with fishing boats bobbing in the water and lobster pots on the dock. The park is always open, and there's no admission charge.

Cross over Boaz and Watford islands to Somerset Island. The largest of all these islets, Somerset Island is fringed on both sides with beautiful secluded coves, inlets, and bays.

㉟ Beside pretty Mangrove Bay, **Somerset Village** is a quiet retreat, quite different from St. George's, Hamilton, and Dockyard. Only one road runs through the village, and the few shops are mostly branches of Hamilton stores. During the low season walks, tour guides concentrate on the area's natural beauty and the unusual and medicinal plants on the island. Somerset Island itself is heavily populated, laced with roads and pathways through quiet residential areas.

Time Out Overlooking Mangrove Bay, the **Somerset Country Squire Restaurant** (Mangrove Bay Rd., tel. 809/234–0105) is an English-style pub with a great atmosphere. Diners can rely on good sandwiches and burgers, as well as such traditional British dishes as steak and kidney pie and bangers (sausages) and mash. Desserts are sensational.

Cambridge Beaches, Bermuda's original cottage colony, sits on its own 25-acre peninsula northwest of Somerset Village. Nestled among the trees near the entrance is a branch of the **Irish Linen Shop** (Cambridge Rd., tel. 809/234–0127). The little cottage was one of the original units of Cambridge Beaches.

㊱ A short distance farther along Cambridge Road is **Long Bay Park and Nature Reserve,** which has a great beach, shallow water, and picnic areas. The Bermuda Audubon Society owns the adjacent nature reserve and its pond, which attracts migrating birds in the spring and fall. Peaceful as this area is now, it was the scene of one of Bermuda's most sensational murders. Skeeters' Corner, at the end of Daniel's Head Road, was the site of a cottage once owned by a couple of the same name. One night in 1878, Edward Skeeters strangled his wife and dumped her in the water. His long, rambling confession revealed that he was irked because she talked too much!

Continue along Cambridge Road (which becomes Somerset Road), until you see the arched gateway leading to the

㊲ Springfield Library and Gilbert Nature Reserve. Set in 5

heavily wooded acres, Springfield is an old plantation home that dates back to around 1700. The restored house and out-buildings—the kitchen, slave quarters, and buttery—are built around an open courtyard. The most interesting rooms are in the main house, which also contains the Somerset branch of the public library. Named after the family that owned the property from 1700 to 1973, the nature re-serve was acquired by the Bermuda National Trust in con-junction with the Bermuda Audubon Society. *Main Rd., Somerset, tel. 809/234–1980. Admission free. Nature re-serve always open. Library open Tues.–Fri. 2–6, Sat. 10–5. Closed public holidays.*

㊳ Somerset Road winds around to the **Somerset Visitors In-formation Centre** (Somerset Rd., tel. 809/234–1388), where you can get information about this area from May through November.

㊴ High atop a promontory against a backdrop of the sea, **St. James Church** is one of the loveliest churches on the island. The entrance on the main road is marked by handsome iron gates that were forged by a Royal Engineer in 1872; the long driveway curls past glistening white tombs in the churchyard. The first church on this site was a wood struc-ture destroyed by a hurricane in 1780. The present church was consecrated in 1789. The tall, slender spire is a faithful replica of the 1880 spire that was hit by lightning and sent crashing down into the church's center aisle in 1937. *Main Rd., Somerset, no phone. Open daily 8–7.*

Shortly after the church, you'll see the entrance to the **㊵ Heydon Trust property,** opposite Willowbank guest house. Among its 43 acres are citrus orchards, banana groves, flower and vegetable gardens, and bird sanctuaries. The quiet, peaceful property has been maintained as undevel-oped "open space"—a reminder of what the island was like in its early days. Pathways dotted with park benches wend through the preserve, affording some wonderful views of the Great Sound. If you persevere along the main path, you'll reach the tiny, rustic **Heydon Chapel,** which dates from before 1620. An old rugged cross is planted in the hill-side, and a welcome mat lies at the door. Inside are a few wooden pews, cedar beams, and an ancient oven and hearth in a small room behind the altar. Services are still held in the chapel. *Somerset Rd., tel. 809/234–1831. Admission free. Open during daylight hours.*

㊶ Just around the bend on your left is **Scaur Hill Fort.** Perched on the highest hill in Somerset, the fort was begun in 1868 and completed in the 1880s. British troops were garrisoned here until World War I. During World War II, American forces from Battery D, 52nd Coast Artillery Battalion, were stationed here. Little remains to be seen here, al-though the 22 acres of gardens are quite pretty, and the view of the Great Sound is fantastic. Almost worth the long climb is the Early Bermuda Weather Stone, the "perfect weather indicator." The plaque reads: "A wet stone means . . . it is raining; a shadow under the stone . . . means the sun is shining; if the stone is swinging, it means there is a strong wind blowing; if the stone jumps up and down it means there is an earthquake; if ever it is white on top . . . believe it or not . . . it is snowing." *Somerset Rd., Ely's Harbour, tel. 809/234-0908. Admission free. Open daily 9–4:30. Closed Christmas and Boxing Day.*

At the bottom of the hilly, twisting road lies spectacular
42 **Ely's Harbour,** with pleasure boats dotting its brilliant turquoise waters. Pronounced "Ee-lees," the small sheltered harbor was once a hangout for smugglers.

Linking Somerset Island with the rest of Bermuda is
43 **Somerset Bridge,** reputed to have the smallest draw in the world. It opens a mere 18 inches, just wide enough to accommodate a sailboat mast. Near the bridge is the Somerset ferry landing, where you can catch a ferry back to Hamilton. Across the bridge, Somerset Road becomes Middle Road, which leads into Southampton Parish (*see* Tour 4: The Parishes, *below*).

Time Out   At the Somerset Bridge Hotel, the **Blue Foam** (162 Somerset Rd, tel. 809/234-2892) is a pleasant lunch spot in a greenhouse setting. In high season, a somewhat more expensive alternative is the casual La Plage restaurant at the **Lantana Colony Club** (Somerset Rd., tel. 809/234-0141). Reservations are necessary at Lantana.

Tour 4: The Parishes

Numbers in the margin correspond to points of interest on the Tour 4: The Parishes map.

Bermuda's other points of interest—and there are many—are scattered across the island's parishes. This final tour takes you across the length and breadth of the colony, commenting only on the major sights. Half the fun of exploring Bermuda, though, is wandering down forgotten lanes or discovering some little-known beach or cove. A moped or bicycle is ideal for this kind of travel, although most of the island is covered by bus and ferry service. It would be foolish to try to see all the sights here in just one day. The tour, which leaves from Hamilton, can easily be broken into two halves: The first half explores those parishes in the eastern part of the island; the second travels through the western parishes. Even so, vacationers may find it more rewarding to do the tour piecemeal—a couple of sites here, a church there, and a day at the beach in between.

44 Follow Cedar Avenue north out of Hamilton to **St. John's Church,** consecrated in 1826 as the parish church of Pembroke. Another church, which dated to 1625, stood on this site before. During a funeral in 1875, the churchyard was

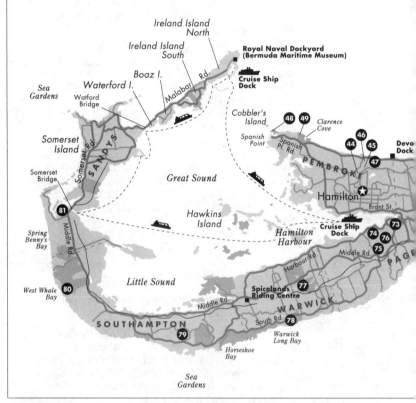

ATLANTIC OCEAN

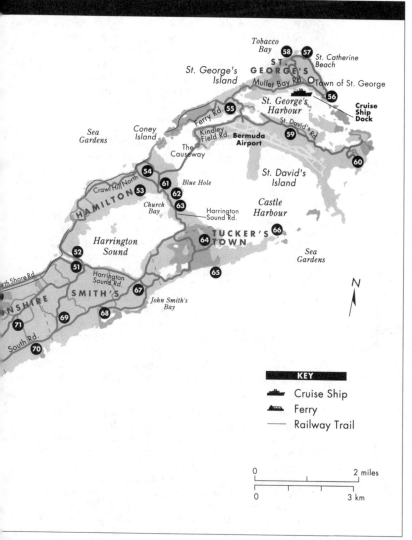

the scene of a verbal duel between the Anglican rector and a Wesleyan minister. The Anglican church insisted that all burial services in parish churchyards be conducted by the rector, but the Wesleyans challenged the church in the case of a deceased woman named Esther Levy. Claiming he'd been asked by her friends to perform the funeral service, a Wesleyan minister appeared in the churchyard despite the efforts of the Anglican rector to stop him. Simultaneous services were held over poor Mrs. Levy's body, with the minister and the adamant Anglican trying to out-shout each other. The rector subsequently filed charges of trespassing against the Wesleyan, and the celebrated case went before the Supreme Court. The jury found for the rector, and fined the minister one shilling. *St. John's Rd., Pembroke. Open daily 8–7.*

By following Marsh Folly Road, which runs between the church and Bernard Park, you'll come to **Black Watch Pass.** The Public Works Department excavated about 2.5 million cubic feet of solid limestone during construction of the pass. The tunnel received its name from **Black Watch Well,** at the intersection of Black Watch Pass and North Shore Road. During a severe drought in 1849, the governor ordered a well dug on government ground to alleviate the suffering of the poor in the area. Excavated by a detachment of the famed Black Watch regiment, the well is marked by a commemorative plaque and shaded by a tiered concrete slab. The site is not particularly inspiring, however, and only the most dedicated well-wishers will want to make the pilgrimage to see it.

From its position on Langton Hill, imposing **Government House** overlooks North Shore Road, Black Watch Well, and the sea. The house is the residence of the governor and is not open to the public. The land was purchased when the capital was transferred from St. George's to Hamilton in 1815. A simple, two-story house served as the governor's home until the present, rather austere mansion was built. Various royals and other distinguished visitors planted the trees and shrubs on the pretty landscaped lawns. Among the guests who have been entertained in Government House are Queen Elizabeth II and Prince Philip, Prince Charles, Winston Churchill, and President Kennedy. The mansion was also the scene of the 1973 assassination of Governor Richard Sharples and his aide, Captain Hugh Sayers.

North Shore Road merges with Spanish Point Road near **Spanish Point,** at the tip of the peninsula. The survivors of the wrecked *Sea Venture* thought they found evidence here of an earlier visit by the Spanish. Apparently they were right: Historians now believe that Captain Diego Ramirez landed here in 1603. There is a small park for picnicking, a sheltered bay for swimming, public facilities, and a lovely view of Somerset across the sound. Cobbler's Island, across Cobbler's Cut from Spanish Point, has a grisly history—executed slaves were exhibited there as a warning to others of the consequences of disobedience.

49 En route to Spanish Point you pass **Admiralty House Park,** a pretty spot with several caves and sheltered coves. Little remains of the house, originally the 19th-century estate of John Dunscombe. Dunscombe, who later became lieutenant governor of Newfoundland, sold the property in 1816 to the Bermuda government, which decided to build a house for the commanding British admiral of the naval base at Dockyard. The house was reconstructed several times over the years, notably in the 1850s by an eccentric admiral with a weakness for subterranean tunnels—he had several caves and galleries cut into the cliffs above the sea. The house was closed when the Royal Navy withdrew in 1951. Within the park, Clarence Cove offers a sheltered beach and pleasant swimming.

Head back along North Shore Road to Devonshire Parish. Ideal for cycling and quiet picnics, Devonshire is a serene part of the island, with much to offer in the way of natural beauty. Locals come to **Devonshire Dock** to buy fresh fish (something to bear in mind if you're staying in a housekeeping apartment).

50 A short distance farther along North Shore Road is **Palmetto House,** an 18th-century cruciform house. It was believed that a house built in the shape of a cross warded off evil spirits. Three rooms, furnished with fine pieces of Bermudian furniture, are on view. *North Shore Rd., tel. 809/ 295–9941. Admission free. Open Thurs. 10–5.*

51 If you continue along North Shore Road, you will reach **Flatts Village,** one of the earliest settlements on the island. The House of Assembly sometimes met in Flatts, although much of the village's activities involved flouting the law rather than making it. Hoping to avoid customs officers, Bermudians returning from the West Indies would sometimes sail into the village in the dead of night to unload their cargoes.

52 The **Aquarium, Museum and Zoo** at Flatts Village is one of the island's most popular attractions. Pick up an audio "wand" at the aquarium entrance for a self-guided tour of the tanks and exhibits. Sea creatures native to Bermudian waters are on display, including sharks, barracuda, and grumpy-looking giant grouper. The natural-history museum features a geology display that explains Bermuda's volcanic origins, and a deep-sea exhibit that documents the half-mile dive of marine biologist Dr. William Beebe in the early 1930s. The odd-looking contraption outside the museum is the bathosphere in which Dr. Beebe made his dive. In the zoo, a reptile walkway gives visitors a close look at alligators, Galapagos tortoises, and lizards. A beehive, octopi, and a touch pool are among the features in the Invertebrate House. There is also a children's Discovery Room, with puzzles and coloring books that pertain to Bermuda. Other attractions include an aviary, a monkey house, and a number of Caribbean flamingos and strutting peacocks. A petting zoo is open only in the summer. *Flatts, tel. 809/293–2727. Admission: $5 adults, $2 senior citizens and children 5–12. Open daily 9–5 (last admission at 4:30). Closed Christmas.*

Near the aquarium is the **Railway Museum,** housed in the old Aquarium Station of the island's erstwhile narrow-guage railroad. The tiny museum is cluttered with photos, signs, wicker chairs from the first class compartment, and other memorabilia. "Old Rattle and Shake," as the railway was known, is so fondly remembered by Bermudians you'll wonder why the line was shut down. *37 North Shore Rd., tel. 809/293–1774. Admission free. Open Tues.–Sat. 9–4.*

Continuing east, North Shore Road climbs **Crawl Hill,** a high point offering spectacular views over the island and sea. "Crawl" derives from the Afrikaans word "kraal," meaning animal enclosure; on Bermuda, the word was applied to several ponds containing turtles and fish. This part of Hamilton Parish was also a site for shipbuilding during the early days of the colony.

53 Turn right on Trinity Church Road to see **Holy Trinity Church.** Built in 1623 as one long room with a thatched roof, it is said to be the oldest Anglican church on Bermuda. The church has been much embellished over the past 368 years, but the original building remains at its core. The small graveyard is encircled by palms, royal poinciana, and cherry trees. *Church Bay, Harrington Sound, no phone. Not open to the public.*

Just off Trinity Church Road is **Mount Wyndham,** the peak from which Admiral Sir Alexander Cochrane surveyed the British fleet prior to its attack on Washington, DC, in 1814.

54 Follow North Shore Road as it dips south to the **Bermuda Perfumery and Gardens.** On a guided tour, visitors learn how the Lili Perfume Factory, which began extracting natural fragrances from the island's flowers in 1929, blossomed into the present perfumery/tourist attraction. The factory is in a 200-year-old cottage with cedar beams, but the biggest draw is the aromatic nature trail that you can walk on your own. A complimentary map helps you sniff your way around the oleanders, frangipani, jasmine, orchids, and passionflower that are the raw material for the factory. *212 North Shore Rd., tel. 809/293–0627. Admission free. Open Apr.–Oct., Mon.–Sat. 9–5, Sun.10–4; Nov.–Mar., Mon.–Sat. 9–4:30, closed Sun. and holidays.*

Time Out   Just up the road, **Bailey's Ice Cream Parlour & Food D'Lites** (Blue Hole Hill, tel. 809/293–9333) offers 40 varieties of freshly made natural ice cream, as well as shakes, sodas, yogurts, and sorbets. For something a bit stronger, cross the road for a rum swizzle and a "swizzleburger" at the **Swizzle Inn** (Blue Hole Hill, tel. 809/293–9300).

Blue Hole Hill leads to the causeway over Castle Harbour. Once on the other side you are in St. George's Parish. Take Kindley Field Road around the airport, turn left onto Mullet Bay Road, and cross Swing Bridge over Ferry Reach. ⑤⑤ The **Bermuda Biological Station for Research** will be of interest to anyone who cares about the environment. Scientists here have conducted research on marine life since 1903. Facilities include ships for ocean research, 13 laboratories, a 250-seat lecture hall, and a 20,000-volume library. Research programs here focus on environmental issues such as global change and the health of Bermuda's reefs. Extensive research has been conducted here on acid rain. Guided tours of the grounds and laboratory are conducted every Wednesday at 10 AM, beginning in the main building. Coffee and snacks are served. *17 Biological La., Ferry Reach, St. George's, tel. 809/297–1880.*

The scenery is magnificent along the stretch of road that runs between Mullet Bay and the sea. A little farther east, Mullet Bay Road becomes Wellington Road, and finally Duke of York Street when you reach St. George's (*see* Tour 2: The Town of St.George, *above*). East of town, Duke of York Street becomes Barrack Hill Road. From the road, the views of the town, St. David's Island, and Castle Harbour are splendid. Barrack Hill Road turns into Cut Road, ⑤⑥ which leads all the way to **Gates Fort.** St. George's has always had the greatest concentration of fortifications on the island. Gates Fort is a reconstruction of a small militia fort dating from the 1620s. Don't expect turrets, towers, and tunnels, however; there is little to see here apart from the sea. The fort and Gates Bay, which it overlooks, were named for Sir Thomas Gates, the first of the survivors of the *Sea Venture* to reach dry land. Upon doing so, he is reputed to have shouted, "This is Gates, his bay!" Public speaking was obviously not his forte, although Gates was by profession a politician—he later became governor of Virginia. *Cut Rd., no phone. Admission free. Open daily 10–4.*

The main camp of the *Sea Venture* survivors is believed to have been in this general area. Leaving Gates Fort via Barry Road, you'll pass **Buildings Bay.** One of the two ships that carried Sir George Somers and his crew to Virginia was built here in 1610, hence the bay's name.

⑤⑦ Continue up Barry Road to **Fort St. Catherine.** Apart from Dockyard, this restored fortress is the most impressive on the island: It has enough cannons, tunnels, and ramparts to satisfy the most avid military historian. One of a host of fortifications constructed in St. George's, the fort was begun around 1614 and work continued on it throughout the 19th century. As you travel through the tunnels, you'll come across some startlingly lifelike figures tucked into niches. Several dioramas depict the island's development, and an audiovisual presentation describes the building and significance of the fort. There is also a small but elaborate display of replicas of the crown jewels of England. *Barry Rd., tel. 809/297–1920. Admission: $2.50 adults, children under 12 free, but must be accompanied by an adult. Open daily 10– 4:30. Closed Christmas.*

St. Catherine's Beach, where the survivors from the Sea Venture scrambled ashore, is a pleasant place for a swim and quiet contemplation of the events of July 28, 1609. Another fine beach, with changing facilities and a refreshment stand, is at nearby **Tobacco Bay,** where the Tuckers secretly loaded the gunpowder bound for Boston in 1775 (*see* Tour 2: The Town of St. George, *above*). Retrace your route through St. George's to Swing Bridge that connects St. George's with St. David's Island. In addition to Bermuda's airport, about 2 square miles of St. David's is occupied by a U.S. Naval Air Station. In 1940, during World War II, Churchill agreed to give the United States a 99-year lease to operate a base on Bermuda in exchange for destroyers. The entire area taken up by the air station is now called St. David's, but construction of the base actually required linking three separate islands—St. David's, Longbird, and Cooper's—with landfills.

Christopher Carter, one of three men left behind when the *Deliverance* and the *Patience* sailed for Jamestown in 1610, was offered St. David's Island in 1612 as a reward for revealing the "Ambergris Plot." Before the ships returned to Bermuda, it seems, one of the three men, Edward Chard, found 80 pounds of ambergris (a precious sperm-whale product used for perfumes) washed up on the beach. In collusion with Carter and the third man, Chard planned to smuggle the ambergris off the island (when a ship arrived) and sell it in London at enormous profit. At the last minute, however, Carter squealed on his co-conspirators to Governor Moore, who had arrived in 1612 with new settlers. Instead of St. David's Island, Carter opted for Cooper's Island, which is also now part of the naval base. Built by Carter's descendants in 1640, **Carter House** is one of the oldest houses in Bermuda and should not be missed. The stone-and-cedar house has been refurbished with new floors and period furnishings, including a 17th-century bedding chest, a mortar and pestle, and an 18th-century tavern table, and is maintained by the naval base as a museum. You can reach Carter House through the main gate of the air station; you'll need a photo identification, and motorbike riders must wear helmets with face masks or protective glasses (this is a hard-hat area). Call to inquire what other restrictions may apply. *Kindley Field Rd., tel. 809/297– 1150 (ask for Ms. Lyndell O'Dey). Admission free. Open Wed. 10–3.*

Apart from the naval base, St. David's is a rustic spot where the inhabitants have always led an isolated life—some are said to have never visited St. George's, let alone the other end of the island. A number of residents had to be relocated when the base was built, but they refused to leave St. David's. Therefore, a section of St. David's called "Texas" was purchased by the government, which built cottages there for the displaced islanders. The area is just off the naval base; you can see Texas Road at the tip of the island near the lighthouse.

⑥ St. David's Lighthouse occupies the highest point on the island's eastern end. Built in 1879 of Bermuda stone, the lighthouse rises 280 feet above the sea. Although only about half the height of Gibbs Hill Lighthouse in Southampton Parish, it nevertheless affords spectacular views: From the balcony you can see St. David's and St. George's, Castle Harbour, and the reef-fringed south shore. The lighthouse is not always open; check with the Visitors Service Bureau in the Visitors Information Centre in Hamilton or St. George's.

Time Out   Right on the water near the lighthouse, the **Black Horse Tavern** (Clarkes Hill, tel. 809/293–9742) is a spot that's popular with the locals. Seafood is the specialty, and shark hash and curried conch stew are featured items. The fish sandwiches are delicious. There are outdoor picnic tables as well as indoor dining.

Head back across the causeway and turn left on Wilkinson Avenue. A network of caves, caverns, and subterranean lakes runs beneath the hills in this part of the island. Two of them are on the property of the nearby Grotto Bay Beach Hotel (*see* Chapter 9, Lodging). Just south of the hotel are **⑥ the Crystal Caves,** discovered in 1907 by two boys playing ball. When the ball disappeared down a hole, the boys burrowed after it and found themselves in a vast cavern 120 feet underground, surrounded by fantastic stalagmite and stalactite formations. Today, the approach is along a wet, sloping walkway and a wood pontoon bridge across the underground lake. After explaining the formation of stalactites and stalagmites, a tour guide uses a lighting system to make silhouettes. People who suffer from claustrophobia will probably want to give the caves a miss, because space can be quite tight. *8 Crystal Caves Rd., off Wilkinson Ave., tel. 809/293–0640. Admission: $3 adults, $1.50 children 5–11, children under 4 free. Open daily 9:30–4:30. Closed Remembrance Day (Nov. 11), Dec. 24–26 and Jan.*

Harrington Sound Road runs along the strip of land between the Sound and Castle Harbour. At Walsingham **⑥ Lane, you'll see a white sign for **Tom Moore's Tavern,** a popular restaurant. The restaurant was originally the home of Samuel Trott, who constructed it in the 17th century and named it Walsingham. (The harbor nearby was named for

Robert Walsingham, a sailor on the *Sea Venture* who apparently became enamored of the bay.) The house is surrounded by woods that are much the same as they were three centuries ago. When Tom Moore, the Irish poet, arrived in Bermuda in 1804, the house was occupied by a descendant of the original owner (also named Samuel Trott) and his family. The Trotts befriended the poet, who became a frequent visitor to the house. In Epistle V, Moore immortalized the Calabash Tree on the Trott estate under which he liked to write his verses. In 1844, the idea for the Royal Bermuda Yacht Club was conceived under the very same tree.

63 Harrington Sound Road leads southward to the **Amber Caves of Leamington,** smaller and less impressive than Crystal Caves. However, they do have their share of stalagmites and stalactites in fanciful formations, one of them an amber-tinted Statue of Liberty. Above ground, the Plantation restaurant (*see* Chapter 8, Dining) serves some of the island's best food—worth a trip whether you visit the caves or not. Lunch at the Plantation ($10 or more per person) entitles one to free admission to the caves. *Harrington Sound Rd., tel. 809/293–1188. Admission: $3 adults, $1.50 children 4–12. Open late Feb.–late Nov., Mon.–Sat. 9:30–4:30. Closed late Nov.–late Feb., Sun., and holidays.*

64 Farther south on Harrington Sound Road is **Tucker's Town,** named for Governor Daniel Tucker, who wanted to abandon St. George's in 1616 in favor of a new settlement on the shores of Castle Harbour. A few streets were laid out and some cottages were built, but the plan was eventually shelved. For 300 years Tucker's Town remained a small fishing and farming community: Cotton was grown for a while, and a few whaling boats operated from here. Dramatic change overtook the community soon after World War I, however. Seeking to raise the island's appeal in order to attract passengers on its luxury liners to Bermuda, a steamship company called Furness, Withy & Co. purchased a large area of Tucker's Town for a new country club. The result was the exclusive Mid Ocean Club, with its fine golf course. Members of the club started building residences nearby, and the Tucker's Town boom began. Today, only members of the club can buy a house in the area, and private residences have been known to sell for more than $2 million.

65 Below the clubhouse on the south shore are the **Natural Arches,** one of the island's oldest and most photographed attractions. Carved over the centuries by the wind and ocean, the two limestone arches rise 35 feet above the beach. Look for the signs near the end of South Shore Road pointing to Castle Harbour Beach and the Natural Arches.

A chain of islands dots the entrance channel to the harbor between St. David's and Tucker's Town Bay. In the colony's early days, these islands were fortified to protect Castle

Harbour from possible enemy attack. Soon after his arrival in 1612, Governor Moore built his first and best fort on **Castle Island.** According to an oft-told tale, two Spanish ships appeared outside the channel in 1614 and attempted to attack the colony. Two shots were fired from the fort: One fell into the water, and the other hit one of the ship's hulls. The Spaniards fled, unaware that the fortress had expended two-thirds of its stock of ammunition—the colonists had one cannonball left.

Touted as Bermuda's first tourist attraction, **Devil's Hole Aquarium** was started by a Mr. Trott in 1830. After building a wall around his fish pond—manifestly to prevent people from fishing in it—Mr. Trott was besieged with questions about what he was hiding. In 1843, yielding to the curiosity of the Bermudians, Mr. Trott permitted people to view his fish pond—at a fee. These days, the deep pool contains about 400 sea creatures, including giant grouper, sharks, and huge turtles. Visitors can play at fishing, using baited—but hookless—lines. *Harrington Sound Rd., tel. 809/293-2072. Admission: $5 adults, $3 children 6-12, 50¢ children 5 years and under. Open Apr.-Oct., daily 9-5; Nov.-Mar., daily 10-4. Closed Sat., Good Friday, and Christmas Day.*

Take steep Knapton Hill Road, which leads westward to South Shore Road and **Spittal Pond.** A showcase of the Bermuda National Trust, this nature park has 60 acres in which visitors can roam, although visitors are requested to keep to the walkways. More than 25 species of waterfowl winter here between November and May. On a high bluff, overlooking the ocean, is an oddity known as Spanish Marks. Early settlers found a rock crudely carved with the date 1543 and other markings that were unclear. It is now believed that a Portuguese ship was wrecked on the island in 1543, and that her sailors built a new ship on which they departed. The carvings are thought to be the initials *RP* (for Rex Portugaline), and the cross to be a badge of the Portuguese Order of Christ. The rock was removed to prevent further damage by erosion, and a plaque now marks the spot. A plaster-of-paris cast of the Spanish Marks is on display at the Museum of Bermuda Historical Society in Hamilton (*see Tour 1: Hamilton, above*). *South Shore Rd., no phone. Admission free. Open daily sunrise-sunset.*

West of Spittal Pond on South Shore Road is the turnoff to **Collector's Hill,** which is a very steep climb indeed. The hill is named for Gilbert Salton, a 19th-century customs collector who lived in a house near the top; the house has long since disappeared.

At the very top of Collector's Hill is **Verdmont,** Bermuda's finest house museum. It was built around 1710, possibly by a prominent shipowner named John Dickinson. At the end of the War of Independence, Verdmont was the home of John Green, an American Loyalist who fled to Bermuda from Philadelphia. Green married one of Dickinson's granddaughters and was appointed judge of the Court of Vice Admiralty. Green was also a portrait painter, and the only furnishings in the house from the 18th century are family portraits by him. The house, which resembles a small English manor house, has an unusual double roof and four large chimneys—all eight rooms have their own fireplace. Elegant cornice moldings and paneled shutters grace the two large reception rooms downstairs, originally the drawing room and formal dining room. The sash windows reflect a style that was fashionable in English manor houses. Although it contains none of the original furnishings, Verdmont is a treasure house of Bermudiana. Some of the furniture is mahogany imported from England—there are two exquisite early 19th-century pianos—but most of it is fine 18th-century cedar, crafted by Bermuda cabinetmakers. In particular, notice the desk in the drawing room, the lid and sides of which are made of single planks. Also displayed in the house is a china coffee service, said to have been a gift from Napoleon to President Madison. The president never received it: The ship bearing it across the Atlantic was seized by a Bermudian privateer and brought to Bermuda. Look carefully, too, at the handmade cedar staircase, with its handsomely turned newels and posts. The newel posts on each landing have removable caps to accommodate candles in the evening. Upstairs is a nursery: It's easy to imagine a child at play with the antique toys, riding the hand-propelled tricycle (circa 1840), or napping in the cedar cradle. The last occupant of Verdmont was an eccentric old woman, who lived here for 75 years without electricity or any other modern trappings. After her death, her family sold the house to the Bermuda Historic Monuments Trust—the forerunner of the Bermuda National Trust—which opened it as a museum in 1956. *Collector's Hill, tel. 809/236-7369. Admission: $3. Open Apr.–Oct., Mon.–Sat. 9:30–4:30; Nov.–Mar., Mon.–Sat. 10–4. Closed holidays.*

Time Out Popular with the locals, **Speciality Inn** (South Shore Rd., foot of Collector's Hill, tel. 809/236-3133) is a simple spot that serves pasta, pizza, sandwiches, soups, shakes, ice cream, and good breakfasts.

70 A singular delight of Devonshire Parish are the gardens at **Palm Grove,** a private estate. There is a splendid pond, within which is a relief map of the island—each parish is divided by carefully manicured grass sections. Desmond Fountain statues stand around the edge, peering into the pond's depths. *South Shore Rd., across from Brighton Hill, no phone. Admission free. Open weekdays 9–5.*

71 Brighton Hill Road, just west of Palm Grove, runs north to Middle Road and the **Old Devonshire Church,** the parish's biggest attraction. A church has stood on this site since 1612, although the original was replaced in 1716. That replacement church was almost completely destroyed in an explosion on Easter Sunday in 1970, and the present church is a faithful reconstruction. A small, simple building of limestone and cedar, it looks much like an early Bermuda cottage. The three-tier pulpit, the pews, and the communion table are believed to be from the original church. Some pieces of church silver date back to 1590 and are said to be the oldest on the island. A cedar chest, believed to have once held the church records, dates from the early 17th century. Other pieces that have survived include an old cedar armchair, a candelabra, a cross, and a cedar screen. *Middle Rd., Devonshire, tel. 809/236–3671. Admission free. Open daily 9–5:30.*

Turn left off Middle Road onto Tee Street, and then right onto Berry Hill Road. One mile farther on the left is the turnoff to Point Finger Road and the **Botanical Gardens,** a landscaped park laced with roads and paths. Information is available in the visitors center, where there are also gift and tea shops. Offices of the Agriculture Department are also on the grounds. The gardens are a fragrant showcase for the island's exotic subtropical plants, flowers, and trees. Within the 36 acres are a miniature forest, an aviary, a hibiscus garden (with more than 150 species of the flower), and a special Garden for the Blind, which is filled with the scent of lemon, lavender, and spices. Ninety-minute walking tours of the gardens leave the visitors center at 10:30 AM on Tuesday, Wednesday, and Friday (Tuesday and Friday only from November 15 to March). *Point Finger Rd., tel. 809/236–4201. Admission free. Open daily sunrise–sunset.*

The pretty white home on the grounds of the Botanical Gardens is **Camden,** the official residence of Bermuda's premier. A large two-story house, Camden is more typical of West Indian estate architecture than traditional Bermudian building. The house is open for tours, except when official functions are scheduled. *Botanical Gardens, tel. 809/236–5732. Admission free. Open Tues. and Fri. noon–2.*

A few minutes away by moped are the offices of the **Bermuda National Trust,** a nonprofit organization that oversees the restoration and preservation of many of the island's gardens and historic homes. The trust is also a wonderful source of information about the island. The offices and "Trustworthy" gift shop are in a rambling 18th-century house built by the Trimingham family. Island crafts, novelties, and Trust logo items are sold in the shop; all proceeds go to the Trust. *"Waterville," 5 The Lane, Paget, tel. 809/236–6483. Open weekdays 9–4:30. Gift shop open Tues.–Sat. 10–4.*

The first half of the tour ends here: Hamilton is just a few hundred yards up the road. The second part of the tour heads west through the parishes of Paget, Warwick, and Southampton.

74 On Harbour Road near the Lower Ferry Landing, **Clermont** is an imposing house noted for its fine woodwork. Once the residence of Sir Brownlow Gray, Chief Justice of Bermuda, the house is also famous for having Bermuda's first tennis courts. During a visit from New York in 1874, Miss Mary Outerbridge learned to play here. Upon her return to the United States, she asked the Staten Island Cricket Club to build a court; armed with her racquet and a book of rules, she introduced tennis to America. This house is not open to the public, although it is sometimes included in the spring House and Gardens Tour (*see* Guided Tours in Chapter 1, Essential Information).

75 Turn left on Valley Road to reach **St. Paul's,** built in 1796 to replace an earlier church on the site. Around the turn of the century, the "Paget Ghost" began to be heard in and around St. Paul's. Nothing could be seen, but the mysterious sound of tinkling bells was plainly audible, coming from several directions. The ghost became quite famous, and a veritable posse—armed with firearms and clubs— gathered to find it; vendors even set up refreshment stands. Finally, a visiting American scientist proclaimed that the tinkling sound came from a rare bird, the fililo. According to the scientist, the fililo was a natural ventriloquist, which explained why the sound jumped around. No one ever saw the fililo, however, and no one saw the ghost either—it disappeared as mysteriously as it had appeared.

76 St. Paul's sits on the edge of **Paget Marsh,** 18 acres of unspoiled woodland that look much as they did when the first settlers arrived. Protected by the Bermuda National Trust, the marsh contains cedars and palmettos, endangered plants, and a mangrove swamp. *Middle Rd., tel. 809/ 236–6483. Admission by arrangement with the Bermuda National Trust.*

From St. Paul's, head west into Warwick Parish along Middle Road. Just after the intersection with Ord Road (opposite the Belmont Hotel, Golf & Country Club), look to your
77 left to see **Christ Church.** Built in 1719, it is reputedly the oldest Presbyterian church in any British colony or dominion.

Turn left off Middle Road onto Camp Hill Road, which winds down to the south shore beaches. Along the way is **Warwick Camp,** built in the 1870s to guard against any enemy landing on the beaches. The camp was used as a training ground and rifle range during World War I. In 1920, Pearl White of *The Perils of Pauline* fame came to Bermuda to shoot a movie, bringing along an entourage that included lions, monkeys, and a host of other exotic fauna. Scenes for the film were shot on Warwick Bay, below the rifle range. Most Bermudians had never seen either a lion or a movie star, and huge crowds collected to watch the filming.

Time Out A moderately priced roadside restaurant, **Tio Pepe's** (South Shore Rd., near the entrance to Horseshoe Bay, tel. 809/238–1897) serves Spanish and Italian foods and pizza to go.

Bermuda's beaches tend to elicit the most effusive travel-writing clichés—simply because they are so good. A 3-mile chain of sandy beaches, coves, and inlets begins at Warwick Long Bay and extends to Horseshoe Bay in the east (*see* Chapter 6, Beaches and Water Sports). Just east of Warwick Bay, **Astwood Park** is a lovely public park with picnic tables and two beaches, one of them ideal for snorkeling.

Two miles west along South Shore Road is the turnoff for Lighthouse Road. High atop Gibbs Hill, **Gibbs Hill Lighthouse** is the second cast-iron lighthouse ever built. Designed in London and opened in 1846, the tower stands 133 feet high and 360 feet above the sea. The original light mechanism had to be wound every three hours, a process that took three minutes. Today, the beam from the 1,500-watt bulb can be seen by ships 40 miles out to sea, and by planes 120 miles away at 10,000 feet. You can climb to the top of the lighthouse, although this is not a trip for anyone who suffers from vertigo. It's a long haul up the 185 spiral stairs—you have to climb another 30 steps just to reach the entrance—but you can stop to catch your breath at platforms along the way, where photographs and drawings of the lighthouse are displayed. At the top you can stroll on the balcony for a spectacular view of Bermuda. The wind may snatch you bald-headed—the tower is known to sway in high winds—and you may find it hard to concentrate on the view knowing that a tiny guard rail is the only thing between you and a swan dive. (An alternative is to inch around with your back pressed against the tower, clinging to it for dear life). *Lighthouse Rd., Southampton, tel. 809/238–0524. Admission: $2 adults, children under 6 free. Open daily 9–4:30. Closed Christmas.*

If you're still feeling adventurous, turn left off Middle Road onto Whale Bay Road (just before the Port Royal Golf & Country Club), and go down the hill to **Whale Bay Fort.** Overgrown with grass, flowers, and subtropical plants, this small 19th-century battery offers little in the way of a history lesson, but it does overlook a secluded pink-sand beach, gin-clear water, and craggy cliffs. The beach is accessible only on foot, but it's a splendid place for a swim. Bear in mind that you have to climb back up the hill to your moped or bike.

Just before Somerset Bridge is a little street with the odd name of **Overplus,** which harks back to the 17th century. When Richard Norwood surveyed the island in 1616, he divided the island into shares and tribes. He allotted 25 acres to each share, and 50 shares to each tribe. When the survey was completed, 200 acres (too small to form a tribe) remained unallotted and were listed as "overplus." Governor

Tucker apparently directed the surveyor to keep an eye peeled for an attractive chunk of territory that could be designated as the surplus land. Norwood recommended a piece of real estate in the western part of the island, whereupon the governor claimed it and built a fine house on it. Upon hearing of the governor's action, the Bermuda Company lodged a complaint, forcing Tucker to return to London to sort everything out. The surplus land was eventually divided into seven parts, with Tucker retaining the section on which his house sat; the remainder was given to the church.

Across Somerset Bridge is the West End (*see* Tour 3: The West End, *above*). If you are traveling by bike or by moped, you can catch a ferry from Somerset Bridge back to Hamilton. Otherwise, take your choice of Middle, Harbour, or South Shore roads, to find your way back to the capital.

Bermuda for Free

Bermuda is an expensive vacation destination. The cost of lodging and food aside, however, many of the island attractions are free. Certainly, Bermuda's greatest attractions— the sea and its beaches—don't cost a penny, but there is also a host of historical sites and museums that don't charge admission fees. Large portions of the exploring tours in this guide can be enjoyed for a few dollars at most. During the low and shoulder seasons (October–April), the government and the Department of Tourism sponsor a whole range of free or inexpensive activities, from walking tours and house tours to fashion shows. Listed below are attractions described in the exploring tours and elsewhere that can be enjoyed for free.

Astwood Park (*see* Tour 4: The Parishes)
Barr's Bay Park (*see* Tour 1: Hamilton)
Beaches (*see* Chapter 6, Beaches and Water Sports)
Bermuda Public Library (*see* Tour 1: Hamilton)
Black Watch Well (*see* Tour 4: The Parishes)
Botanical Gardens (*see* Tour 4: The Parishes)
Cabinet Building and Sessions House (*see* Tour 1: Hamilton)
Camden (*see* Tour 4: The Parishes)
Carter House (*see* Tour 4: The Parishes)
City Hall (*see* Tour 1: Hamilton)
Featherbed Alley Printery (*see* Tour 2: The Town of St. George)
Fort Hamilton (*see* Tour 1: Hamilton)
Gates Fort (*see* Tour 4: The Parishes)
Heydon Chapel (*see* Tour 3: The West End)
Old Rectory (*see* Tour 2: The Town of St. George)
Par-la-Ville Park (*see* Tour 1: Hamilton)
St. Peter's Church (*see* Tour 2: The Town of St. George)
Scaur Hill Fort (*see* Tour 3: The West End)

What to See and Do with Children

Although Bermuda has no amusement parks, fairs, and such, the island is becoming more user-friendly for children. In addition to the obvious attractions of surf and sand, and several hotels that offer day care and children's activities, the aquarium has a children's Discovery Room, and children visiting the Bermuda Maritime Museum are given a free book that helps them understand what the Royal Naval Dockyard is all about. Other books are available that can make exploring the island with children much easier. The first, *The Bermuda Coloring Book*, by Diana Watlington Ruetenik, is an educational book with historical sites for small children to color. The second, *A Child's History of Bermuda*, by E. M. Rice, puts the island's history into words that are easy to understand. Both books are available at A. S. Cooper & Son (59 Front St., Hamilton, 809/295–3961). Listed below are some of the attractions in the exploring tours and elsewhere that will appeal to children.

Aquarium, Museum and Zoo (*see* Tour 4: The Parishes)
Beaches (*see* Chapter 6, Beaches and Water Sports)
Bermuda Maritime Museum (*see* Tour 3: The West End)
Botanical Gardens (*see* Tour 4: The Parishes)
Ferries (*see* Getting Around Bermuda in Chapter 1, Essential Information)
Glass-bottom boat ride (*see* Guided Tours in Chapter 1, Essential Information)

Off the Beaten Track

The **Railway Trail** is a secluded 18-mile track that runs the length of the island along the route of the old Bermuda Railway. Restricted to pedestrians, horseback riders, and cyclists, the trail is a delightful way to see the island, away from the traffic and noise of the main roads. The Bermuda Department of Tourism has published *The Bermuda Railway Trail Guide*, which is available at all Visitors Service Bureaus and Information Centres. The pamphlet includes seven separate walking tours, ranging from about two to four hours, and an outline of what you can expect to see along the way. (For more information about sights along the way, refer to the appropriate section of the exploring tours, above. See also "Following in the Tracks of the Bermuda Railway," in Chapter 2, Portraits of Bermuda.) It should be noted that many of the trails are quite isolated, and none is heavily trafficked. Although Bermuda has no major crime problem, unpleasant incidents do sometimes occur; women travelers especially should avoid striking out on remote trails alone. Apart from reasons of safety, the Railway Trail is much more enjoyable shared with a companion.

The history of the railway that ran along this trail is fascinating. Aside from horse-drawn carriages, boats, and bikes, the Bermuda Railway—"Old Rattle and Shake" as it was called—was the primary means of transportation on the island from 1931 to 1948. As early as 1899, however, the Bermuda Public Works Department bandied about proposals for a railroad. In 1922, over the objections of livery stable owners, the Bermuda Parliament finally granted permission for a narrow-gauge railroad to run from Somerset to St. George's.

The laying of the tracks was a formidable undertaking, requiring the construction of long tunnels and swing bridges. By the time it was finished in 1931, the railway had cost the investors $1 million. Mile for mile it was the most expensive railroad ever built, and the construction, which proceeded at a somnolent 2½ miles per year, was the slowest ever recorded. Nevertheless, on October 31, 1931, the little train got off to a roaring start with festive opening ceremonies at Somerset Bridge.

Passengers in the first-class carriages sat in wicker chairs, and the second-class cars were outfitted with benches. An American visitor reported in glowing terms of her first train ride in Bermuda, waxing lyrical about rolling cedar-covered hills, green velvet lawns, and banks of pink oleanders. Certainly, it was a vast improvement over the 19th-century horse buses that lumbered from Somerset to St. George's, carrying freight as well as passengers. Not everyone was happy, however. One writer groused that the train was "an iron serpent in the Garden of Eden." "Old Rattle and Shake" began going downhill during World War II. While the train was put to hard use by all the military personnel on the island, it proved impossible to obtain the necessary maintenance equipment. At the end of the war, the government acquired the distressed railway for £115,000. After the arrival of the automobile on Bermuda in 1946, the government sold the railway in its entirety to British Guiana (now Guyana).

Sightseeing Checklists

Historical Buildings and Sights

"Birdcage" (*see* Tour 1: Hamilton)
Black Watch Well (*see* Tour 4: The Parishes)
Bridge House (*see* Tour 2: The Town of St. George)
Cabinet Building (*see* Tour 1: Hamilton)
Camden (*see* Tour 4: The Parishes)
Cenotaph (*see* Tour 1: Hamilton)
City Hall (*see* Tour 1: Hamilton)
Clermont (*see* Tour 4: The Parishes)
Deliverance II (*see* Tour 2: The Town of St. George)

Featherbed Alley Printery (*see* Tour 2: The Town of St.George)
Gibbs Hill Lighthouse (*see* Tour 4: The Parishes)
Government House (*see* Tour 4: The Parishes)
Old Rectory (*see* Tour 2: The Town of St. George)
Old State House (*see* Tour 2: The Town of St. George)
Palmetto House (*see* Tour 4: The Parishes)
Perot Post Office (*see* Tour 1: Hamilton)
Printer's Alley (*see* Tour 2: The Town of St. George)
Royal Bermuda Yacht Club (*see* Tour 1: Hamilton)
Sessions House (*see* Tour 1: Hamilton)
St. David's Lighthouse (*see* Tour 4: The Parishes)
Tom Moore's Tavern (*see* Tour 4: The Parishes)
Town Hall (*see* Tour 2: The Town of St. George)
White Horse Tavern (*see* Tour 2: The Town of St. George)

Churches

Cathedral of the Most Holy Trinity (*see* Tour 1: Hamilton)
Christ Church (*see* Tour 4: The Parishes)
Heydon Chapel on the grounds of the Heydon Trust property (*see* Tour 3: The West End)
Holy Trinity Church (*see* Tour 4: The Parishes)
Old Devonshire Church (*see* Tour 4: The Parishes)
St. James Church (*see* Tour 3: The West End)
St. John's Church (*see* Tour 4: The Parishes)
St. Paul's (*see* Tour 4: The Parishes)
St. Peter's Church (*see* Tour 2: The Town of St. George)
St. Theresa's Church (*see* Tour 1: Hamilton)
Unfinished Church (*see* Tour 2: The Town of St. George)

Forts

Castle Island (*see* Tour 4: The Parishes)
Fort Hamilton (*see* Tour 1: Hamilton)
Fort St. Catherine (*see* Tour 4: The Parishes)
Gates Fort (*see* Tour 4: The Parishes)
Royal Naval Dockyard (*see* Tour 3: The West End)
Scaur Hill Fort (*see* Tour 3: The West End)
Warwick Camp (*see* Tour 4: The Parishes)
Whale Bay Fort (*see* Tour 4: The Parishes)

Museums and Galleries

Aquarium, Museum and Zoo (*see* Tour 4: The Parishes)
Bank of Bermuda (*see* Tour 1: Hamilton)
Bermuda Public Library and Museum of the Bermuda Historical Society (*see* Tour 1: Hamilton)
Carriage Museum (*see* Tour 2: The Town of St. George)
Carter House (*see* Tour 4: The Parishes)
Confederate Museum (*see* Tour 2: The Town of St. George)
Maritime Museum (*see* Tour 3: The West End)
Railway Museum (*see* Tour 4: The Parishes)

St. George's Historical Society Museum (*see* Tour 2: The Town of St. George)
Tucker House (*see* Tour 2: The Town of St. George)
Verdmont (*see* Tour 4: The Parishes)

Parks and Gardens

Admiralty House Park (*see* Tour 4: The Parishes)
Albuoy's Point (*see* Tour 1: Hamilton)
Astwood Park (*see* Tour 4: The Parishes)
Barr's Bay Park (*see* Tour 1: Hamilton)
Botanical Gardens (*see* Tour 4: The Parishes)
Gilbert Nature Reserve (*see* Tour 3: The West End)
Heydon Trust property (*see* Tour 3: The West End)
Lagoon Park (*see* Tour 3: The West End)
Long Bay Park and Nature Reserve (*see* Tour 3: The West End)
Paget Marsh (*see* Tour 4: The Parishes)
Palm Grove (*see* Tour 4: The Parishes)
Par-la-Ville Park (*see* Tour 1: Hamilton)
Somers Garden (*see* Tour 2: The Town of St. George)
Spittal Pond (*see* Tour 4: The Parishes)
Victoria Park (*see* Tour 1: Hamilton)

5 Shopping

By Honey Naylor   If you're looking for colorful street markets where you can haggle over the price of low-cost goods and souvenirs, find another island. Shopping in Bermuda is characterized by sophisticated department stores and boutiques that stock top-quality—and expensive—merchandise. Bargains are a rarity (though Bermudians are alarmed at the proliferation of Front Street T-shirt shops), and only products actually made in Bermuda (and antiques more than 100 years old) can be sold duty-free. If you're accustomed to shopping in Saks Fifth Avenue, Neiman-Marcus, and Bergdorf-Goodman, the prices in Bermuda's elegant shops won't come as a surprise. Actually, the prices on many items in Bermuda's stores are discounted, but a $600 dress discounted by 20% is still $480. Bermuda shopkeepers have felt the effect of the growing number of discount stores in the United States. It would be wise to check discount prices at home and then compare Bermuda prices on items that are of interest to you. The quality of goods in Bermuda is quite good, and if you are looking for high-end merchandise, Bermuda does offer substantial savings on many items, particularly British-made clothing. Woolens and cashmere are good buys, especially in February when there is a host of sales during which many stores offer two-for-one sweater deals. Bermuda shorts are hot items, obviously, as are kilts.

European-made crystal and china—Wedgwood, Royal Crown Derby, Villeroy & Boch, Waterford, and Orrefors, to name a few—are available at prices at least 25% lower than those in the United States. Figurines from Lladro, Royal Doulton, and Hummel are also sold at significantly discounted prices. European fragrances and cosmetics are priced about 20%–25% less than in the United States, as are Rolex, Tissot, Patek Philippe, and other watches.

Bermuda has a thriving population of artists and artisans, whose work ranges from sculpture and paintings to miniature furniture, hand-blown glass, and dolls (*see* Arts and Crafts, *below*). Bermuda also has a number of noteworthy products to offer. Outerbridge's Sherry Peppers condiments add zip to soups, stews, drinks, and chowders. The original line has been expanded to include Bloody Mary mix, pepper jellies, and barbecue sauce; gift packs are available all over the island.

Bermuda rum is another popular item, and a variety of rum-based liqueurs is available, including Bermuda Banana, Banana Coconut Rum, and Bermuda Gold. Gosling's Black Seal Rum is excellent mixed with ginger beer to make a Dark 'n' Stormy, a famous Bermuda drink that should be treated with respect and caution. Rum is also found in quantity in Horton's Rum Cakes, which are made from a secret recipe and sold island-wide. U.S. citizens aged 21 or older, who have been out of the country for 48 hours, are allowed to bring home one liter of duty-free liquor each (*see* Customs and Duties in Chapter 1, Essential Information).

In a bizarre catch-22, however, Bermuda requires a minimum purchase of two liters. Some liquor stores tell tourists that they must buy a minimum of four or five bottles to qualify for in-bond (duty-free) prices, but it isn't true. Although liquor prices are identical island-wide, some stores allow customers to create their own mixed packs of various liquors at in-bond prices, while others offer a selection of prepackaged sets (the five-pack is most common). Duty-free liquor must be purchased at least 24 hours before your departure, and it can be picked up only in the airport departure lounge or on board your cruise ship. The airport has no duty-free shop of its own. Below are some sample prices at press time for one liter of liquor: Tia Maria, $14; Grand Marnier, $27.50; Chivas Regal, (12-year-old) $26.50; J&B Rare, $13.10; Johnnie Walker Black, $23; Stolichnaya vodka, $9.30; Beefeater gin, $13; and Bermuda rum, $8.

Panatel VDS has produced several half-hour videos, including "Bermuda Highlights," "Dive Bermuda," and "Bermuda Bound, Paradise Found." Priced at $29.95, and available for both North American and European systems, the videos are sold at several stores and shops around the island.

Comparison shopping is probably a waste of time in Bermuda because the merchants' association keeps prices almost identical island-wide. However, it's worth checking the price of items at home—especially crystal and china—before you embark on a shopping spree in Bermuda. Ask your local department store if any sales are scheduled and check the prices of designer and name-brand products at local factory outlets. Remember that Bermuda, unlike most U.S. states, has no sales tax, which means that the price on the tag is the price you pay.

Although the numbering of houses is becoming more common (houses have traditionally been known only by their picturesque names rather than numbers), buildings in Hamilton are still numbered rather whimsically. If you check the phone directory for a store address, you may find a listing on Front Street or Water Street, for example, but no street number. In fact, some Front Street buildings have two numbers, one of them an old historic address that has nothing to do with the building's present location. Fortunately, almost all Bermudians can give you precise directions.

In general, shops are open Monday–Saturday 9–5 or 9–5:30, and close on Sunday and public holidays. Several Hamilton shops stay open on Friday until 9 from the end of November until Christmas Eve. In the two weeks before Christmas many stores stay open until 9 most nights. When cruise ships call (Apr.–Oct.), some Front Street shops stay open until 10:30 and are open also on Sunday.

In most cases in this chapter, if a store has several branches or outlets, only the main branch phone number has been listed. Unless otherwise noted the shops listed below accept American Express, MasterCard, and Visa.

Shopping Districts

Hamilton boasts the greatest concentration of shops in Bermuda, and **Front Street** is its pièce de résistance. Lined with small, pastel-colored buildings, this most fashionable of Bermuda's streets houses sedate department stores and snazzy boutiques, with several small arcades and shopping alleys leading off it. A smart canopy shades the entrance to the **55 Front Street Group,** which houses several upmarket boutiques. **The Emporium** on Front Street, a renovated old building arranged around an open atrium, is home to an eclectic collection of dress and jewelry shops. The statue on top of the atrium fountain is of Bermudian Gina Swainson, who ruled as Miss World in 1979–80. **Windsor Place** is a modern mall on Queen Street where you can get anything from running shoes, sunblock, and greeting cards to haircuts, handblown glass, and cash (there's an ATM machine on the lower level).

In St. George's, **Water Street, Duke of York Street, and Somers Wharf** are the site of numerous renovated buildings that now house boutiques and branches of Front Street stores. **King's Square** is also dotted with shops selling everything from dresses to sweaters and ties. In the West End, **Somerset Village** has a few shops, but they hardly merit a special shopping trip. However, the Clocktower Mall at Royal Naval Dockyard has a plethora of shops, including branches of Front Street shops and specialty boutiques. Dockyard is also home to the Craft Market, the Bermuda Arts Centre, and Island Pottery, where local artisans display their wares and visitors can sometimes watch them at work. Several other small plazas are sprinkled over the island, featuring a few shops, and often a grocery store and post office.

Department Stores

Bermuda's three leading department stores are A. S. Cooper & Son, Trimingham's, and H. A. & E. Smith's, the main branches of which are on Front Street in Hamilton. These elegant, venerable institutions are operated by the third or fourth generation of the families that founded them, and customers stand a good chance of being waited on by a Cooper, a Trimingham, or a Smith. In addition, many of the salespeople have worked at the stores for two or three decades; they tend to be unobtrusive, but polite and helpful when you need them.

A. S. Cooper & Son (59 Front St., Hamilton, tel. 809/295–3961) is best known for Wedgwood bone china. A five-piece

Hamilton Shopping

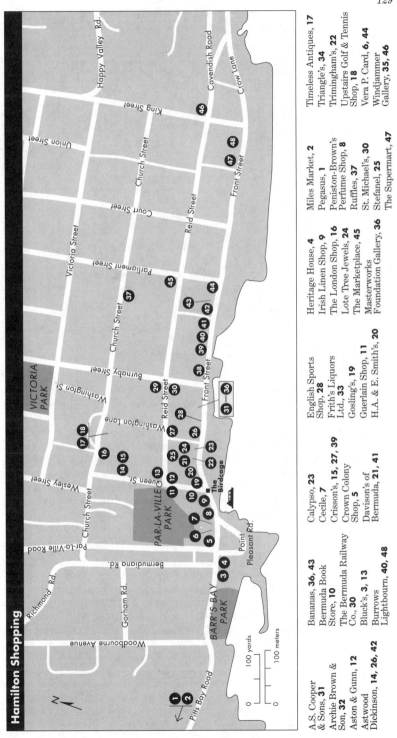

A.S. Cooper
& Sons, **31**
Archie Brown &
Son, **32**
Astwood
Dickinson, **14, 26, 42**

Bananas, **36, 43**
Bermuda Book
Store, **10**
The Bermuda Railway
Co., **30**
Bluck's, **3, 13**
Burrows
Lightbourn, **40, 48**

Calypso, **23**
Cecile, **7**
Crisson's, **15, 27, 39**
Crown Colony
Shop, **5**
Davison's of
Bermuda, **21, 41**

English Sports
Shop, **28**
Frith's Liquors
Ltd., **33**
Gosling's, **19**
Guerlain Shop, **11**
H.A. & E. Smith's, **20**

Heritage House, **4**
Irish Linen Shop, **9**
The London Shop, **16**
Lote Tree Jewels, **24**
The Marketplace, **45**
Masterworks
Foundation Gallery, **36**

Miles Market, **2**
Pegasus, **1**
Peniston-Brown's
Perfume Shop, **8**
Ruffles, **37**
St. Michael's, **30**
Stefanel, **25**
The Supermart, **47**

Timeless Antiques, **17**
Triangle's, **34**
Trimingham's, **22**
Upstairs Golf & Tennis
Shop, **18**
Vera P. Card, **6, 44**
Windjammer
Gallery, **35, 46**

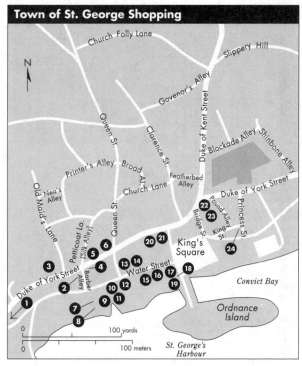

Town of St. George Shopping

place setting of the Wedgwood Wild Strawberry pattern costs $105, or $131.35 (including duty, freight, and insurance) if you want it shipped to the United States. Prices on other well-known brands of china, as well as crystal, are similarly attractive. The store's own private-label collection of clothing can be found in the well-stocked men's and women's departments. Shoppers can have breakfast, lunch, or afternoon tea at Romancing the Scone, a tiny balcony restaurant just off the second floor that has a magnificent view of the harbor. It's open Mon.–Sat. 9–4. Other branches of the department store can be found in all major hotels and in St. George's at 22 Water Street.

H. A. & E. Smith's (35 Front St., Hamilton, tel. 809/295–2288), founded in 1889 by Henry Archibald and Edith Smith, is arguably the best men's store in Bermuda—and exclusive agents for Burberry and Alan Paine. Burberry raincoats are priced from $385–$595, and Alan Paine cable-knit sweaters sell for about $375; a Chester Barrie cashmere jacket costs around $650, a madras jacket around $230. You can buy Harris Tweed jackets for $180, men's 100% cashmere topcoats for $395, and Italian silk ties for $30. There is a large selection of Shetland sweaters, which go for about $30 each. Smith's is also a good place to buy kilts. Ladies can find Christian Dior handbags for about $300, and ladies' cashmere-lined leather gloves cost $65 (un-

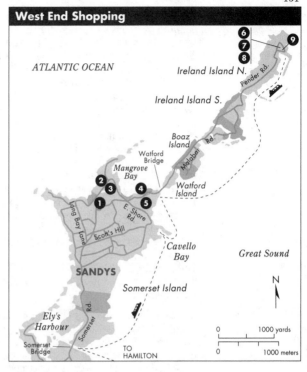

West End Shopping

lined $45). Unfortunately, the store's confusing layout makes it easy to get lost. The staff here is especially genteel, however, and they will help orient you. Branches can be found in the Belmont and Southampton Princess hotels and at 18 York Street in St. George's.

St. Michael's (10 Reid St., Hamilton, tel. 809/295–0031), an offshoot of Britain's Marks & Spencer, is called Marks and Sparks by everyone in Bermuda. This large store is usually filled with thrift-minded Britons attracted by its moderate prices for men's, women's, and children's clothing. Summer wear, including swimsuits, cotton jerseys, and polo shirts, is a good buy. High-quality men's and women's cashmere and woolen sweaters are also sold at substantial discounts.

Trimingham's (37 Front St., Hamilton, tel. 809/295–1183) has been a Hamilton fixture since 1842. The first store in the world to tailor madras for Western clothing, this is the place to look for men's colorful madras blazers and trousers. The store also has its own line of sportswear, and Bermuda shorts are good buys. In womenswear, savings can be found on Shetland and lamb's wool sweaters, but prices for Dean's of Scotland woolens are about the same, or even a bit less, in the United States. Liberty of London and Hermès scarves are definitely worth a look. The store has an impressive display of perfumes and cosmetics, and it is the exclusive Bermuda distributor for Tiffany and Boucheron fragrances. La

Prairie, the beauty treatment from Montreux, is discounted by about 20%. Head for the excellent gift boutique to buy Outerbridge's Sherry Pepper Sauce or a box of Trimingham's hand-baked assorted cookies. Trimingham branches have sprouted up all over the island, including at Somers Wharf in St. George's and in Somerset Village.

Grocery Stores

Most of the accommodation on Bermuda, from cottage colonies to guest houses and housekeeping apartments, offers guests the opportunity to do their own cooking. Self-catering vacations are cheaper than those where you pay full board or dine out at every meal; considering how expensive Bermuda is, this option has widespread appeal for both families and budget travelers. Don't expect the same prices as at home, however—foodstuffs in Bermuda are also quite expensive. For example, a dozen large eggs costs $2.85, a six-pack of Coke is $4.35, a 13-ounce can of coffee is $3.56, a 10-ounce box of shredded wheat is $3.29, and a quart of Tropicana orange juice $3.45. Listed below are some of the major supermarkets in Bermuda.

A-1 Fine Food Market (South Shore Rd., Paget, tel. 809/236–0351) features a take-out counter that serves inexpensive ($6–$9) chicken dinners, french fries, burgers, hot dogs, and sandwiches. The store is near Barnsdale Guest Apartments and the Sky Top Cottages, but you will need a vehicle to carry heavy groceries up the hill.

The Giant Store (Middle Rd., Warwick, tel. 809/236–1344) is a medium-size convenience store within walking distance of the Pretty Penny guest house.

Harrington Hundreds Grocery & Liquor Store (South Rd., Smith's, tel. 809/293–1635) is near Spittal Pond, not far from Angel's Grotto apartments; it may be too far to walk, however.

The Marketplace (Reid St., near Parliament St., Hamilton, tel. 809/292–3163) is part of a moderately priced chain with stores around the island. Customers can get hot soups to go.

Miles Market (Pitts Bay Rd., near The Princess, Hamilton, tel. 809/295–1234) has expensive steaks and Häagen-Dazs ice cream. The market makes deliveries anywhere on the island.

The Supermart (Front St., near King St., Hamilton, tel. 809/292–2064) has a well-stocked salad bar, prepackaged sandwiches, and hot coffee. This store and Miles Market are a five-minute ferry ride across the harbor from the Greenbank Cottages and Salt Kettle House.

Specialty Stores

Antiques **Heritage House** (2 W. Front St., Hamilton, tel. 809/295–2615). Browsers will find it difficult to tear themselves away from this small shop, which features an array of both antique and modern pieces. Among the antiques recently featured were an early 19th-century, mahogany corner washstand for $1,795; several handmade chess sets (one of them with Battle of the Alamo chess pieces) at around $875; an 1800 walnut chest of drawers, $3,500; a wind-up gramophone for $1,200; a Cartier silver dressing case (London, 1930) for $960; and a charming collection of miniature cottages by British sculptor David Winter. Prices range from $22.50 for a small cottage to $644 for an elaborate Castle in the Air. The original works of several local artists are also on display. Shoppers who don't want to make a major purchase can search through bins of prints. The shop has its own framing department.

Pegasus (63 Pitts Bay Rd., Hamilton, tel. 809/295–2900). A Dickensian place with creaky wood floors, this store has racks and racks of antique prints and maps. In particular, look for the "original" *Vanity Fair* caricatures that were published between 1869 and 1914 ($40–$100) and the Dickens characters by 19th-century artist Frederick Barnard ($50–$100). Among the antique maps are some 18th-century representations of the United States priced at $300, and others showing the castles of Ireland, Scotland, and England. There are several racks of children's books (about $5.50) by British authors, as well as a good selection of postcards, whimsical greeting cards, and wrapping paper. Shoppers can browse here to their hearts' content. Diners Club cards are accepted here in addition to those credit cards mentioned above.

Timeless Antiques (26 Church St., Hamilton, tel. 809/295–5008, fax 809/295–8306). Across the street and down the steps from City Hall, you'll find this small, Old World shop, where the walls are lined with 200- to 300-year-old grandfather (or long-case) clocks. Among the store's collection of antiques are carved Early English oak tables, chests, chairs, candelabra, and exquisite reproductions of medieval tapestries. Time is of the essence here, however, and clock aficionados will want to spend hours talking with proprietor Peter Durhager. If $8,000 for a long-case clock is a little too rich for your blood, take a look at the collection of antique pocket watches.

Arts and Crafts Buying artwork by someone you know is always more satis-
Artists fying than buying it blind, and some of Bermuda's resident artists encourage visits to their studios. Call ahead first, however, to find out if it's convenient to stop by, and be sure to check which credit cards each artist accepts. Remember that there are no duties levied on Bermudian arts and crafts.

Celia and Jack Arnell (tel. 809/236–4646). The miniature cedar furniture crafted by this husband-and-wife team is displayed in a dollhouse at the Craft Market (*see below*). The fine details on the breakfronts and chests of drawers include tiny metal drawer knobs, and the wonderful four-poster bed comes complete with a canopy. A breakfront sells for $140; the four-poster bed for $100; and chairs for $27.

Kathleen Kemsley Bell (tel. 809/236–3366). A director of the Bermuda Arts Centre, Ms. Bell creates exquisite dolls of a particular person or period in Bermuda's history. Each doll is researched for historical accuracy and is unique. The bodies are sculpted of papier-mâché and hand-painted. The faces of the dolls are marvelously expressive, and the costumes are all hand-stitched. The base of each doll is signed and carries a description of the historical period on which the doll's fashions are based. Ms. Bell works on commission and will visit your hotel with samples of her work. Prices start at $185.

Alfred Birdsey Studio ("Stowe Hill," Paget, tel. 809/236–6658). An island institution, Mr. Birdsey is a recipient of the Queen's Certificate of Honour and Medal in recognition of "valuable services given to Her Majesty for more than 40 years as an artist of Bermuda." His watercolors of Bermuda hang in the Bank of Bermuda and Cambridge Beaches cottage colony, as well as in the building at 2 Wall Street in New York. His studio is open weekdays 9–5.

Liz Campbell (tel. 809/236–8539). Lovely stained-glass butterflies, mirrors, panels, and boxes created by Ms. Campbell are displayed at the Dockyard Craft Market (*see below*). Prices range from $30 to about $200 for larger, more elaborate pieces.

Ronnie Chameau (tel. 809/292–1387). Ms. Chameau creates Christmas angels and dolls from dried palm, banana, and grapefruit leaves gathered from her yard. The 9-inch dolls ($35), with palmetto leaf baskets and hats, Spanish moss hair, and pecan heads with painted faces, are intended as table ornaments, while the dainty little 4-inch angels ($5–$20) are designed to hang on the Christmas tree. The angels and dolls are available year-round at Trimingham's (*see above*) and at Carole Holding's studio in St. George's (*see below*).

Joan Forbes (Art House, 80 South Shore Rd., Paget, tel. 809/236–6746, fax 809/236–5525). Watercolors and lithographs are the specialty of Ms. Forbes, whose work focuses on Bermudian architecture, horticulture, and seascapes. Her lithographs sell for $10–$45. She also produces cards, notepaper, and envelopes.

Desmond Fountain (tel. 809/292–3955, by appointment only). This award-winning sculptor's works are on display all over the island, whether it's a life-size bronze statue perched beside a lagoon or a lolling figure seated in a garden chair. Fountain created the *Land Ho!* statue of Sir George Somers on Ordnance Island in St. George's, and other of his works can be seen in the Sculpture Gallery on the mezzanine of the Southampton Princess (tel. 809/238–8840, fax 809/292–0630). Prices start at about $5,000 for a small bronze and soar to dizzying heights.

Carole Holding Studio (3 Featherbed Alley, St. George's, tel. 809/297–1833 or 809/236–6002 after hours). Ms. Holding uses pastel watercolors to paint the flowers and homes of Bermuda. In addition to her own watercolors, signed prints, and limited editions, her studio displays works, including cedar crafts, by local artists. Housed in the slave quarters of an 18th-century home that now serves as the St. George's Historical Society, Holding's studio is open to the public Monday–Saturday 10–4. She also has a shop in the Clocktower Mall at Dockyard (tel. 809/234–3800; open Mon.–Sat. 10–5, Sun. 11–5).

Graeme Outerbridge (tel. 809/238–2411). A photographer who contributed to the acclaimed *Day in the Life* book series, Mr. Outerbridge captures Bermuda in original photographic prints, silk screens, and posters.

Mary Zuill (10 Southlyn La., Paget, tel. 809/236–2439). In a tiny studio attached to her house, Ms. Zuill paints delightful watercolors of Bermuda's flowers, alleyways, and cottages. She accepts commissions and will either design a painting or work from a photograph you've taken in Bermuda. Original watercolors cost from $60 to $600. She welcomes visitors Tuesday–Friday from April to November only.

Galleries and Crafts Shops **Bermuda Arts Centre** (Dockyard, Ireland Island, tel. 809/234–2809). Sleek and modern, with well-designed displays of local art, this gallery is housed in one of the stone buildings of the former naval yard. The walls are adorned with pictures and photographs, and glass display cases contain costume dolls, jewelry, and other crafts. Visitors are provided with a printed list with descriptions and prices of the various works. Changing exhibits are frequently held.

Bermuda Glass-Blowing Studio & Show Room (16 Blue Hole Hill, Hamilton Parish, tel. 809/293–2234). A Bermuda cottage in the Bailey's Bay area houses this glassblower's studio. Glass plates, bowls, cups, and ornaments are created here in vibrant, swirling colors. Prices range from $15 to more than $200. Shoppers can watch glassblowers at work daily, and attend a workshop the last Sunday of each month (call for details).

Bridge House Gallery (1 Bridge St., St. George's, tel. 809/297–8211). Housed in a Bermuda mansion that dates to 1700, this gallery is of historical and architectural interest in its own right. In the 18th century, the two-story white building was the home of Bermuda's governors; today it is maintained by the Bermuda National Trust. Displayed amid 18th- and 19th-century furnishings are works of Bermudian artists: original paintings, hand-blown glass, Bermuda costume dolls, antique bottles and maps, jewelry, and books.

Craft Market (The Cooperage, Dockyard, Ireland Island, tel. 809/234-3208). Occupying part of what was once the cooperage, this large stone building dates to 1831. Some lovely work is to be found here—miniature cedar furniture, stained glass, and costume dolls, in particular—although the setting itself is plain and simple.

Island Pottery (Dockyard, Ireland Island, tel. 809/234-3361). Pottery is turned out in a large stone building at Dockyard, where artisans toil over potter's wheels. The end results are sold in the Dockyard shop, as well as in the Emporium outlet at 69 Front Street, Hamilton (tel. 809/295-8185).

Masterworks Foundation Gallery (41 Front St., Hamilton, tel. 809/295-5580). Formed in 1987, the foundation showcases the works of well-known American, Canadian, British, and French artists whose works were inspired by Bermuda. The Bermudiana Collection contains over 100 works in watercolor, oil, and other media, as well as original prints, and miniature cedar furniture. Selected works from this collection can be seen in the "Festival of Colour" exhibits in the Bermuda National Gallery, City Hall.

Windjammer Gallery (King and Reid Sts., Hamilton, tel. 809/292-7861). A cluttered, three-room shop on the ground floor of a small cottage, this is the place to go to find out about upcoming art shows. The staff can help you choose from the huge range of prints, lithographs, oils, watercolors, and photographs that fill the walls and bins. Jewelry and sculpture—most notably by Desmond Fountain—are also on display. There is also a gallery at 95 Front Street, and a "print pocket" outlet in Walker Arcade, which wanders between Front and Reid Streets.

Bookstores **Bermuda Book Store** (Queen and Front Sts., Hamilton, tel. 809/295-3698). Book lovers, beware! Once you set foot inside this musty old place, you'll have a hard time tearing yourself away. Stacked on a long table are a host of books about Bermuda. The proprietor can probably answer any questions you have about the island.

Boutiques **Archie Brown & Son** (51 Front St., Hamilton, tel. 809/295-2928). Top-quality woolens, Pringle of Scotland cashmeres, Shetland and lamb's wool sweaters, and 100% wool tartan kilts are among the specialties at this store.

Aston & Gunn (2 Reid St., Hamilton, tel. 809/295-4866). An upmarket member of the English Sports Shops that dot the island, this handsome shop carries men's and women's clothing and accessories. Women's two-ply cashmere pull-

over sweaters are $160, and men's cashmere jackets are
$275. Pure lambswool scarves are $30; Pierre Balmain
dress shirts are $40, while Aston & Gunn dress shirts sell
for $30. Good-quality soft leather carry-on bags are $245.

Bananas (93 W. Front St., 7 E. Front St., Hamilton, and 3
King's Sq., St. George's, tel. 809/295–1106 or 809/297–
0351). Sportswear and T-shirts make this place a teenag-
er's dream. Brightly colored Bermuda umbrellas cost about
$25.

The Bermuda Railway Co. (Reid and Burnaby Sts., Hamilton, tel. 809/295–4830; Clocktower Mall, Dockyard; 29
Mangrove Rd., Somerset; 8 Kings Sq., St. George's; 90
South Shore Rd., Paget, Crystal Cave; Wilkinson Ave.,
Hamilton Parish). The main Hamilton location is called
"Grand Central Station," the various branches are "stations," and some of the items sold bear the logo of "Old Rattle and Shake." This apparel shop carries accessories and
casual color-coordinated separates for men, women, and
children. In addition to skirts, shirts, shorts, and the like,
belt buckles and even beach towels are sold. A best-selling
item is the Bermuda Railway cap.

Calypso (45 Front St., Hamilton, tel. 809/295–2112). Available only in Bermuda, owner Polly Hornburg's ladies' fashions are created from splashy fabrics imported from
Europe, India, and Africa. Her casually elegant dresses
sell for $145 and more. The store has an exclusive arrange-
ment to sell Louis Vuitton merchandise in Bermuda. Expect to shell out $180 for a small wallet; $1,145 for an
attaché case.

Cecile (15 Front St., Hamilton, tel. 809/295–1311). Specializing in upscale off-the-rack ladies' fashions, this shop carries designer labels such as Ciao and Ciaosports, Nina
Ricci, Geiger of Austria, and Louis Feraud of Paris. There's
a good selection of swimwear, too, including swimsuits by
Gottex. Leslie Fay petites are also featured. The shop also
carries accessories (scarves, jewelry, handbags, belts).
Check the rooms in the back of the store for sale dresses.

Constable's of Bermuda (Duke of York St., St. George's, tel.
809/297–1995). Icelandic woolen clothing is the specialty of
this store, and prices are generally 30%–50% lower than
those in the United States. This is *the* place to come for
heavy woolen coats, ski sweaters, ponchos, jackets, and
skirts in smoky colors. Travel blankets are also a hot item.

Cow Polly (Somers Wharf, St. George's, tel. 809/297–1514).
Phoebe and Sam Wharton's store is an upscale novelty shop
that carries only imported items. You won't find their unusual pottery, jewelry, or men's ties sold anywhere else on
the island.

Davison's of Bermuda (27 and 73 Front St., Hamilton, tel.
809/292–2083; Water St., St. George's). Good-quality cot-

ton sportswear items include sweaters and slacks, tennis and sailing clothing, golf and tennis hats, and children's sportswear. They also carry gift packages of Bermuda Fish Chowder ($15), and a collection of deliciously vicious-looking stuffed trolls—a huge, perfectly horrid one guards the doorway and claims to "bite" if touched.

English Sports Shop (95 Front St., Hamilton, tel. 809/295–2672). Bermuda has several branches of this store, which specializes in British woolens: Harris Tweed jackets for men cost $175, while Shetland woolen sweaters are priced at $45; more expensive cashmere sweaters go for $99. The Crown Colony Shop (1 Front St., Hamilton, tel. 809/295–3935), a branch of the store that focuses on women's clothing, sells Lady Clansmen Scottish Shetland sweaters for $45 and silk dresses made in Hong Kong for about $300.

Frangipani (Water St., St. George's, tel. 809/297–1357). Exotic men's and women's clothing from Greece and Indonesia give this little shop a distinctly non-Bermudian feel. Colorful cotton sweaters from Greece come in more than 100 designs. The shop also has a collection of unusual jewelry.

The London Shop (22 Church St., Hamilton, tel. 809/295–1279). This small, cluttered shop has shelves piled high with Pierre Cardin dress shirts for about $35 and sweaters for $45. Countess Mara short-sleeve sport shirts are priced at $19, and herringbone caps cost $35.

Ruffles (48 Reid St., Hamilton, tel. 809/295–9439). This small, chic shop carries upscale women's casual dresses and separates, and elegant, glittering formal wear. The staff here is especially friendly and helpful.

Stefanel (12 Reid St., Hamilton, tel. 809/295–5698). This very smart, very expensive boutique stocks the snazzy cotton knits of Italian trendsetter Carlo Stefanel. Imported from Italy, the clothing includes men's cotton and linen suits and cotton dress shirts; women's patterned wool skirts with handknit, contrasting jackets; and children's sweaters and sweats.

Triangle's (55 Front St., Hamilton, tel. 809/292–1990). The star attractions of this boutique are Diane Freis's original, colorful, and crushable mosaic dresses, priced between $220 and $260—almost half what they cost in the United States.

Upstairs Golf & Tennis Shop (26 Church St., Hamilton, tel. 809/295–5161). As befits Bermuda's role as a golfing paradise, this store stocks clubs and accessories from some of the best brands available including Hogan, Ping, MacGregor, and Spalding. Tennis players can choose a racquet by Head, Wilson, Square Two, or Nike. Men's and women's sportswear is also available.

Crystal, China, and Porcelain **Bluck's** (4 W. Front St., Hamilton, tel. 809/295–5367, Reid and Queen Sts., Hamilton, Clocktower Mall, Dockyard; Somers Wharf and Water St., St. George's). A dignified establishment that has been in business for more than 140 years, this is the only store on the island devoted exclusively to the sale of crystal and china. Royal Doulton, Royal Copenhagen, Villeroy & Boch, Herend, Lalique, Minton, Waterford, Baccarat, and others are displayed on two floors in the main Front Street location. Villeroy & Boch Siena is $80.80 ($646.60 for eight five-piece place settings). The courteous staff will provide you with price lists upon request. As an example, a five-piece place setting of Hermés Peonies is $198.40 ($1,587.20 for eight place settings).

Vera P. Card (11 Front St., and 102 Front St., Hamilton; 9 Water St. and 13 York St., St. George's, tel. 809/295–1729, fax 809/295–2833). Lladro and Royal Doulton's "Reflections" figurines are widely available all over the island at almost identical prices, but this store has the most extensive selection. The shop's collection of Hummel figurines is, without a doubt, the best on the island.

Jewelry **Astwood Dickinson** (83–85 Front St., the Southampton Princess Hotel, and Walker Arcade, Hamilton, tel. 809/292–5805). In addition to 18-karat gold Omega watches that sell for $7,125, this store carries less expensive items such as Le Clip Swiss quartz watches ($40) and alarm Le Clips ($65). Most interesting of all, however, is the store's Bermuda Collection of 18-karat gold mementos that sell for $50–$600. The collection includes the Bermuda dinghy pendant for $300 (earrings are $230), a tall ship pin or pendant for $600, a Bermuda Island pendant for $50, and a Gibbs Hill Lighthouse tie-pin for $150.

Crisson's (71 Front St., 20 Reid St., Hamilton, and seven other locations, tel. 809/295–2351). The exclusive Bermuda agent for Rolex, Cartier, and Raymond Weil, this upscale establishment offers discounts of 20%–25% on expensive merchandise, but don't expect to find cheap Timex or Swatch watches. The gift department carries English flatware, Saint Louis crystal, and imported baubles, bangles, and beads.

Lote Tree Jewels (Walker Arcade, Hamilton, tel. 809/292–8525). Opened by owner Mary Walker in 1980 to showcase her own Marybeads—14-karat gold beads intertwined with semiprecious gems or freshwater pearls—the shop now emphasizes ethnic jewelry from around the world: African trade beads combined with tooled silver beads from Afghanistan, Bali, and India; and handmade, hand-painted Peruvian clay beads strung with hand-carved stone beads from Ecuador. There are baskets of bangles from Burkina Faso, Mali, and Kenya; and tribal jewelry from Afghanistan that features lapis lazuli and silver chokers, earrings, rings, and brooches. Marybeads are still available—a 14-karat necklace sells for $495.

Linens **Irish Linen Shop** (31 Front St., Hamilton, tel. 809/295–4089; Cambridge Rd., Somerset, tel. 809/234–0127). In a cottage that looks as though it belongs in Dublin, the Hamilton branch is *the* place for Irish linen double damask tablecloths. Prices range from $40 to $500 (not including napkins), although antique tablecloths can cost as much as $1,600. A 52″ × 52″ linen damask tablecloth is $75 (matching napkins $12.50 each). From Madeira come exquisite hand-embroidered handkerchiefs ($20); cotton and organdy pillowcases; and cotton organdy christening robes with slip and bonnet, hand embroidered with garlands and tiers of Valenciennes lace ($220 to upwards of $800). Pure linen hand-rolled handkerchiefs from Belgium with Belgian lace are priced under $20, while Le Jacquard Français cotton kitchen towels cost less than $12. The shop's Bermuda Cottage Collection includes quilted place mats, tea cozies, and pot holders—most for less than $15. The store has an exclusive arrangement with Souleiado, maker of the vivid prints from Provence that are available in skirts, dresses, place mats, bags, as well as by the yard.

Liquors and The following liquor stores sell at identical prices, each has
Liqueurs branches sprinkled around the island from St. George's to Somerset, and each will allow you to put together your own package of Bermuda liquors at in-bond (duty-free) prices: **Burrows Lightbourn** (Front St., Hamilton, tel. 809/295–0176), **Frith's Liquors Ltd.** (57 Front St., Hamilton, tel. 809/295–3544, fax 809/295–1049), **Gosling's** (33 Front St., Hamilton, tel. 809/295–1123, fax 809/292–9463).

Perfumes **Bermuda Perfumery** (212 North Shore Rd., Bailey's Bay, tel. 809/293–0627 or 800/527–8213, fax 809/293–8810). This highly promoted perfumery is on all the taxi-tour itineraries. Guided tours of the facilities are given continuously, during which you can see how the fragrances of flowers are distilled into perfume and take a walk through the ornamental gardens. At the Cobweb gift shop you can purchase the factory's Lili line of fragrances.

Peniston-Brown's Perfume Shop (23 W. Front St., Hamilton, tel. 809/295–0570) and the **Guerlain Shop** (19 Queen St., Hamilton, tel. 809/295–5535 and 6 Water St., St. George's, tel. 809/297–1525), which is the exclusive agent for Guerlain products, stock more than 127 lines of French and Italian fragrances, as well as soaps, bath salts, and bubble bath.

Perfume & Cosmetic Boutique (55 Front St., tel. 809/295–1183) is Trimingham's fragrance boutique, which is the exclusive agent for Chanel No. 5, Laura Ashley No. 1, Elizabeth Taylor's Passion and White Diamonds, and Calvin Klein's Obsession, among others. Skin care products from Elizabeth Arden, Estée Lauder, Givenchy, and Clarins are also sold, and skin consultants and "beauty therapists" are on hand.

Miscellaneous   **Hodge Podge** (3 Point Pleasant Rd., Hamilton, tel. 809/295–0647). Just around the corner from the Ferry Terminal and Visitors Center in Hamilton, this cluttered little shop offers pretty much what its name implies: postcards, sunblock, sunglasses, film, and T-shirts.

6 Water Sports and Beaches

So, you're getting away from it all.

Just make sure you can get back.

Here's a travel tip that will make it easy to call back to the States. Dial the access number for the country you're visiting and connect right to AT&T **USADirect**® Service. It's the quick way to get English-speaking operators and can minimize hotel surcharges.

If all the countries you're visiting aren't listed above, call **1 800 241-5555** before you leave for a free wallet card with all AT&T access numbers. International calling made easy—it's all part of **The i Plan.**℠

THE i PLAN™

AT&T

All The Best Trips Start with Fodor's

Fodor's Affordables

Titles in the series: Caribbean, Europe, Florida, France, Germany, Great Britain, Italy, London, Paris.

"Travelers with champagne tastes and beer budgets will welcome this series from Fodor's." — *Hartford Courant*

"These books succeed admirably; easy to follow and use, full of cost-related information, practical advice, and recommendations...maps are clear and easy to use." — *Travel Books Worldwide*

Fodor's Bed & Breakfast and Country Inn Guides

Titles in the series: California, Canada, England & Wales, Mid-Atlantic, New England, The Pacific Northwest, The South, The Upper Great Lakes Region, The West Coast.

"In addition to information on each establishment, the books add notes on things to see and do in the vicinity. That alone propels these books to the top of the heap."— *San Diego Union-Tribune*

The Berkeley Guides

Titles in the series: California, Central America, Eastern Europe, France, Germany, Great Britain & Ireland, Mexico, The Pacific Northwest, San Francisco.

The best choice for budget travelers, from the Associated Students at the University of California at Berkeley.

"Berkeley's scribes put the funk back in travel." — *Time*

"Hip, blunt and lively." — *Atlanta Journal Constitution*

"Fresh, funny and funky as well as useful." — *The Boston Globe*

Exploring Guides

Titles in the series: Australia, California, Caribbean, Florida, France, Germany, Great Britain, Ireland, Italy, London, New York City, Paris, Rome, Singapore & Malaysia, Spain, Thailand.

"Authoritatively written and superbly presented, and makes worthy reading before, during or after a trip." — *The Philadelphia Inquirer*

"A handsome new series of guides, complete with lots of color photos, geared to the independent traveler." — *The Boston Globe*

Visit your local bookstore or call 1-800-533-6478 24 hours a day.

Fodor's The name that means smart travel.

By Peter Oliver

Peter Oliver is a New York–based freelance writer, specializing in sports and the outdoors. His articles have appeared in Backpacker, The New York Times, Skiing, *and* Travel-Holiday.

Bermuda boasts that it has "water scientifically proven to be the clearest in the western Atlantic." Whether this is true or not, the water is certainly clear enough to make Bermuda one of the world's great centers for snorkeling and scuba diving. Clear water also gives fishermen a distinct advantage—a fish has almost nowhere to hide in the island's shallow, translucent water. For whatever reasons, however, the water around Bermuda was apparently *not* clear enough to allow many ship captains to see the barrier reefs encircling the island. Consequently, the reefs today are a veritable smorgasbord of marine wreckage, guaranteed to whet the appetite of any diving enthusiast. Some wrecks are in less than 30 feet of water and are accessible even to snorkelers. The reefs also help keep the water close to shore relatively calm, acting as a fortress wall against the pounding swells of the Atlantic and reducing beach erosion. And Bermuda's beaches are definitely worth saving—fine-grain sand tinted pink with crushed coral. But Bermuda's reefs remain as dangerous as ever. Boat rentals are available at several island locations, but only the most experienced yachtsmen should venture beyond the safe waters of Great Sound, Harrington Sound, and Castle Harbour. To go anywhere else without a full knowledge of Bermuda's considerable offshore hazards is pure folly.

Thanks to Bermuda's position close to the Gulf Stream, the water stays warm year-round, although Bermudians consider anything under 75°F frigid. In summer, the ocean is usually above 80°F, and even warmer in the shallows between the reefs and shore. In winter, the water temperature only occasionally drops below 70°F, but it seems cooler because the air temperature is usually in the mid-60s—a wet suit is recommended for anyone who plans to spend an extended period of time in the water. Lack of business, more than a drop in water temperature, is responsible for the comparative dearth of water-sports activity during the winter months. The winter does tend to be windier, however, which means water conditions can be less than ideal. Rough water creates problems anchoring or stabilizing fishing and diving boats, and visibility underwater is often clouded by sand and debris. High season runs from April through October, during which time fishing, diving, and yacht charters fill up quickly. Most boats carry fewer than 20 passengers, so it's advisable to sign up early. March–April and October–November are shoulder seasons, and December–February is the off-season, when many operators close to make repairs and perform routine maintenance. During these months, a few operators stay open on a limited basis, scheduling charters only when there are enough people to fill a boat; if too few people sign up, the charter is canceled. For this reason, water-sports enthusiasts have to be flexible during the winter months.

Take advantage of the activities director at your hotel or your ship's cruise director—he or she can make arrangements for you long before you arrive. **"What to Do in Bermuda: Information and Prices,"** a 20-page brochure available free from the Bermuda Department of Tourism (*see* Chapter 1, Essential Information), has extensive listings and information on all water sports in Bermuda; it's worth obtaining a copy before you make any plans.

Water Sports

Boating and Sailing

Visitors to Bermuda can either rent their own boat or charter a boat with a skipper. Rental boats, which are 17 feet at most, range from sailboats (typically tiny Sunfish) to motorboats (typically 13-foot Boston Whalers), glass-bottom boats, kayaks, and pedal boats. Such vessels are ideal for exploring the coves and harbors of the sounds or, in the case of motorboats, waterskiing. In **Great Sound,** several small islands, such as Hawkins Island and Long Island, have tiny secluded beaches that are usually empty during the week. If the wind is fresh, the islands are about a half hour's sail from **Hamilton Harbour** or **Salt Kettle.** These beaches are wonderful places to have a picnic, although many are privately owned and visitors are not always welcome. Check with the boat-rental operator before planning an island outing.

The trade winds pass well to the south of Bermuda, so the island does not have predictable air currents. Channeled by islands and headlands, the winds around Hamilton Harbour and the Great Sound can be particularly unpredictable; **Mangrove Bay** has far more reliable breezes. The variability of the winds has no doubt aided the education of Bermuda's racing skippers, who are traditionally among the world's best. To the casual sailor, however, wind changes can be troublesome, although you can be fairly confident you won't be becalmed: The average summer breeze is 10–15 knots, usually out of the south or southwest. Encircled by land, **Harrington Sound** has the calmest water, ideal for novice sailors, pedal boaters, and waterskiers. Anyone wanting a small taste of open water should head for **Pompano Beach Club Watersports Centre** (36 Pompano Rd. Southampton, tel. 809/234–0222) on the western ocean shore.

Boat Rentals Rates for small powerboats start at about $45 for one or two hours, or about $110 for a full day; sailboat rentals begin at $25 for one or two hours, or $50–$85 for a full day. A refundable deposit of about $50 is usually required. Sailboats and powerboats can be rented at **South Side Scuba Water Sports** (tel. 809/293-2915), which has outlets at **Marriott's Castle Harbour Resort** (Paynters Rd., Hamilton Parish), the **Sonesta Beach Hotel & Spa** (Sinky Bay Rd., Southampton), and the **Grotto Bay Beach Hotel** (11 Blue Hole Hill, Hamilton Parish). Rentals are also available at **Mangrove Marina**

(Cambridge Rd., Sandys, tel. 809/234–0914), **Robinson's Marina** (Somerset Bridge, Sandys, tel. 809/234–0709), **Pompano Beach Club Watersports Centre** (36 Pompano Rd., Southampton, tel. 809/234–0222), **Harbour Road Marina** (Newstead, Paget, tel. 809/236–6060), and **Salt Kettle Boat Rentals** (off Harbour Rd., Salt Kettle Rd., Paget, tel. 809/236–4863).

Charter Boats More than 20 large power cruisers and sailing vessels, piloted by local skippers, are available for charter. Typically between 35 and 50 feet long, charter sailboats can carry up to 18 passengers, with overnight accommodations available in some cases. Meals and drinks can be included on request, and a few skippers offer dinner cruises for the romantically inclined. Rates generally range between $230 and $300 for a half-day cruise, or $400–$600 for a full-day cruise, with additional per-person charges for large groups. Where you go and what you do—exploring, swimming, snorkeling, cruising—is up to you and your skipper. In most cases, cruises travel to and around the islands of Great Sound. Several charter skippers advertise year-round operations, but the off-season (December–February) schedule can be haphazard. Skippers devote periods of the off-season to maintenance and repairs or close altogether if bookings lag. Be sure to book well in advance. A full listing of charter-boat operators is included in the "What to Do in Bermuda: Information and Prices" brochure available from the Bermuda Department of Tourism (*see* Chapter 1, Essential Information).

Diving

Bermuda has all the ingredients necessary for classic scuba diving—reefs, wreckage, underwater caves, a variety of coral and marine life, and clear, warm water. Although diving is possible year-round, the best months are May–October, when the water is calmest and warmest. No prior certification is necessary; novices can learn the basics and be diving in water up to 25 feet deep on the same day. Three-hour resort courses ($75), which teach the basics in a pool or on the beach and culminate in a reef or wreck dive are offered by **South Side Scuba Water Sports** (at the Grotto Bay Beach Hotel, 11 Blue Hole Hill, Hamilton Parish; tel. 809/293–2915 and Marriott's Castle Harbour, Hamilton Parish, tel. 809/293–2040); **Fantasea Diving** (Darrells Wharf, Harbour Rd., Paget, tel. 809/236–6339); **Nautilus Diving** (Southampton Princess Hotel, off South Rd., Southampton, tel. 809/238–2332); **Blue Water Divers** (Robinson's Marina, Somerset Bridge, Sandys, tel. 809/234–1034 or 809/234–2922 evenings before 9); and **Dive Bermuda** (Dockyard Terrace, Royal Naval Dockyard, Sandys, tel. 809/234–0225). The easiest day trips, offered by South Side Scuba Water Sports and Nautilus Diving Ltd. involve exploring the south-shore reefs that lie close inshore. These reefs

Beaches and Water Sports

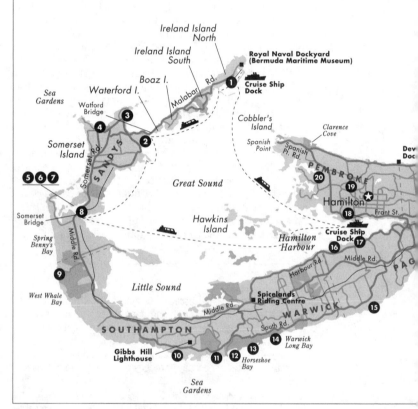

ATLANTIC OCEAN

Ireland Island North
Ireland Island South
Boaz I.
Waterford I.
Royal Naval Dockyard (Bermuda Maritime Museum)
Cruise Ship Dock
Sea Gardens
Watford Bridge
Cobbler's Island
Clarence Cove
Somerset Island
Spanish Point
Spanish Pt. Rd.
Dev Doc
PEMBROKE
Great Sound
Hamilton
Front St.
Somerset Bridge
Hawkins Island
Cruise Ship Dock
Spring Benny's Bay
Hamilton Harbour
West Whale Bay
Little Sound
PAG
Middle Rd.
Harbour Rd.
Spicelands Riding Centre
Middle Rd.
WARWICK
Gibbs Hill Lighthouse
South Rd.
Warwick Long Bay
SOUTHAMPTON
Horseshoe Bay
Sea Gardens

Beaches
Chaplin Bay, **13**
Elbow Beach Hotel, **15**
Horseshoe Bay Beach, **12**
John Smith's Bay, **23**
St. Catherine Beach, **28**
Shelley Bay Beach, **21**
Somerset Long Bay, **4**
Tobacco Bay Beach, **27**
Warwick Long Bay, **14**

Water Sports
Bermuda Waterski Centre, **5**
Bermuda Water Skiing, **24**
Bermuda Water Tours Ltd., **18**
Blue Water Divers Ltd., **7**
Bronson Hartley's Underwater Wonderland, **22**
Dive Bermuda, **1**

Fantasea, **20**
Four Winds Fishing Tackle, **19**
Greg Hartley's Under Sea Adventures, **2**
Harbour Road Marina, **17**
Mangrove Marina, **3**
Nautilus Diving Ltd., **11**
Pitman's Snorkeling, **8**

Pompano Beach Club Watersports Centre, **9**
Robinson's Marina, **6**
Salt Kettle Boat Rentals, **16**
South Side Scuba, **10**
South Side Scuba (at Grotto Bay Beach Hotel), **25**
Tobacco Bay Beach House, **26**

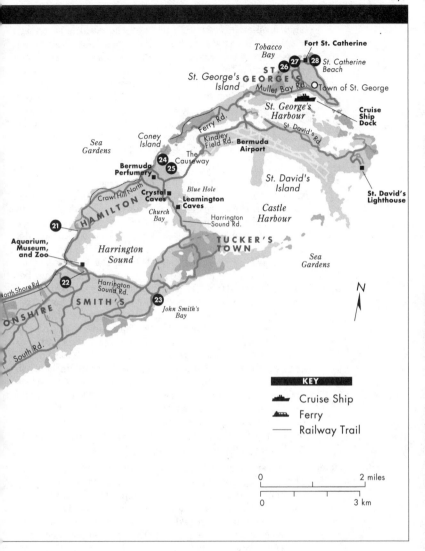

may be the most dramatic in Bermuda: In places, the ocean-side drop-off exceeds 60 feet, and the coral is so honey-combed with caves, ledges, and holes that exploratory possibilities are infinite. Also infinite are the chances of be-coming lost in this coral labyrinth, so it is important to stick with your guide. Despite concerns in recent years about dy-ing coral and fish depletion, most of Bermuda's reefs are still in good health—anyone eager to swim with multicol-ored schools of fish or the occasional barracuda will not be disappointed. In the interest of preservation, however, the removal of coral or coral objects is illegal.

Prominently displayed in any dive shop in Bermuda is a map of nautical carnage, showing the outlying reef system and wreck sites. The map shows 38 wrecks spanning three cen-turies, but these are only the larger wrecks that are still in good condition. There are reportedly more than 300 wreck sites in all, many of them well preserved. As a general rule, the more recent the wreck or the more deeply submerged it is, the better its condition. Most of the well-preserved wrecks are to the north and east, and dive depths range be-tween 25 and 80 feet. Several wrecks off the western end of the island are in relatively shallow water—30 feet or less—making them accessible to novice divers and even snorkelers. The major dive operators for wrecks on the western side of the island are Blue Water Divers Ltd. (*see above*); and **Dive Bermuda;** for wrecks off the east coast, contact South Side Scuba (*see above*). Costs range from $45 for a one-tank dive to $70 for introductory dives for novices or two-tank dives for experienced divers. With two tanks, divers can explore two or more wrecks during the same four-hour outing. Rates usually include all equipment—mask, fins, snorkel, scuba apparatus, and wet suit (if neces-sary). Some operators also offer night dives.

Helmet Diving A different, less technical type of diving that is popular in Bermuda is "helmet diving." Underwater explorers, wear-ing helmets that are fed air through hoses leading to the surface, walk along the sandy bottom in 15 feet of water or less. Although cruises last three hours or more, actual un-derwater time is about a half hour. Underwater videos and portraits are available for an extra charge. A morning or af-ternoon tour costs $40. Contact **Greg Hartley's Under Sea Adventure** (Village Inn dock, Bridgeview La., Sandys, tel. 809/234–2861) or Greg's father, Bronson Hartley, who op-erates the **Underwater Wonderland** (Flatts Village, Smiths, tel. 809/292–4434).

Fishing

Fishing in Bermuda falls into three basic categories: shore or shallow-water fishing, reef fishing, and deep-sea fishing. No license is required, although some restrictions apply, particularly regarding the prohibition against spear guns and the fish you can keep (for instance, only Bermudians with commercial fishing licenses are permitted to take lobsters). In recent years, some concern has been expressed about the decline in the number of reef and shore fish in Bermudian waters. New government measures to restore fish populations have adversely impacted some commercial fishers, but sportfishing has been largely unaffected. Indeed, the deep-sea fishing for which Bermuda is famed remains as good as ever.

Shore Fishing The principal catches for shore fishers are pompano, bonefish, and snapper. Excellent sport for saltwater fly-fishing is the wily and strong bonefish, which is found in coves, harbors, and bays—almost anywhere it can find food and shelter from turbulent water. Among the more popular spots for bonefish are **West Whale Bay** and **Spring Benny's Bay,** which feature large expanses of clear, shallow water, protected by reefs close inshore. Good fishing holes are numerous along the south shore, too, although fishing is not permitted on major south-shore swimming beaches. Fishing in the calm waters of the **Great Sound** and **St. George's Harbour** can be rewarding, but enclosed **Harrington Sound** is less promising. Ask at local tackle shops about the latest hot spots and the best baits to use. Rod and reel rentals for shore fishing are available for about $10 a day ($20–$30 deposit required) from **Four Winds Fishing Tackle** (2 Woodlands Rd., Pembroke, tel. 809/292–7466), **Harbour Road Marina** (Newstead, Paget, tel. 809/236–6060), and **Mangrove Marina** (Cambridge Rd., Somerset, tel. 809/234–0914). **Salt Kettle Boat Rentals** (off Harbour Rd., Salt Kettle Rd., Paget, tel. 809/236–4863) rents rod, reel, and tackle only with motorboat rental. Rental arrangements can also be made through hotel activities directors.

Reef Fishing Three major reef bands lie at various distances from the island: The first is anywhere from a half mile to 5 miles offshore; the second, the Challenger Bank, is about 15 miles offshore; the third, the Argus Bank, is located about 30 miles offshore. As a rule, the farther out you go, the larger the fish—and the more expensive the charter. Most charter fishers work the reefs and deep water to the north and northwest of the island, because most of Bermuda's harbors face in those directions. Catches over the reefs include snapper, amberjack, grouper, and barracuda. Of the most sought-after deep-water fish—marlin, tuna, wahoo, and dolphin—wahoos are the most common and blue marlin the least. Trolling is the usual method of deep-water fishing, and charter-boat operators offer various tackle set-ups, with test-line weights ranging from 20 to 130 pounds. The boats, which range between 35 and 55 feet long, are fitted with a wide array of gear and electronics to track fish, including depth sounders, lorans, video fish finders, radar, and computer scanners. Half-day or full-day charters are offered by most operators, but full-day trips offer the best chance for a big catch, because the boat can reach waters that are less frequently fished. Rates vary widely, as do policies about keeping the catch. The Bermuda Game Fishing Association runs a year-long **Game Fishing Tournament,** open free to all fishers. Catches of any of 26 game varieties can be registered with the Bermuda Department of Tourism, and prizes are awarded at the end of the year. Charter bookings can be arranged through three organizations: the **Bermuda Charter Fishing Boat Association** (Box SB 145, Sandys SB BX, tel. 809/292–6246), the **Bermuda Sport Fishing Association** ("Creek View House," 8 Tulo La., Pembroke HM 02, tel. 809/295–2370), and the **St. George's Game Fishing & Cruising Association** (Box GE 107, St. George's GE BX, tel. 809/297–1622). In addition, several independent charter boats operate out of Hamilton Harbour and harbors in Sandys at the western end of the island. For more information about chartering a fishing boat in Bermuda, obtain a copy of the "What to Do in Bermuda: Information and Prices" brochure from the Bermuda Department of Tourism (*see* Chapter 1, Essential Information).

Snorkeling

The clarity of the water, the stunning array of coral reefs, and the shallow resting places of several wrecks make snorkeling in the waters around Bermuda—both close inshore and offshore—particularly rewarding. Snorkeling is possible year-round, although a wet suit is advisable for anyone planning to spend a long time in the water in winter, when the water temperature can dip into the 60s. During the winter, too, the water tends to be rougher, often restricting snorkeling to the protected areas of Harrington Sound and Castle Harbour. Underwater caves, grottoes, coral formations, and schools of small fish are the highlights of these areas. When Bermudians are asked to name a favorite snorkeling spot, however, **Church Bay** is invariably ranked at or near the top of the list. A small cove cut out of the coral cliffs, this protected bay is full of nooks and crannies in the coral, and the reefs are relatively close to shore. Snorkelers should exercise caution here, as they should everywhere along the south shore, because the water can be rough. Other popular snorkeling areas close inshore are the beaches of **John Smith's Bay** at the eastern end of the south shore, and **Tobacco Bay** at the eastern end of the north shore. Despite its small size, **West Whale Bay** is also worth a visit.

Having a boat at your disposal can improve your snorkeling experience immeasurably. Otherwise, long swims are necessary to reach some of the best snorkeling sites from shore, while other sites are inaccessible from anything but a boat. Small boats, some with glass bottoms, can be rented by the hour, half day, or day (*see* Boat Rentals, *above*). As the number of wrecks attests, navigating around Bermuda's reef-strewn waters is no simple task, especially for inexperienced boaters. If you rent a boat yourself, stick to the protected waters of the sounds, harbors, and bays. For trips to the reefs, let someone else do the navigating—a charter-boat skipper (*see* Charter Boats, *above*) or one of the snorkeling-cruise operators (*see* Snorkeling Cruises, *below*). Some of the best reefs for snorkeling, complete with shallow-water wrecks, are to the west. Where the tour guide or skipper goes, however, often depends on the tide, weather, and water conditions. For snorkelers who demand freedom of movement and privacy, a boat charter (complete with captain) is the only answer, but the cost is considerable—$450 a day or more. Divided among eight or more passengers, however, the expense may be worthwhile. By comparison, half-day snorkeling cruises (*see* Snorkeling Cruises, *below*) generally cost $35 or less, including equipment and instruction.

Snorkeling equipment is available for rental at most major hotels; the **Grotto Bay Hotel, Sonesta Beach Hotel,** and **Southampton Princess** have dive operators on site. Rates for mask, flippers, and snorkel are usually $6 per hour, or $18 per day from the dive operators; however, snorkels and masks can be rented for $3 an hour at the concession stand at **Horseshoe Bay Beach** (tel. 809/238–0572). Equipment, including small boats and underwater cameras, can also be rented at several dive shops or marinas. The two best places for equipment rentals on the western end of the island are **Blue Water Divers Ltd.** (Robinson's Marina, Somerset Bridge, Sandys, tel. 809/234–1034) and **Mangrove Marina** (Cambridge Rd., Sandys, tel. 809/234–0914), both of which also rent small boats. In the central part of the island, boats and gear can be rented at **Salt Kettle Boat Rentals** (off Harbour Rd., Salt Kettle Rd., Paget, tel. 809/236–4863), and **Harbour Road Marina** (Newstead, Paget, tel. 809/236–6060). At the eastern end of the island, contact **Tobacco Bay Beach House** (Tobacco Bay, Naval Tanks Hill, St. George's, tel. 809/293–9711).

Snorkeling Cruises Snorkeling cruises, which are offered from May to November, may be too touristy for many visitors. Some boats carry 20 passengers or more, and feature music and bars (complimentary beverages are usually served on the return trip from the reefs). Smaller boats limit capacity to 10 passengers, but they offer few amenities and their travel range is shorter. To make sure you choose a boat that's right for you, ask for all the details before booking. Half-day snorkeling tours cost approximately $35. **Bermuda Water Tours Ltd.** (Albuoy's Point, Hamilton, tel. 809/295–3727) operates two boats out of Hamilton, and **Pitman's Snorkeling** (Somerset Bridge Hotel, Main Rd., Sandys, tel. 809/234–0700) offers half-day and shorter evening cruises, departing from the Somerset Bridge Hotel dock next to Robinson's Marina. Half-day cruises are also available from **Salt Kettle Boat Rentals** (off Harbour Rd., Salt Kettle Rd., Paget, tel. 809/236–4863).

Waterskiing

Winds on the island vary considerably, making it difficult to predict when the water will be calmest, although evening breezes are usually the lightest. Head for the **Great Sound** when the winds are coming from the south or southwest, the prevailing winds on Bermuda. In the event of northerly winds, however, **Castle Harbour** and **Harrington Sound** are protected bodies of water. If possible, make friends with a Bermudian with a boat—many visitors are invited boating by Bermudians they have only recently met. Otherwise, contact **Bermuda Water Skiing** (Grotto Bay Hotel, 11 Blue Hole Hill, Hamilton Parish, tel. 809/293–8333, ext. 37) or **Bermuda Waterski Centre** (Robinson's Marina, Somerset Bridge, Sandys, tel. 809/234–3354). Rates fluctuate with fuel costs, but average $50 per half hour, $85 per hour, lessons included.

Windsurfing

Great Sound, Somerset Long Bay, Mangrove Bay, and **Harrington Sound** are the favorite haunts of board sailors in Bermuda. For novices, the calm, enclosed waters of Harrington Sound are probably the best choice. The Great Sound, with its many islands, coves, and harbors, is good for board sailors of all abilities, although the quirky winds that sometimes bedevil yachts in the sound obviously affect sailboards as well. When the northerly storm winds blow, the open bays on the north shore are popular among wave-riding enthusiasts. Only experts should consider windsurfing on the south shore. Wind, waves, and reefs make the south shore so dangerous that rental companies are prohibited from renting boards there. Experienced board sailors might want to try their luck in the open races at **Salt Kettle** from April through mid-October every Thursday at 6 PM.

Even the most avid board sailors should rent sailboards rather than attempt to bring their own. Transporting a board around the island is a logistical nightmare: There are no rental cars on Bermuda, and few taxi drivers are willing to see their car roofs scoured with scratches in the interest of sport. Rental rates range between $15 and $20 an hour, or about $80 a day. Contact **South Side Scuba** (Grotto Bay Hotel, 11 Blue Hole Hill, Hamilton Parish and Marriott's Castle Harbour, Hamilton Parish, tel. 809/293–2915), **Mangrove Marina** (Cambridge Rd., Sandys, tel. 809/234–0914), or **Pompano Beach Club Watersports Centre** (36 Pompano Rd., Pompano Beach Club, Southampton, tel. 809/234–0222). **South Side Scuba** and **Mangrove Marina** offer 90-minute beginner lessons, including equipment and dry land simulators, at a cost of $50 for private lessons and $35 per person for group lessons (maximum of three people).

Beaches

The beaches of Bermuda fall into two categories: those on the south shore and those on the north shore. The water on the south-shore beaches tends to be a little rougher, because the prevailing winds come from the south and southwest. However, most people would agree that the typical south-shore beach is also more scenic—fine pinkish sand, coral bluffs topped with summer flowers, and gentle, pale-blue surf. Most Bermudian beaches are relatively small compared with ocean beaches in the United States. Although sizes vary considerably, an average Bermudian beach might be 300 yards long and 30 yards wide. In winter, when the weather is more severe, beaches may erode—even disappear—only to be replenished as the climate eases into spring.

The Public Transportation Board provides a free "Bermuda's Guide to Beaches," available in all visitors centers and most hotels. A combination bus schedule and map, the guide shows locations of beaches and how to reach them by bus. Information about the submarine *Enterprise*, ferries, taxis, and moped rentals is also included.

Bermudian beaches offer little shade, either in the way of palm trees or thatched shelters, so bring hats, umbrellas, and plenty of sunscreen. Below are reviews of the major beaches on the island that are open to the public. (For information about the many private beaches owned by hotels on the south shore, *see* Chapter 9, Lodging.)

South-Shore Beaches

Chaplin Bay. In a secluded bay east of Horseshoe Bay (*see below*), this tiny beach disappears almost entirely at high tide or after a storm. Its most distinguishing feature is a high coral wall that reaches across the beach to the water, perforated by a 10-foot high, arrowhead-shaped hole. Like Horseshoe Bay, the beach fronts South Shore Park. *Off South Rd., Southampton. Bus 2 or 7 from Hamilton.*

Elbow Beach Hotel. The $3 fee for nonguests ensures that this beach remains relatively quiet, even on weekends. (Nonguests must call first.) Shielded from big ocean swells by reefs, the beach has almost no surf, except in heavy winds. The Elbow Beach Surf Club sells refreshments, and has umbrellas and beach chairs to rent; toilet facilities are available. A free public beach lies adjacent. *Off South Rd., Paget, tel. 809/236–3535. Bus 2 or 7 from Hamilton.*

Horseshoe Bay Beach. Horseshoe Bay has everything you would expect of a Bermudian beach: A ¼-mile crescent of pink sand, clear water, a vibrant social scene, and an uncluttered backdrop provided by South Shore Park. This is the most popular beach with visitors and locals alike, a place where adults arrive with coolers and teenagers come to check out the action. The presence of lifeguards during summer months—the only other beach with lifeguards is John Smith's Bay (*see below*)—and a variety of rentals, a snack bar, and toilet facilities add to the beach's appeal; in fact, it can become uncomfortably crowded here on summer weekends. Parents should keep a close eye on their children in the water: The undertow can be strong, especially when the wind is blowing. *Off South Rd., Southampton, tel. 809/ 238-2651. Bus 2 or 7 from Hamilton.*

John Smith's Bay. Backed by houses and South Road, this beach consists of a pretty strand of long, flat, open sand. The presence of a lifeguard in summer makes this an ideal place to bring children. As the only public beach in Smith's Parish, John Smith's Bay is also popular among locals. *South Rd., Smith's. Bus 1 from Hamilton.*

Warwick Long Bay. Very different from covelike Chaplin and Horseshoe bays, this beach features the longest stretch of sand—about ½ mile—of any beach on the island. And instead of a steep backdrop, low grass- and brush-covered hills slope away from the beach, exposing the beach to the wind. Despite the wind, the waves are rarely big here because the inner reef is close inshore. An interesting feature of the bay is a 20-foot coral outcrop, less than 200 feet offshore, that looks like a sculpted boulder balancing on the surface of the water. The emptiness of South Shore Park, which surrounds the bay, heightens the beach's sense of isolation and serenity. *Off South Rd., Southampton. Bus 2 or 7 from Hamilton.*

North-Shore Beaches

Shelley Bay Beach. As at Somerset Long Bay (*see below*), the water at this beach near Flatts is well protected from prevailing southerly winds. In addition, a sandy bottom and shallow water make this a good place to take small children. Shelley Bay also boasts shade trees—something of a rarity at Bermudian beaches. A beach house has rest rooms, showers, and changing areas. One drawback is the traffic noise from busy North Shore Road, which runs nearby. *North Shore Rd., Hamilton Parish, tel. 809/293-1327. Bus 10 or 11 from Hamilton.*

Somerset Long Bay. Popular with Somerset locals, this beach sits on the quiet northwestern end of the island—far from the airport, the bustle of Hamilton, and major tourism hubs. In keeping with the area's rural atmosphere, the beach is low-key and unprepossessing. Undeveloped parkland shields the beach from light traffic on Cambridge Road. The main beach is crescent-shaped and long by Bermudian standards—nearly a ¼-mile from end to end. Instead of the great coral outcroppings common on the south shore, grass and brush make up the main backdrop here.

Although exposed to northerly storm winds, the bay water is normally calm and shallow—ideal for children. However, the bottom is not sandy everywhere nor is it even. *Cambridge Rd., Sandys. Bus 7 or 8 from Hamilton.*

Tobacco Bay Beach. The most popular beach near St. George's, this small north-shore beach is huddled in a coral cove similar to those found along the south shore. Like Shelley Bay (*see above*), Tobacco Bay has a beach house with a snack bar, equipment rentals, toilets, showers, and changing rooms. *Naval Tanks Hill, St. George's, tel. 809/293–9711 (public phone). Bus no. 10 or 11 from Hamilton.*

7 Sports and Fitness

By Peter Oliver

When high jumper Nicky Barnes won a gold medal in the 1990 Commonwealth Games, Bermuda welcomed him home with a degree of adoration normally reserved for martyrs and deities. Bermudians champion their sports heroes, but—more significantly—they champion sports, both as participants and spectators. Every taxi driver seems to be a single-handicap golfer; tennis courts outnumber banks by more than three to one; and runners, cyclists, and horseback riders fill the roads and countryside in the mornings, especially on weekends. Bermuda might not have the world's fittest population but, at sunrise on Saturday, it certainly seems that way.

Washed by the Atlantic, Bermuda is probably best known as a beach destination, offering a host of water sports and activities (*see* Chapter 6, Beaches and Water Sports). However, the island is also a golfing center—eight courses are jammed onto this tiny island—and the popularity of tennis, squash, and riding are a further testament to Bermudians' love affair with land-based sports. Britain's oldest colony tends to favor pursuits with a British flavor. In addition to several golf tournaments, cricket, soccer, rugby, field hockey, equestrian events, and even badminton are popular spectator sports in season. Visitors can enter some of these events, primarily races and golf and tennis tournaments, although it is usually necessary to qualify.

Perhaps more than any other single factor, climate is what makes Bermuda such a sporting hive. In winter (December–February), temperatures hover between 50°F and 70°F, often climbing higher. While this might prove too chilly for many water sports, the cool air is ideal for activities on land. And although it is not immune to the occasional hurricane or storm, Bermuda does not have an extended storm season. Island residents like to boast, with some justification, that if you enjoy sport, you can enjoy it here 365 days of the year.

Most visitors can arrange sporting activities (tee times, for example) through their hotel's or ship's activities director, although arrangements can be made independently as well. For this purpose, the Bermuda Department of Tourism issues two excellent publications, the "Golfer's Guide" and the brochure "What to Do in Bermuda: Information and Prices." Available through the Department of Tourism (*see* Government Tourist Offices in Chapter 1, Essential Information), the guides offer descriptions of sports facilities and golf courses on the island, addresses, phone numbers, and prices.

Participant Sports

Bicycling

In Bermuda, bicycles are called pedal or push bikes, to distinguish them from the more common motorized two-wheelers. Many of the cycle liveries around the island (*see* Chapter 1, Essential Information) also rent three-speed and 10-speed pedal bikes, but they can be difficult to find—it makes sense to reserve a bike a few days in advance. Rental rates start at $10–$15 for the first day, and $5 per day thereafter.

Bermuda is not the easiest place in the world to bicycle. Riders should be prepared for some tough climbs—the roads running north–south across the island are particularly steep and winding—and the wind can sap even the strongest rider's strength, especially along South Road in Warwick and Southampton parishes. Bermudian roads are narrow, with heavy traffic (especially near Hamilton during rush hours) and no shoulder. Most motorists are courteous to cyclists—arbitrary horn-honking is against the law—and stay within 10 mph of the 20-mph speed limit. Despite the traffic, bicycle racing is a popular sport in Bermuda, and club groups can regularly be seen whirring around the island on evening and weekend training rides. Bermudian roads are no place for novice riders, however, and parents should think twice before allowing preteen children to hop on a bike.

Bermuda's premier cycling route, the Railway Trail (*see* Chapter 4, Exploring Bermuda), requires almost no road riding. Restricted to pedestrian and bicycle traffic, the paved trail runs intermittently for almost the length of the island along the route of the old Bermuda Railway. The Bermuda Department of Tourism publishes "The Bermuda Railway Trail Guide," a free pamphlet that features a series of short exploring tours along the trail. The pamphlet is available at all Visitors Service Bureaus and Information Centres.

Tribe roads—small side roads that are often unpaved—are also good for exploring, although don't be surprised if many of these roads, which date back to the earliest settlement of Bermuda, are dead ends. Well-paved South Road has relatively few climbs and some excellent ocean views, although it is one of Bermuda's most heavily traveled thoroughfares. The "Bermuda Handy Reference Map," also available at Visitors Service Bureaus and Information Centres, is quite good, but even better is the *Bermuda Islands Guide*, a paperback available at the Bermuda Book Store in Hamilton. It is a detailed atlas showing every thoroughfare, lane, and alleyway.

Golf

Bermuda is justifiably renowned for its golf courses. The scenery is spectacular, and the courses are challenging. However, visitors should not expect the manicured, soft fairways and greens typical of U.S. courses. Just as courses in Scotland have their own identity, the same is true of courses on this Atlantic isle. Bermudian golf courses are distinguished by plenty of sand, firm fairways and greens, relatively short par fours, and wind—*especially* wind. Elsewhere, golf courses are usually designed with the wind in mind—long downwind holes and short upwind holes. Not so on Bermuda's eight courses, where the wind is anything but consistent or predictable. Quirky air currents make a Bermudian course play differently every day. On some days, a 350-yard par four may be driveable; on other days, a solidly hit drive may fall short on a 160-yard par three. Regardless, the wind puts a premium on being able to hit the ball straight; any slice or hook becomes disastrously exaggerated in the wind.

The island's water supply is limited, so irrigation is done sparingly and the ground around the green tends to be quite hard. For success in the short game, therefore, players need to run the ball to the hole, rather than relying on high, arcing chips, which require plenty of club face under the ball. Typically, Bermudian greens are elevated and protected by sand traps rather than thick grass. Most traps are filled with the pulverized coral that has made the island's beaches so famous. Such fine sand may be unfamiliar to visiting golfers, but it tends to be consistent from trap to trap and from course to course.

Greens are usually seeded with Bermuda grass and then overseeded with rye. Golfers putt on Bermuda grass during the warmer months (March–November) and on rye when the weather cools and the Bermuda grass dies out. Greens are reseeded anytime from late September to early November, according to the weather. (Castle Harbour Golf Club's greens are reseeded in early January.) Some courses use temporary greens for two to four weeks; others keep the greens in play while reseeding and resurfacing. Greens in Bermuda tend to be much slower than the bent-grass greens prevalent in the United States, and putts tend to break less.

Another characteristic of Bermudian courses is the preponderance of rolling, hummocky fairways, making a flat lie the exception rather than the rule. Little effort has been made to flatten the fairways, because much of the ground beneath the island's surface is honeycombed with caves; bulldozer and backhoe operators are understandably uneasy about doing extensive landscaping.

How should golfers prepare for a Bermuda trip? In anticipation of the wind, practice hitting lower shots—punching

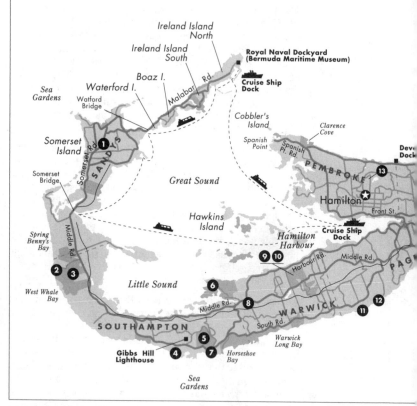

ATLANTIC OCEAN

Ireland Island
North

Ireland Island
South

Boaz I.

Waterford I.

**Royal Naval Dockyard
(Bermuda Maritime Museum)**

**Cruise Ship
Dock**

*Sea
Gardens*

Watford
Bridge

Malabar Rd.

*Cobbler's
Island*

*Clarence
Cove*

*Somerset
Island*

SANDYS

Somerset Rd.

*Spanish
Point*

*Spanish
Pl. Rd.*

PEMBROKE

**Dev
Dock**

*Somerset
Bridge*

Great Sound

Hamilton

Front St.

Middle Rd.

*Spring
Benny's
Bay*

*Hawkins
Island*

*Hamilton
Harbour*

**Cruise Ship
Dock**

*West Whale
Bay*

Little Sound

Harbour Rd.

Middle Rd

PAG

Middle Rd.

WARWICK

SOUTHAMPTON

South Rd.

**Gibbs Hill
Lighthouse**

*Horseshoe
Bay*

*Warwick
Long Bay*

*Sea
Gardens*

Golf Courses

Belmont Golf &
Country Club, **9**

Castle Harbour Golf
Club, **19**

Mid Ocean Club, **20**

Ocean View Golf &
Country Club, **14**

Port Royal Golf &
Country Club, **3**

Princess Golf Club, **5**

Riddell's Bay Golf &
Country Club, **6**

St. George's Golf
Club, **22**

**Tennis and Squash
Courts**

Belmont Hotel, Golf &
Country Club, **10**

Bermuda Squash
Club, **17**

Coral Beach & Tennis
Club, **11**

Elbow Beach Hotel, **12**

Government Tennis
Stadium, **13**

Marriott's Castle
Harbour Resort, **18**

Pompano Beach
Club, **2**

Port Royal Golf &
Country Club, **3**

Sonesta Beach Hotel
& Spa, **4**

Southampton
Princess Hotel, **7**

Horseback Riding

National Equestrian
Centre, **15**

Spicelands Riding
Centre, **8**

Spectator Sports

National Sports
Club, **16**

St. George's Cricket
Club, **21**

Somerset Cricket
Club, **1**

Tobacco Bay

Fort St. Catherine

St. Catherine Beach

ST. GEORGE'S

St. George's Island

22

Town of St. George

Mullet Bay Rd.

21

St. George's Harbour

Cruise Ship Dock

Ferry Rd.

St. David's Rd.

Sea Gardens

Coney Island

Kindley Field Rd.

The Causeway

Bermuda Airport

St. David's Lighthouse

Bermuda Perfumery

HAMILTON

Crawl Hill North

Crystal Caves

Blue Hole

Leamington Caves

St. David's Island

Castle Harbour

Church Bay

Harrington Sound Rd.

18

19

TUCKER'S TOWN

Aquarium, Museum, and Zoo

Harrington Sound

20

Sea Gardens

North Shore Rd.

17

Harrington Sound Rd.

SMITH'S

15 16

ONSHIRE

John Smith's Bay

South Rd.

N

KEY

Cruise Ship

Ferry

Railway Trail

0   2 miles

0   3 km

the ball or playing it farther back in the stance may be helpful. Working on chip-and-run shots (a seven iron is ideal for this), especially from close-cropped lies, should also help. You can save yourself some strokes, too, by practicing iron shots from awkward, hillside lies. On the greens, a long, firm putting stroke may save you from the bugaboo that haunts many first-time visitors: gently stroked putts dying short of the hole or drifting off-line with the grain of the Bermuda grass. As Allan Wilkinson, the former professional at the Princess Golf Club, has said. "In Bermuda, ya gotta slam 'em into the back of the cup."

Tournaments for pros, seniors, juniors, women, and mixed groups fill Bermuda's golfing schedule from February through December. Some competitions, such as the Bermuda Open in early October, are high-level competitions with prize money for professional participants. Handicap limits are usually imposed for the more serious tournaments, and entry fees range between $90 and $120 (not all events are open to non-Bermudian players). A schedule, with entry forms, is available from the **Bermuda Golf Association** (Box HM 433, Hamilton HM BX, tel. 809/238–1367). A low-key event for golfers of all abilities is the **Bermuda Golf Festival,** a two-week affair in late February that gives players a chance to compete on several of the island's courses. Greens fees are reduced for festival participants, and several hotels offer reduced package rates. For more information, contact the Bermuda Golf Festival (c/o NYT Event Sports Marketing, 5520 Park Ave., Box 395, Trumbull, CT 06611, tel. 203/373–7163 or 800/321–1947). Another easygoing tournament in mid-February is the **Valentine's Mixed Foursomes,** for which tournament/hotel packages are also available. For information or entry forms, contact the Tournament Chairman (Bermuda Golf Company, Box GE 304, St. George's GE BX, tel. 809/297–8067).

Be sure to pack proper golf attire—long pants (no jeans) or Bermuda shorts (no cutoffs) are required for men. Lessons, available at all courses, usually cost $25–35 for a half hour, and club rentals range between $10 and $24. Caddies are a thing of the past, except at the Mid Ocean Club. Below are reviews and ratings of all eight of Bermuda's golf courses. The ratings, devised and administered by the United States Golf Association (USGA), "represent the expected score of an expert amateur golfer based upon yardage and other obstacles." For example, a par-72 course with a rating of 68 means that a scratch golfer would hit a four-under-par round—and ordinary hackers would probably score a little better, too. Ratings below are given for the blue tees (championship), white tees (men's), and red tees (women's).

Belmont Golf and Country Club
Length: 5,777 yards from the blue tees
Par: 70
Rating: blue tees, 68.9; white tees, 67.9; red tees, 69.1

Of Bermuda's eight courses, the layout of the public Belmont Golf & Country Club is perhaps the most maddening. The first two holes, straight par fours, are a false preview of what lies ahead—a series of doglegs and blind tee shots. Playing with an experienced Belmont player, who knows where to hit drives on such blind holes as the sixth, 11th, and 16th, and how best to play a dogleg hole such as the eighth, can help a newcomer trim six or more shots from a round. Despite the layout, Belmont remains one of Bermuda's easier courses, and it is ideal for inexperienced players. Belmont is an inland course and has few ocean panoramas. Instead, most holes overlook pastel houses with white roofs, a few of which have taken a beating from errant golf balls. A new irrigation system has improved the course dramatically in recent years. Fairway grass tends to be denser—and the clay soil moister—than the grass on the close-cropped, sandy fairways typical of other Bermudian courses. The rough, too, is generally deeper, snaring any wild tee shots. For this reason, and because Belmont is a short course (only one par four in more than 400 yards), it makes sense to use a three or five wood, or even a low iron, from the tee. Belmont's chief drawback, especially on the weekend, is slow play—weekend rounds of five hours or more are common.

Highlight hole: The par-five 11th features a severe dogleg left, with a blind tee shot—Belmont in a nutshell. A short but straight drive is the key; trying and failing to cut the corner can be disastrous. The approach to the green is straight, although a row of wispy trees on the left awaits hooked or pulled shots. *Belmont Rd., Warwick, tel. 809/ 236–1301, fax 809/236–6867. Greens fees: $45 for the public; free to hotel guests. Cart rentals, $32; hand carts, $7.*

Castle Harbour Golf Club **Length:** 6,440 yards from the blue tees
Par: 71
Rating: blue tees, 71.3; white tees, 69.2; red tees, 69.2

The only course on Bermuda that requires players to use golf carts is the Castle Harbour Golf Club—with good reason. The only flat areas on the course, it seems, are the tees. The first tee, a crow's-nest perch by the clubhouse, offers an indication of things to come: Looking out over the fairway, with the harbor beyond, is like peering onto a golf course from a 20th-story window. Wind can make this course play especially long. Although most par fours feature good landing areas despite all the hills, holes such as the second, 16th, and 17th require players to drive over fairway rises. A wind-shortened drive can mean a long, blind shot to the green. Carrying the rise, on the other hand, can mean a relatively easy short shot, especially on the second and 17th holes. Elevated greens are a common feature of Castle Harbour. The most extreme example is the 190-yard, par-three 13th, with the green perched atop a steep, 100-foot embankment. Balls short of the green inevitably roll back down into a grassy basin between the tee and the green. On the other hand, sand traps at Castle Harbour are mercifully few and far between by Bermudian standards; 10 holes feature two or fewer bunkers around the green.

Castle Harbour is one of Bermuda's most expensive courses; however, the money is clearly reinvested in the course. Greens are well maintained—firm, consistently cropped, and generally faster than most Bermudian greens. The course also rewards golfers with several spectacular views, such as the hilltop panorama from the 14th tee, where blue water stretches into the distance on three sides.

Highlight hole: The 235-yard, par-three 18th is the most difficult finishing hole on Bermuda, especially when the wind is blowing from the northwest. On the right are jagged coral cliffs rising from the harbor; on the left are a pair of traps. When the course was revamped a few years ago, a small, flower-lined pond was added on the front right of the green, making this hard hole even harder. *Marriott's Castle Harbour Hotel, Paynters Rd., Hamilton Parish, tel. 809/293-0795, fax 809/293-1051. Greens fees: $75 ($47 after 4:30 PM), plus mandatory $35 cart rental. Shoe rentals.*

Mid Ocean Club **Length:** 6,547 yards from the blue tees
Par: 71
Rating: blue tees, 72; white tees, 70; red tees, 72

It isn't Bermuda's oldest course—that honor belongs to Riddell's Bay—and other Bermudian courses are equally difficult, but the elite Mid Ocean Club is generally regarded as one of the top 50 courses in the world. Quite simply, this course has charisma, embodying everything that is golf in Bermuda—tees on coral cliffs above the ocean, rolling fairways lined with palms and spice trees, doglegs around water, and windswept views. It is rich in history, too. At the dogleg fifth hole, for example, Babe Ruth is said to have splashed a dozen balls in Mangrove Lake in a futile effort to drive the green. The course rewards long, straight tee shots and deft play around the green, while penalizing—often cruelly—anything less. The fifth and ninth holes, for example, require that tee shots (from the blue tees) carry 180 yards or more over water. And while length is not a factor on two fairly short par fives, the 465-yard second and the 487-yard 11th, accuracy is: Tight doglegs ensure that any wayward tee shot ends up in trees, shrubbery, or rough. The course may have mellowed with age, however. The course lost hundreds of trees to a tornado in 1986 and was battered again by Hurricane Emily in 1987. The tight, tree-lined fairways have become more open as a result, and the rough less threatening.

Highlight hole: The 433-yard fifth is a par-four dogleg around Mangrove Lake. The elevated tee overlooks a hillside of flowering shrubbery and the lake, making the fairway seem impossibly far away. Big hitters can take a short cut over the lake (although the green is unreachable, despite the Babe's heroic efforts), but anyone who hits the fairway has scored a major victory. To the left of the green, a steep embankment leads into a bunker that is among the hardest in Bermuda from which to recover. *Mid Ocean Dr., off South Rd., Tucker's Town, tel. 809/293–0330, fax 809/ 293–8837. Greens fees: $90 ($40 when accompanied by a member). Nonmembers must be introduced by a hotel activities director or a club member; nonmember starting times available only on Mon., Wed., and Fri. Caddies, $20 per bag (tip not included).*

Ocean View Golf and Country Club
Length: 3,000 yards (nine holes) from the blue tees
Par: 35; ladies, 37
Rating: none

Work on the Ocean View Golf & Country Club is still in progress. Founded nearly 40 years ago as a club for blacks, the nine-hole course fell into neglect as other courses in Bermuda began admitting black players. In 1988, the Bermudian government took over management of Ocean View and committed roughly $3 million to its refurbishment. In addition to restoring the course to good playing condition and altering a few holes, the government's plans include a new clubhouse, possibly to be finished by the end of 1994. Also under consideration is the addition of a second nine holes. Although the old clubhouse is indeed a dank place, the course is better—and in far better shape—than its reputation would suggest. Several holes challenge and intrigue: The second is a tough par four that runs up and along the side of a hill; the sixth is a wind-buffeted par five, with a 40-foot coral wall on one side, and a slope leading down to the Great Sound on the other. Some holes have as many as six tees, offering players the opportunity for considerable variation. Locals crowd the course on weekends, although Ocean View is relatively empty on weekdays. That could change, however, if the course continues to improve as expected.

Highlight hole: The green on the 177-yard, par-three fifth hole has been cut out of a coral hillside draped with flowering vines, giving players the sensation of hitting into a grotto. Club selection can be tricky—winds off the Great Sound might seem insubstantial on the tee, but they can be much stronger over the coral wall near the green. *Off North Shore Rd., Devonshire, tel. 809/236–6758, fax 809/236– 9193. Greens fees: $22 for 9 or 18 holes ($18 when playing with a member, $10 after 4). Cart rental, $13 per 9 holes, $26 per 18 holes; hand carts, $5.*

Port Royal Golf and Country Club
Length: 6,565 yards from the blue tees
Par: 71; ladies, 72
Rating: blue tees, 72; white tees, 69.7; red tees, 72.5

Such golfing luminaries as Jack Nicklaus rank the Port Royal Golf & Country Club among the world's best public courses. A favorite among Bermudians as well, the course is well laid out, and the greens fees are modest. By Bermudian standards, Port Royal is also relatively flat. Although there are some hills, on the back nine in particular, the course has few of the blind shots and hillside lies that are prevalent elsewhere. Those holes that do have gradients tend to run either directly uphill or downhill. In other respects, however, Port Royal is classically Bermudian, with close-cropped fairways, numerous elevated tees and greens, and holes raked by the wind, especially the eighth and the 16th. The 16th hole, one of Bermuda's most famous, is frequently pictured in magazines. The green sits on a treeless promontory overlooking the blue waters and pink-white sands of Whale Bay, a popular boating and fishing area. When the wind is blowing hard onshore, as it frequently does, a driver may be necessary to reach the green, which is 163 yards away. One complaint often raised about Port Royal is the condition of the course, which can become chewed up by heavy usage—more than 55,000 rounds a year.

Highlight hole: Like the much-photographed 16th hole, the 371-yard, par-four 15th skirts the cliffs along Whale Bay. In addition to the ocean view, the remains of Whale Bay Battery, a 19th-century fortification, lie between the fairway and the bay. Only golf balls hooked wildly from the tee have any chance of a direct hit on the fort. The wind can be brutal on this hole. *Off Middle Rd., Southampton, tel. 809/ 234–0974, fax 809/234–3562. Greens fees: $36; discount rates after 4 PM; 5-day Golf Package weekdays only, $130, greens fees only. Except for groups, tee times can be arranged no more than 2 days in advance. Cart rental, $26; hand cart, $6. Shoe rentals.*

Princess Golf Club **Length:** 2,684 yards from the blue tees
Par: 54
Rating: none

The Princess Golf Club unfolds on the hillside beneath the Southampton Princess. The hotel has managed to sculpt a neat little par-three course from the steep terrain, and players who opt to walk around will find their mountaineering skills and stamina severely tested. The vertical drop on the first two holes alone is at least 200 feet, and the rise on the fourth hole makes 178 yards play like 220. Kept in excellent shape by an extensive irrigation system, the course is a good warm-up for Bermuda's full-length courses, offering a legitimate test of wind and bunker play with a minimum of obstructions and hazards. Ocean views are a constant feature of the front nine, although the looming presence of the hotel does detract from the scenery.

Highlight hole: The green of the 174-yard 16th hole sits in a cup ringed by pink-blooming oleander bushes. Less than a mile away, the Gibbs Hill Lighthouse dominates the back-drop. *Southampton Princess, South Rd., tel. 809/238-0446, fax 809/238-8245. Greens fees: $32 ($28.50 for hotel guests). Cart rental: $28 ($25 for hotel guests), hand carts $5. Shoe rentals.*

Riddell's Bay Golf and Country Club **Length:** 5,588 yards from the blue tees
Par: 69; ladies, 71
Rating: blue tees, 67.7; white tees, 66.4; red tees, 70.6

Built in 1922, the Riddell's Bay Golf & Country Club is Bermuda's oldest course. In design, however, it more nearly approximates a Florida course—relatively flat, with wide, palm-lined fairways. You don't need to be a power hitter to score well here, although the first four holes, including a 427-yard uphill par four and a 244-yard par three, might suggest otherwise. The par fours are mostly in the 360-yard range, and the fairways are generously flat and open. Despite the course's position on a narrow peninsula between Riddell's Bay and the Great Sound, water only comes into play on holes eight through 11. With the twin threats of wind and water, these are the most typically Bermudian holes on the course, and accuracy off the tee is important. This is especially true of the par-four eighth, a 360-yard right dogleg around the water. With a tail wind, big hitters might try for the green, but playing around the dogleg on this relatively short hole is the more prudent choice. As at the Belmont course, a few tees are fronted with stone walls—an old-fashioned touch that harks back to the old courses of Great Britain. Like Mid Ocean, Riddell's is a private club that is open to the public only at certain times, but the clubbish atmosphere is much less pronounced here.

Highlight hole: The tees on the 340-yard, par-four 10th are set on a grass-topped quay on the harbor's edge. The fairway narrows severely after about 200 yards, and a drive hit down the right-hand side leaves a player no chance to reach the green in two. Two ponds guard the left side of a sloped and elevated green. The hole is rated only the sixth most difficult on the course, but the need for pinpoint accuracy probably makes it the hardest to par. *Riddell's Bay Rd., Warwick, tel. 809/238-1060, fax 809/238-8785. Greens fees: $36 ($18 when accompanied by a member). Cart rental, $30; hand carts, $5.*

St. George's Golf Club **Length:** 4,502 yards from the blue tees
Par: 64
Rating: blue tees, 62.8; white tees, 61.4; red tees, 62.8

Built in 1985, St. George's Golf Club dominates a secluded headland at the northeastern end of the island. The 4,502-yard course is short, but it makes up for its lack of length with sharp teeth. No course in Bermuda is more exposed to wind, and no course has smaller greens—some are no more than 25 feet across. To make matters trickier, the greens are hard and slick from the wind and salty air. Many of the holes have commanding views of the ocean, particularly the eighth, ninth, 14th, and 15th, which run along the water's edge. Wind—especially from the north—can turn these short holes into club-selection nightmares. Don't let high scores here ruin your enjoyment of some of the finest views on the island. The scenery, the course's shortness, and the fact that it gets little play midweek, make St. George's Golf Club a good choice for couples or groups of varying ability.

Highlight hole: Pause to admire the view from the par-four 14th hole before you tee off. From the elevated tee area, the 326-yard hole curls around Coot Pond, an ocean-fed cove, to the green on a small, treeless peninsula. Beyond the neighboring 15th hole is old Fort St. Catherine's, and beyond that lies the sea. With a tail wind, it's tempting to hit for the green from the tee, but Coot Pond leaves no room for error. *1 Park Rd., St. George's, tel. 809/297–8067 or 809/297–8148, fax 809/297–2273. Greens fees: $26; $13 after 3 on weekdays, after 4 on weekends. Cart rental, $26; hand carts, $5.*

Horseback Riding

Bermuda has strict regulations regarding horseback riding, particularly on public beaches. Visitors may only rent horses for supervised trail rides.

Because most of the land on Bermuda is residential, opportunities for riding through the countryside are few. The chief exception is **South Shore Park,** between South Road and the Warwick beaches. Sandy trails, most of which are open only to riders or people on foot, wind through stands of dune grass and oleander, along beaches, and over coral bluffs. Nearby is the **Spicelands Riding Centre** (Middle Rd., Warwick, tel. 809/238–8212 or 809/238–8246), the main riding facility on the island. The center's most popular trail ride is the two-hour south-shore breakfast ride, departing at 7 AM; breakfast is included in the $37.50 fee. The daily 10 AM trail ride ($25) is a leisurely one-hour trek. Evening rides ($30) are also offered weekly May–September; call for schedules. Spicelands also offers instruction in its riding ring.

Jogging and Running

Many of the difficulties that cyclists face—hills, traffic, and wind—also confront runners in Bermuda. The presence of pedestrian sidewalks and footpaths along roadsides, however, does make the going somewhat easier. Runners who like firm pavement will be happiest on the Railway Trail (*see* Bicycling, *above*) or on South Road, a popular route. For those who like running on sand, the trails through **South Shore Park** are relatively firm, while the island's beaches obviously present a much softer surface. **Horseshoe Beach** is frequented by a large number of runners, although their interest in the beach may be more social than physical, because Horseshoe Beach is where the action is. A better beach for running is ½-mile Warwick Long Bay, the longest uninterrupted stretch of sand on the island. By using South Shore Park trails to skirt coral bluffs, runners can create a route that connects several beaches, although trails in some places can be winding and uneven.

The big race on the island is the **Bermuda International Marathon & 10K Race,** held in mid-January. The race attracts world-class distance runners from several countries, but it is open to everyone. For information, contact the Race Committee (Box DV 397, Devonshire DV BX). The association can also provide information on other races held throughout the year. Another event for fitness fanatics is the **Bermuda Triathlon** in late September. Held in Southampton, the event combines a 1-mile swim, a 15-mile cycling leg, and a 6-mile run. For information, contact the Bermuda Triathlon Association (Box HM 1002, Hamilton HM DX). Less competitive—and certainly less strenuous—are the 2-mile **"fun runs,"** sponsored by the Mid-Atlantic Athletic Club (Box HM 1745, Hamilton HM BX) and held every Tuesday evening from April through October. Runs begin at 6 PM in front of Camden House on Berry Hill Road, Botanical Gardens. No entry fee is charged. Additional information about jogging and running is available from the Bermuda Track & Field Association (Box DV 397, Devonshire DV BX).

Squash

The **Bermuda Squash Club** (Middle Rd., Devonshire, tel. 809/292–6881) makes its four courts available to nonmembers between 9 AM and 11 PM by reservation. A $5 fee per person includes racquet, ball, towel, and 40 minutes of play. Softball players will enjoy the two English courts (larger than U.S. courts) at the **Coral Beach & Tennis Club** (South Rd., Paget, tel. 809/236–2233. Introduction by a member or an associated hotel or guest house is required at Coral Beach.) In mid-November, the Bermuda Squash Racquets Association (tel. 809/292–6881) sponsors the **Bermuda Open Squash Tournament,** in which top international players compete.

Tennis

Bermuda has a tennis court for every 600 residents, a ratio that even the most tennis-crazed countries would find difficult to match. Many of the tennis courts are private, but the public has access to more than 80 courts in 20 locations island-wide. Courts are inexpensive and seldom full. Hourly rates for nonguests are about $10–$15. Bring along a few fresh cans of balls, because balls in Bermuda cost $6–$7 per can—about three times the rate in the United States. Among the surfaces used in Bermuda are Har-Tru, clay, cork, and hard composites, of which the relatively slow plexipave composite is the most prevalent. Considering Bermuda's British roots, it's surprising that there are no grass courts on the island.

Wind, heat (in summer), and humidity are the most distinguishing characteristics of Bermudian tennis. From October through March, when daytime temperatures rarely exceed 80°F, play is comfortable throughout the day. In summertime, however, the heat radiating from the court (especially hard-surface ones) can make play uncomfortable between 11 AM and 3 PM. At such times, the breezes normally considered a curse in tennis can become a cooling blessing. Early morning or evening tennis presents players with an entirely different problem, when tennis balls grow heavy with moisture from Bermuda's humid sea air, always at its wettest early and late in the day. On clay courts, the moist balls become matted with clay, making them even heavier. In strong winds, inland courts, such as the clay and all-weather courts at the **Government Tennis Stadium** (Cedar Ave. and St. John's Rd., Pembroke, tel. 809/292–0105) or the clay courts at the **Coral Beach & Tennis Club** (off South Rd., Paget, tel. 809/236–2233 or 809/236–6495) are preferable. Despite their position at the water's edge, the plexipave courts of the **Southampton Princess Hotel** (South Rd., Southampton, tel. 809/238–1005) are reasonably well shielded from the wind (especially from the north), although the breeze can be swirling and difficult. High on a bluff above the ocean, the courts at the **Sonesta Beach Hotel & Spa** (off South Rd., tel. 809/238–8122) offer players one of the more spectacular settings on the island, but the courts are exposed to summer winds from the south and southwest. Other hotels with good tennis facilities open to the public are the **Elbow Beach Hotel** (South Shore, Paget, tel. 809/236–3535), with five courts, and **Marriott's Castle Harbour Resort** (Paynters Rd., Hamilton Parish, tel. 809/293–2040), with six cork courts. All of the above facilities have some floodlit courts for night play, as do the **Pompano Beach Club** (off Middle Rd., Southampton, tel. 809/234–0222) and the **Belmont Hotel, Golf & Country Club** (Belmont Rd., Warwick, tel. 809/236–1301). Guests at the Pompano Beach Club have complimentary use of the four clay courts at the neighboring **Port Royal Club** (Southampton, tel. 809/234–0974). Others pay $5; ball and racquets are loaned, and two courts are lighted for night play. An additional fee of $2–$5 is usually charged to play under lights. Most tennis facilities offer lessons, ranging from $15 to $25 for 30 minutes of instruction, and racquet rentals for $3–$5 per hour (a few hotels lend racquets to hotel guests for free).

Spectator Sports

Bermuda is a great place for sports enthusiasts seeking relief from an overdose of baseball, football, and basketball—sports that mean little to Bermudians. In addition to golf and tennis, the big spectator sports here are cricket, rugby, soccer, field hockey, and yacht racing. The Bermuda Department of Tourism (*see* Government Tourist Offices in Chapter 1, Essential Information) can provide exact dates and information about all major sporting events.

Cricket Cricket is the big team sport in summer, and the **Cup Match Cricket Festival** is *the* event on Bermuda's summer sports calendar. Held in late July or early August at the Somerset Cricket Club (Broome St., off Somerset Rd., 809/234–0327) or the St. George's Cricket Club (Wellington Slip Rd., tel. 809/297–0374), the competition features teams from around the island. Although cricket is taken very seriously, the event itself is a real festival, attended by thousands of colorful picnickers and party goers. Admission is free. The regular cricket season runs from April through September.

Field Hockey Hockey games between local teams can be seen at the National Sports Club (Middle Rd., Devonshire, tel. 809/236–6994) on weekends from October through April. In early September, the National Sports Club is the site of the **Hockey Festival,** a tournament with teams from Bermuda, the United States, Great Britain, Holland, and Germany. Admission is free.

Golf Golf tournaments are held throughout the year at various courses on the island. The highlight of the golf year is the **Bermuda Open** in early October, which attracts a host of professionals and amateurs. A schedule of events is available from the Bermuda Golf Association (*see* Golf in Participant Sports, *above*).

Horseracing Equestrian events are held throughout the year at the **National Equestrian Club** (Vesey St., Devonshire, tel. 809/234–0485). Harness races take place twice monthly from September through April. The horsey set also turns out in October for the FEI/Samsung Dressage Competition and Show Jumping events. For additional information contact the Bermuda Equestrian Federation (Box DV 583, Devonshire DV BX, tel. 809/295–4434).

Rugby The **Easter Rugby Classic** is the final event in Bermuda's rugby season, which runs from September to April. Held at the National Sports Club (Middle Rd., Devonshire, tel. 809/236–6994), the competition attracts teams from Great Britain, France, New Zealand, and Australia, as well as Bermuda. Admission is $5. During the rest of the season, matches between local teams can be seen on weekends at the National Sports Club.

Soccer In late March or early April, teams from countries around the Atlantic, including the United States, Canada, Great Britain, and several Caribbean nations, compete for the **Diadora Youth Soccer Cup.** Teams play in three age divisions, and games are held on fields around the island. Contact the Bermuda Department of Tourism (tel. 809/292–0023).

Tennis Tennis tournaments are played year-round, although most of the major ones are in the fall and winter. Included among them are September's **Grotto Bay Open,** a 12-day tournament played on hard courts at the Grotto Bay Beach Hotel & Tennis Club (Hamilton Parish, tel. 809/293–8333, ext. 1914); October's **All Bermuda Tennis Club Tournament,** played on clay courts (Government Tennis Stadium, Pembroke Parish, tel. 809/292–0105) and **Pomander Gate Tennis Club Tournament,** a closed tournament at which spectators are welcome (Paget, tel. 809/236–5400); and the **Bermuda Lawn Tennis Club Invitational,** played on clay courts at the Coral Beach Tennis Club (Paget, tel. 809/236–2233). For full information about other tournaments, contact the Bermuda Lawn Tennis Association, Box HM 341, Hamilton HM BX, no tel., fax 809/295–3056).

Yachting Bermuda has a worldwide reputation as a yacht-racing center. Spectators, particularly those on land, may find it difficult to follow the intricacies of a race or regatta, but the sight of the racing fleet, with brightly colored spinnakers flying, is always striking. The racing season runs from March to November. Most races are held on weekends in the Great Sound, and several classes of boats usually compete. Good vantage points for viewing races are around Spanish Point, Hamilton Harbour, and the islands northeast of Somerset. Anyone wanting to get a real sense of the action, however, should be aboard a boat near the race course.

In late June, Bermuda acts as the finish for oceangoing yachts in two major races beginning in the United States—the **Newport–Bermuda Race** and the **Annapolis–Bermuda Race.** Of the two, the Newport–Bermuda Race is considered the more prestigious, but both provide the spectacular sight of the island's harbors filled with yachts, which range in length from 30 to 100 feet. For those more interested in racing than expensive yachts, the **Omega Gold Cup International Match Racing Tournament** is the event to see. Held in late October or early November in Hamilton Harbour, the tournament pits visiting America's Cup Match Racing skippers against Bermudians in one-on-one races for prize money.

8 Dining

By John DeMers

Updated by
Judith Wadson

With 140 restaurants from which to choose, visitors to this tiny island will have little difficulty satisfying their cravings for everything from traditional English fare to French, Italian, Japanese, Indian, and Chinese. A quest for Bermudian food, however, is likely to be as extended and elusive as the search for the Holy Grail. And if you persist, you'll discover the single greatest truth about Bermudian cuisine: There's not much to it, but everybody on the island loves it. Waiters, in particular, prove inspirational. While heaping your plate, they will wax lyrical about their mother's conch stew, their late uncle's fish chowder, or their great aunt's codfish and potatoes. And no islander seems to remember ever tasting anything better than a mysterious concoction called hash shark or—more intelligibly—shark hash.

In moments of candor, islanders will confide that Bermudian cuisine is really a collection of dishes showing English, American, and West Indian influences. But whatever the origins of the recipes, the island's cuisine begins and ends with Bermudian ingredients—and therein lies the island's culinary identity. Seafood is extraordinary here, especially the local lobster that may only be eaten from September through March, due to fishing laws. This is the spiny lobster familiar in the Caribbean, usually prepared with a minimum of seasoned stuffing, broiled, and served drizzled with butter. Menus also feature Bermuda rockfish, the flesh of which is firm and white; red snapper, often served with onions and potatoes; shark; and mussels steamed in white wine or made into a pie with a curry seasoning. You should also try the fish chowder, laced at the table with local black rum and sherry peppers (sherry in which hot peppers have been marinated). The result is unforgettable. Conch fritters, too, are a good bet when you can find them. Unless you venture to St. David's Island on the island's East End, you may never get to taste shark hash. The best approach is to hang around the Black Horse Tavern or Dennis's Hideaway until somebody announces that the hash is ready. The passion that East Enders hold for this dish means the pot won't be full for long.

Without doubt, the most famous vegetable is the Bermuda onion, hailed by onion lovers as a more heavenly version of the sweet Vidalia onion from Georgia. It is most commonly found in onion pie and cheese and onion sandwiches, and glazed in sugar and rum. Bermuda's soil works miracles with most common vegetables. Don't be put off if your meal is accompanied by potatoes, broccoli, or even carrots. Rarely will these vegetables taste better or fresher in their natural flavors.

In addition to onion pie and mussel pie, cassava pie is a tradition dating back three centuries. Made from dough of eggs, sugar, and ground cassava root, this savory meat pie is a Christmas standard, nearly always paired with a traditional turkey and dressing. Other island dishes turn up just

American Express offers Travelers Cheques built for two.

American Express® Cheques *for Two*. The first Travelers Cheques that allow either of you to use them because both of you have signed them. And only one of you needs to be present to purchase them.

Cheques *for Two* are accepted anywhere regular American Express Travelers Cheques are, which is just about everywhere. So stop by your bank, AAA* or any American Express Travel Service Office and ask for Cheques *for Two*.

AMERICAN EXPRESS **Travelers Cheques**®

when you despair of ever finding any. At Sunday breakfast, ask for codfish and bananas, made with the salt cod commonly known as Portuguese bacalao. Revived by soaking in water, the cod is served with boiled potatoes, fresh bananas, sliced avocado, and either a creamed egg sauce or, occasionally, a savory tomato topping. Hoppin' John, a Bermudian dish that's also popular in the Carolinas, is rice cooked with chicken, beans or peas, bacon, onion, and thyme. Another traditional favorite is syllabub, a sweet treat of guava, wine, and cream served either as a liquid or a jelly.

For the most part, however, dining on the island is fairly non-Bermudian, and expensive: Dinner at the best restaurants can cost as much as $100 per person, excluding a 15% service charge. During the summer season, reservations are essential at these restaurants. Of course, if you are staying in one of the major resorts, you can usually choose from several restaurants without ever leaving the property, and most hotels and cottage colonies offer a variety of meal plans ranging from full board to Continental breakfasts (*see* Chapter 9, Lodging).

Dining in Bermuda tends to be rather formal. In the more upscale restaurants, men should wear jackets and ties, and women should be comparably attired. Credit cards are widely accepted in the major hotels and restaurants, while the small taverns and lunch spots only take cash.

Highly recommended restaurants are indicated by a star ★.

Category	Cost*
Very Expensive	over $50
Expensive	$36–$50
Moderate	$20–$35
Inexpensive	under $20

per person, excluding drinks and service (a 15% service charge is sometimes added)

The following credit card abbreviations are used: AE, American Express; D, Discover; DC, Diners Club; MC, MasterCard; V, Visa.

Asian

Expensive **Bombay Bicycle Club.** The culinary scene of any British colony would be woefully incomplete without a curry house. Named after a private gentleman's club in the waning days of the Raj, this burgundy-hued restaurant captures the flavor of the subcontinent without becoming a caricature. All the traditional Indian favorites are offered here and prepared remarkably well. Order the *peeaz pakora* (onion fritters) and mulligatawny soup as starters, then opt for the

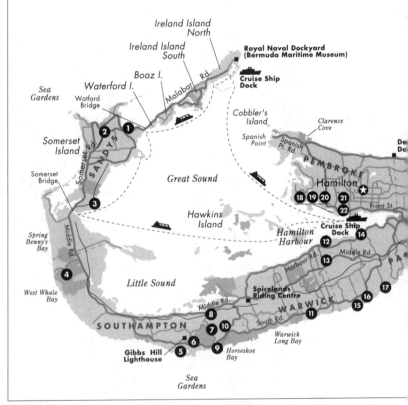

ATLANTIC OCEAN

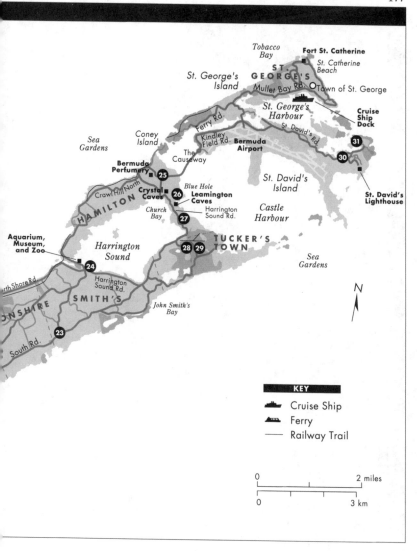

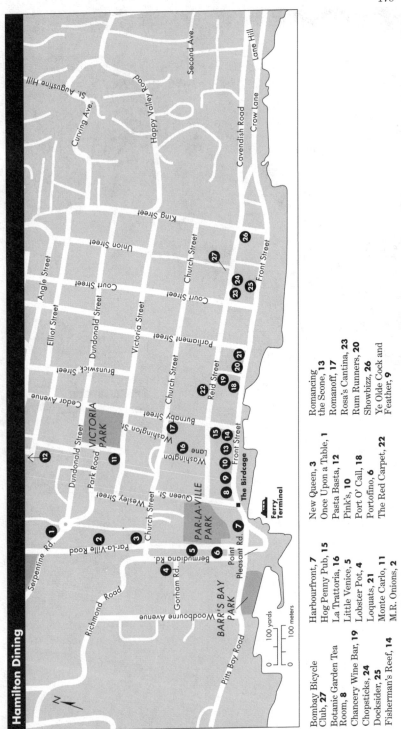

Hamilton Dining

Bombay Bicycle Club, **27**
Botanic Garden Tea Room, **8**
Chancery Wine Bar, **19**
Chopsticks, **24**
Docksider, **25**
Fisherman's Reef, **14**

Harbourfront, **7**
Hog Penny Pub, **15**
La Trattoria, **16**
Little Venice, **5**
Lobster Pot, **4**
Loquats, **21**
Monte Carlo, **11**
M.R. Onions, **2**

New Queen, **3**
Once Upon a Table, **1**
Pasta Basta, **12**
Pink's, **10**
Port O' Call, **18**
Portofino, **6**
The Red Carpet, **22**

Romancing the Scone, **13**
Romanoff, **17**
Rosa's Cantina, **23**
Rum Runners, **20**
Showbizz, **26**
Ye Olde Cock and Feather, **9**

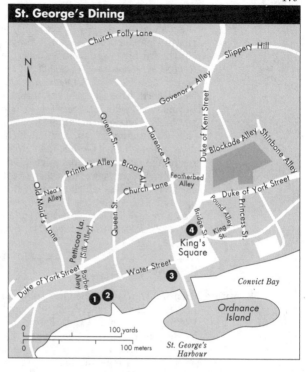

St. George's Dining

jhinga vindaloo (shrimp in hot curry), *mutton saagwala* (braised lamb in creamy spinach), or anything from the clay tandoor oven. *Nan, paratha,* and *papadums* are terrific breads and snacks to accompany the meal. *Reid St., Hamilton, tel. 809/292-0048 or 809/292-8865. Reservations suggested. Dress: casual but neat. AE, DC, MC, V.*

Mikado. This fun restaurant in Marriott's Castle Harbour Hotel brings Japanese cooking to very English Bermuda. The decor is stark, using simple lines and colors to great effect. As at many Japanese-style steak houses, the enjoyment lies less in the food than in the dazzling flash of twirling knives, slapping mallets, and airborne salt and pepper shakers—it's like judo you can eat. Although à la carte dining is available, you're better off with one of the complete dinners: a shrimp or scallop appetizer with ginger sauce, miso or *tori* soup, a seafood or beef entrée selection, salad, steamed rice, *teppan-yaki* vegetables, and Japanese tea. The sushi bar here is the only one on the island. *Marriott's Castle Harbour Hotel, Tucker's Town, tel. 809/293-2040. Reservations required. Dress: casual but neat. AE, DC, MC, V.*

Moderate **Chopsticks.** An alternative to New Queen (*see below*) at the east end of Hamilton, this Chinese restaurant features an intelligent mix of Szechuan, Hunan, and Cantonese favorites. The decor is very pink and mercifully devoid of calendars depicting Hong Kong's skyline. Top selections include the mandarin butterfly steak, lemon chicken Macau, and ribs in a mandarin orange sauce. For dessert, order nothing but the freshly baked pastries described as "Betty's pies." *Reid St. E, Hamilton, tel. 809/292–0791. Reservations suggested. Dress: casual but neat. AE, DC, MC, V.*

New Queen. This Chinese restaurant is an old favorite of Bermudians, who flock here for the hot and spicy fare. The emphasis is on the food rather than the decor, but the interior is attractive, clean, and subdued. Try the Szechuan duck, steamed until tender, then pressed with black mushrooms and potato flour, deep-fried, and served with a peppery mushroom sauce. Another great choice is *wor suit* chicken—boneless chicken pressed with minced meat, lightly battered and fried, and served on a bed of vegetables. *Par-la-Ville Rd., Hamilton, tel. 809/295–4004 or 809/292–3282. Reservations suggested. Dress: casual but neat. AE, DC, MC, V.*

Bermudian

Expensive **Glencoe.** The Salt Kettle ferry from Hamilton drops you off just two minutes' walk from this popular restaurant overlooking the harbor in Paget. Part of a cottage colony owned by Reggie and Margot Cooper, the restaurant offers truly stylish dining: Lunch is served on the patio in good weather, and dinner is in an impressive manor house that dates back to the 1700s. The lunch menu is in English, and the dinner menu in French—a sure sign that the dining becomes fussier after sunset. Start with the *gaspacho Andaluz* (chilled vegetable soup) in summer or the fish chowder in any season. The vichyssoise is excellent as a special at dinner, too, as are the local fish in a sauce of tomatoes, capers, and white wine, and the crispy roast duckling in a dark cherry sauce. Another dish worth considering is the chicken breast wrapped around a lobster tail, served in a red-wine sauce. *Salt Kettle, Paget, tel. 809/236–5274. Reservations required. Dress: casual but neat. AE, MC, V.*

★ **Plantation.** Chris and Carol West call their trendy, clublike establishment a "truly Bermudian restaurant"; if that means the emphasis is on fresh seafood, they are absolutely right. Island wicker, flickering candles, and a glass-enclosed atrium filled with plants give the restaurant a cool, exotic look that works well with the ambitious, tropical menu. Some of the dishes can be overly exotic; however, panfried fish-of-the-day served with fried Bermuda bananas or roast lamb with a delicate rosemary sauce seem right at home here. *Bailey's Bay, Hamilton Parish, tel. 809/293–1188. Reservations suggested. Dress: casual but neat; men are asked to wear a collared shirt. AE, DC, MC, V.*

Moderate **Black Horse Tavern.** Long a secret among Bermudians who
★ flock here for the good, plentiful food, this place was finally discovered by Americans from the next-door Naval Air

Station. Nothing has changed much as a result. A menacing shark, with jaws agape, still hangs on the white-plaster wall, along with an assortment of other mounted island fish. And islanders still fill the casual dining room and the six outside picnic tables to savor the culinary magic of chef Bernel Pitcher. Curried conch stew with rice is a favorite, as are Pitcher's straightforward renderings of amberjack, rockfish, shark, tuna, wahoo, and—in season—Bermuda lobster. For lunch, the fish sandwich is a taste sensation. If you want to try a Bermuda original, ask for shark hash, the chef's most popular specialty—the kitchen can never keep it in stock. *St. David's Island, tel. 809/293-9742. Reservations unnecessary. Dress: casual. No credit cards.*

Loquats. A popular lunch spot for businesspeople, this chic restaurant becomes far more romantic at night, serving well-prepared meals to the accompaniment of a pianist. Bright colors and eye-catching graphics will appeal to the MTV generation. The extensive menu is thoroughly international, but the best dishes have a Bermudian touch. In other words, choose the conch fritters over the Norway or Canada prawn cocktail, the fish chowder over the onion soup, and the broiled Bermuda rockfish over the so-called scampi tempura. *Front St., Hamilton, tel. 809/292-4507. Reservations suggested. Dress: casual but neat. AE, DC, MC, V.*

Inexpensive
★

Dennis's Hideaway. Of all the eccentric characters who call St. David's home, Dennis Lamb may be the most eccentric. Piratical in appearance, he hunches over his pots grousing about everything from the plumbing and the government to the fate of man. The place consists of little more than a ramshackle pink building, a scattering of homemade picnic tables, and a few yapping dogs, but it serves probably Bermuda's best local dishes. Don't come here if you're a stickler for cleanliness, however—the place is decidedly grubby. Dennis's son does most of the cooking these days, but Dennis still potters around the kitchen. If you want to make Dennis's day, order his "fish dinner with the works"—$28.50 for a feast of shark hash on toast, conch fritters, mussel stew, conch stew, fish chowder, fried fish, conch steak, shark steak, shrimp, scallops, and perhaps a bit of mussel pie. He may even include some bread-and-butter pudding for good measure. *Cashew City Rd., St. David's, tel. 809/297-0044. Reservations necessary weekend evenings. Dress: casual. No credit cards.*

British

Expensive

Carriage House. Hearty English food is the daily bread of this attractive slice of the Somers Wharf restoration. With its exposed brick walls, the interior looks rather like the exterior; try to secure a table by a window so you can watch the action on the docks. The price of dinner can add up quickly, especially if you choose something like the Bermuda Triangle—shrimp, filet Mignon, and chicken breast, each prepared with its own sauce. Don't overlook the fresh Bermuda rockfish. On Sunday, a much less expensive brunch features a generous buffet of eggs, pancakes, meat and seafood entrées, pastas, salads, and desserts. There's even unlimited wine. A well-stocked salad bar makes calorie-counting possible. *Somers Wharf, St. George's, tel. 809/297-1270. Reservations suggested. Jacket required at dinner. AE, DC, MC, V.*

Henry VIII. As popular with locals as it is with tourists from the nearby Southampton resorts, this lively restaurant affects an Old England look that stops just short of "wench" waitresses and contrived Tudor styling. The food is terrific, an eclectic mix of English and Bermudian favorites. Order the mussel pie if it's offered, or opt for the lighter steamed mussels in wine. The fish chowder is wonderful, as are the very British lamb, beef, and steak and kidney pies. Save room for the dessert of bananas flamed in dark rum. *South Shore Rd., Southampton, tel. 809/238-1977. Reservations suggested. Dress: casual but neat. AE, DC, MC, V.*

Moderate **Colony Pub.** A favorite meeting place for Hamilton's busi-
★ ness and government communities, this cozy nook is an excellent place for visitors to gain an understanding of how Bermuda works. Tourists are readily accepted by the lunching locals, although more as honored spectators than participants. Part of the Princess Hotel, the pub is redolent of Britain and the history of this tiny island. Rich shades of brown and green, and plenty of polished brass, give the restaurant an appealing clublike atmosphere. Food at the luncheon buffet is unpretentious but good, and the prices are very reasonable. *Princess Hotel, Hamilton, tel. 809/295-3000. Reservations unnecessary. Dress: casual. AE, DC, MC, V.*

Hog Penny Pub. Veterans of a London pub crawl might wonder about some of the dishes offered at this atmospheric watering hole off Front Street in Hamilton—"escargots pub-style" is, after all, something of an oxymoron. Nevertheless, die-hard aficionados of British cooking (if such animals actually exist) will also be rewarded with shepherd's pie, steak and kidney pie, and bangers (sausages) and mash; there's even a small but passable sampling of curries. But look for good fun more than good food: Sunburned strangers mingle freely in this dark and smoky den, and entertainment is offered nightly. *Burnaby Hill, Hamilton, tel. 809/292-2534. Reservations suggested. Dress: casual. AE, DC, MC, V.*

Port Royal Golf Club. This white dining room featuring light wicker furniture, on the 19th hole of the Port Royal Golf Club, overlooks the golf course through large plate-glass windows. Ask for a steak sandwich and English beer, although don't hesitate to order something more sophisticated from the main menu—the food is quite good. *Port*

Royal, Southampton, tel. 809/234–0236. Reservations suggested. Dress: casual. No credit cards. Open until dusk.

Pub on the Square. After a morning wandering around St. George's, this pub on King's Square is perfect for a slaking pint of English beer. The draft beer is better than anything that comes from the kitchen, although hamburgers and fish-and-chips are reasonably prepared. Warehouse brick and plenty of dark wood give the pub a warm atmosphere. *King's Sq., St. George's, tel. 809/297–1522 or 809/293–9704. Reservations unnecessary. Dress: casual. AE, MC, V.*

Somerset Country Squire. Overlooking Mangrove Bay in the West End, this typically English tavern is all dark wood and good cheer, with a great deal of malt and hops in between. The food isn't good enough to warrant a special trip across the island, but you won't be disappointed if you do stop by. Steak and kidney pie is fine, but the curried mussel pie is much better. Desserts are excellent: The hot apple pie with whipped cream approaches mythical status. *Mangrove Bay, Somerset, tel. 809/234–0105. Reservations necessary weekend evenings. Dress: casual. AE, MC, V.*

Wharf Tavern. Like most dockside restorations in Bermuda, this English-style watering hole is nondescript, with a stale atmosphere; it should be much better than it is. The mainstays are a selection of so-called Black Beard's pizzas (of which the privateer would surely disapprove) and an equally varied selection of burgers. The quality is typical of a pub, but the menu and prices are what you would expect in a proper restaurant, and service is often slow. *Somers Wharf, St. George's, tel. 809/297–1515. Reservations unnecessary. Dress: casual. MC, V (with a $25 minimum).*

Ye Olde Cock and Feather. One of the busiest spots along Front Street in Hamilton, this is a favorite meeting place for locals. Patrons sit either in a room that is a cross between a British pub and a Key West–style tropical outpost or on the upstairs balcony overlooking the harbor. Food here is served pub-style, but the eclectic menu spans several cuisines and continents, from gazpacho Andaluz to steak and kidney pie and chicken Kiev. Live entertainment is featured nightly April through November. *Front St., Hamilton, tel. 809/295–2263. Reservations suggested. Dress: casual. MC, V.*

Inexpensive **Botanic Garden Tea Room.** One of Bermuda's most pleasant traditions is afternoon tea here at Trimingham's department store in Hamilton. Like many tearooms, it has seen better days, but its faded elegance is now part of its appeal. The tearoom also serves light lunches. A wide variety of teas, coffee, and soft drinks are available. *Front St., Hamilton, tel. 809/295–1183. Reservations unnecessary. Dress: casual. No credit cards.*

Docksider. This Front Street hangout boasts that it has the widest selection of draft beers on the island, which says a lot about its priorities and the priorities of its young clientele. However, that's no reason to steer clear of the fish-

and-chips or the hamburgers. The club sandwiches are a good bet, too, although taste just won't matter once you've drunk your way through the bar's large selection of European brews. The interior is crowded with hundreds of beer bottles, labels, and beer paraphernalia. *Front St., Hamilton, tel. 809/292–4088. Reservations unnecessary. Dress: casual. AE, MC, V.*

Romancing the Scone. Unless docked cruise ships are in the way, the dozen-or-so tables at this restaurant offer a terrific view of Hamilton Harbour. Perched on the veranda of one of the island's oldest department stores (but operated independently), this is a favorite aprés-shopping stop, and—view or not—a great place for breakfast, lunch, or a snack of coffee with biscuits or scones. Try the croissant sandwich or the chef's salad. *Front St., in A.S. Cooper & Sons, Ltd., Hamilton, tel. 809/295–3961. Reservations unnecessary. Dress: casual. No credit cards. No dinner.*

French

Very Expensive   **Newport Room.** With its nautical theme, this lovely restaurant in the Southampton Princess has occupied a special place in the hearts of the island's elite for several years. French cuisine is the specialty. Glistening teak and models of previous America's Cup winners set the tone for some culinary winners, especially the free-range chicken roasted with vegetables in natural juices, and the venison medallions with red currant and raspberry sauce. *South Shore Rd., Southampton, tel. 809/238–8167. Reservations suggested. Jacket and tie required. AE, DC, MC, V. Dinner only.*

Tiara Room. After something of an identity crisis, the gourmet restaurant in Bermuda's historic Princess Hotel has rediscovered those elements of dining that make for fine cuisine and theater. The dining room has a fresh look, utilizing clean lines and bright colors (particularly mauve), but the highlight remains the stunning view of Hamilton Harbour. The emphasis is on classic French cuisine and service that can be overwhelming. Whenever possible, dishes are finished by your table, often flambéed dramatically. These tableside theatrics may not be chic in Paris or New York nowadays, but they work in these surroundings. The rack of lamb carved tableside is always an excellent choice, as are the cherries Jubilee and the crepes suzette. *Princess Hotel, Hamilton, tel. 809/295–3000. Reservations suggested. Jacket and tie required. AE, DC, MC, V.*

★   **Waterlot Inn.** Housed in a graceful, two-story manor house that dates back to 1670, this restaurant is a Bermudian treasure. Like most Bermudian restaurants, it has good days and bad, but it works hard to live up to its reputation and age. Chef Regis Neaud watches over the kitchen, while the dining room staff has just enough island exuberance to take the edge off their European-style training. The menu's French selections are far superior to most of the cuisine that passes for French on the island, although the chef seldom misses an opportunity to prepare dishes indigenous to Bermuda. Waterlot serves one of the best fish chowders on the island, while the fillet of fresh Bermuda fish filled with mushrooms and herbs, wrapped in cabbage leaves and served with a bell-pepper butter sauce is spectacular. For dessert, try the chocolate domino—white chocolate mousse in a domino of dark chocolate. One of the island's best Sunday brunches is served here to the sounds of first-rate local jazz musicians. *Middle Rd., Southampton, tel. 809/238-0510. Reservations suggested. Jacket and tie required. AE, DC, MC, V.*

Expensive   **Lantana Colony Club.** French classical cuisine of a high order indeed is served at this resort on the tip of the island, just past the Somerset Bridge. Surrounded by a rainbow of hibiscus and wild lemon trees, you can settle in for an à la carte lunch or a six-course prix-fixe dinner. Your best bet among the first courses is the poached salmon in Pommerey mustard sauce over linguine. Among entrées, the escalope of veal coated in almonds with a mild curry sauce, and the wahoo with orange peppercorn sauce are hard to beat. *Somerset Bridge, adjacent to the ferry stop, tel. 809/234-0141. Reservations required. Jacket and tie required at dinner indoors, casual but neat for patio. AE, DC, MC, V.*

Monte Carlo. Southern French cooking is the trademark of this bright restaurant just behind City Hall in Hamilton. Beams of old Bermuda cedar add a touch of local color, as does the unusual original artwork on the walls. There is a good selection of pizzas, but the main emphasis is on a sprightly collection of hot and cold appetizers. The carpaccio (thinly sliced raw beef served with lemon) and the stuffed mussels are superb. Favorite entrées include roast duck in mango sauce, and veal breaded with Parmesan and served with two sauces. *Victoria St., Hamilton, tel. 809/295-5453 or 809/295-5442. Reservations suggested. Dress: casual but neat. AE, MC, V.*

★ **Waterloo House.** A private home a century ago, this restaurant/guest house on Hamilton Harbour serves Bermudian and Continental cuisine. Guests can eat either on the waterside patio adjoining the flower-shaded buildings, or in the uncluttered English dining room, where a fire is kept burning during the winter. Chef Bruno Heeb usually offers a special or two, but don't overlook such appetizers as crab tartare wrapped in salmon with a dill cucumber sauce, and linguine with shrimp and a basil-and-white-wine sauce. For an entrée, consider one of the stranger dishes on the island: Bermuda fresh fish with passion fruit and yogurt coulis. *Pitt's Bay Rd., Pembroke, Hamilton, tel. 809/295-4480. Reservations suggested. Jacket and tie required at dinner. AE, MC, V.*

International

Very Expensive
Fourways Inn. This restaurant has risen to preeminence on the island in recent years, as much for its lovely 18th-century surroundings as anything coming out of the kitchen. The decor is evocative of a wealthy plantation home, with plenty of expensive china, crystal, and silver. Order the local mussels simmered in white wine and cream, and any of the sautéed veal dishes. The Caesar salad is a good choice, too, but leave enough room for strawberry soufflé. For a slightly different cocktail, try a Fourways Special, made with the juice from the Bermuda loquat and other fruits, and a dash of bitters. *1 Middle Rd., Paget, tel. 809/236-6517. Reservations suggested. Jacket and tie required. AE, MC, V.*

Romanoff. Elegant European meals served in a theatrical Russian setting are the specialty of this restaurant run by Anton Duzavic. A collection of faux-naif landscape paintings hang on the walls, and a deep rich red is the restaurant's predominant color, providing a dramatic backdrop for the vodka and black caviar that Duzavic himself presents to each diner. Stick to the well-known dishes or select a seafood special from the cart that is wheeled around the tables. *Church St., Hamilton, tel. 809/295-0333. Reservations suggested. Jacket and tie required. AE, DC, MC, V.*

Expensive
★
'Brellas. Overlooking Hamilton Harbour from a hillside in Paget, this outdoors-only restaurant on a plant-filled terrace is open in good weather from June to early October, and serves food that brightens even the less-than-dazzling days. The cold fruit soup and Bermuda fish chowder are excellent; recommended entrées include the fresh Bermuda fish, and roast lamb with delicately steamed vegetables. Both are served with cassava pie—a traditional meat pie made for special holidays in Bermuda. *In Newstead Hotel, Harbour Rd., Paget, tel. 809/236-6060. Reservations necessary. Dress: casual but neat. AE, MC, V.*

Cafe Lido. Located on the beachfront terrace at the Elbow Beach Hotel, with waves breaking just below, this is one of the island's most romantic settings. The creative menu offers plenty of inventive taste treats. Start with the grilled Portobello mushroom with avocado and red onion salsa or fresh Maine lobster with a champagne cocktail sauce served in a coconut shell. Main course winners are the scallops with green peppercorns and lime juice, the panfried soft shell crab, and the escalop of veal sauteéd in wine sauce with bacon, mushroom, and pine nuts. *Elbow Beach Hotel, off Shore Rd., Paget, tel. 809/236-3535. Reservations required. Dress: casual but neat. AE, DC, MC, V.*

Norwood Room. Don't be put off that this restaurant in the Stonington Beach Hotel is run by students of the Bermuda Department of Hotel Technology. Under the supervision of their mentors, the students offer a dining experience notable for the high quality of the food and superb service. The kitchen uses local ingredients and European culinary techniques to create a whole range of bright, fresh tastes. Seafood is the best bet here, well prepared and served with excellent sauces. Enjoy a preprandial cocktail at the sunken bar overlooking the swimming pool. *South Shore Rd., tel. 809/236-0607 or 809/236-5416. Reservations suggested. Jacket and tie required. AE, DC, MC, V.*

★ **Once Upon a Table.** Hailed by many Bermudians as the finest restaurant on Bermuda, this delightful restaurant offers elegant service in an 18th-century island home, complete with fine china and crystal. Dinner here is theatrical—the restaurant is not unlike a theme park in its use of costumes and setting to create a sense of a bygone era. From the menu, consider fillets of venison with an Armagnac and juniperberry chocolate sauce, rack of lamb, roast duckling, or pork, although you can also order a dinner of Bermudian specialties with 48-hours' notice. Low-cholesterol dishes such as broiled chicken breast with steamed vegetables and rice, and paillard of veal with cucumbers are also served. *Serpentine Rd., Hamilton, tel. 809/295-8585. Reservations recommended. Jacket and tie required. Dinner only. AE, DC, MC, V.*

Tom Moore's Tavern. Set in an old home that dates to 1652, this restaurant overlooking Bailey's Bay clearly enjoys its colorful past. Irish poet Tom Moore visited friends here frequently during his stay on the island in 1804 and wrote several of his odes under the nearby calabash tree. Today, fireplaces, casement windows, and copper appointments capture a sense of the building's history. The cuisine, however, labors under none of history's baggage—it is fresh, light, and innovative. Seafood lovers should try the Treasures of St. David's Island, a marriage of local fish, flame fish, and lobster tail. *Bailey's Bay, Hamilton Parish, tel. 809/293-8020. Reservations suggested. Jacket required. AE, MC, V.*

Windsor. Overlooking Castle Harbour Resort, this elegant dining room in Marriott's Castle Harbour Hotel features an international blend of cuisines with a strong European underpinning. Try the salmon, seafood pasta, filet mignon, or lamb. A good gravlax is served as an appetizer. Don't expect much innovation, however; as a hotel dining room, the restaurant must hedge its culinary bets. Nevertheless, with its unhurried atmosphere, live piano music, and view of Castle Harbour, the Windsor makes for a fine night out. *Castle Harbour Resort, Tucker's Town, tel. 809/293-2040. Reservations required. Jacket required. AE, DC, MC, V. No lunch.*

Moderate **Chancery Wine Bar.** This place changes its menu seasonally but is a perennial favorite with locals. Throughout the year start out with the fish chowder or, in summer, the terrine of Bermuda fish. Entrées such as breast of duck with blueberries or ratatouille and grilled Bermuda fish with mustard on roasted peppers are sure winners. Outdoor dining is in an enclosed courtyard with Cinzano umbrella topped tables set in white gravel; indoors it's a wine cellar–like room with a vaulted ceiling. *Chancery lane, off Front St., Hamilton, tel. 809/295–5058. Reservations required. Dress: casual. AE, MC, V.*

Harbourfront. Few of the restaurants along Front Street have the courage to be so inventively Continental or ambitious as this thoroughly modern restaurant, where unusual architectural elements clash with a tropical decor. The menu has recently traded its Mediterranean flavors for more basic European fare; the lamb chops with minted sauce are superb as is chicken breast served Satay–style with peanut sauce. *Front St., Hamilton, tel. 809/295–4207. Reservations recommended. Dress: casual but neat; jacket recommended at dinner. AE, DC, MC, V.*

The Inlet. With beautiful views over Harrington Sound, this restaurant in the Palmetto Hotel is filled with sunlight and fresh air. None of the dishes is likely to find its way into a gourmet magazine, but the quality is reasonable and guests have a wide selection from which to choose. In winter, there are good steaks and rack of lamb. *Palmetto Hotel, Flatts Village, tel. 809/293–2323. Reservations suggested. Jacket and tie required. AE, DC, MC, V.*

M. R. Onions. The Bermudian equivalent of TGIFriday, this fun restaurant got its name from the phrase "Him are Onions," meaning "he's one of us" (Bermudians are referred to as Onions, after the sweet onion that grows on the island). Friendly service and good spirits (both from the heart and the bar) make for an enjoyable evening here. Finger foods, such as potato skins, zucchini sticks, and breaded mushrooms, are especially good, although don't hesitate to order anything from fish chowder to charbroiled fish, steaks, and barbecued ribs. A special children's menu is available 5–7 PM, but children are discouraged any later than that. A $12.50 early-bird dinner menu is offered 5–6:30. *Par-la-Ville Rd. N, Hamilton, tel. 809/292–5012. Reservations suggested. Dress: casual. AE, DC, MC, V.*

★ **Paw-Paws.** This bistro offers seating either outdoors on a patio overlooking busy South Shore Road or in a cozy dining room with colorful wall murals of Italian garden scenes. The varied and unusual menu features Bermudian, European, and North American dishes. For starters try the Danish specialty of deep-fried Camembert with lingonberries and fried parsley, or the Bermuda fish chowder. The *ravioli d'homard et saumon* (homemade lobster ravioli in herb cream sauce with strips of smoked salmon) and *brochette des legumes* (grilled veggies on rice with basic provençal sauce) are not-to-be-missed main courses, and the Bermuda fish fillet with fennel and garlic butter is also superb. The lunchtime menu offers soups, salads, burgers, and such sandwiches as the grilled goat cheese with spinach and melted mozzarella on multi-grain bread. The wide selection of desserts comes from the adjacent bakery shop. *South Shore Rd., Warwick, tel. 809/236–7459. Reservations suggested. Dress: casual. MC, V.*

Rum Runners. This popular Front Street restaurant assumes different personalities throughout the day. It is at its most formal at dinner, when it becomes a full-service restaurant with terrific seafood. The best bets are the seafood brochette and the crab legs with sirloin, both combination plates of immense proportions. Meat patrons will be amply satisfied by the mixed English grill. Lunch is far more casual, with traditional pub fare as well as sandwiches, salads, and the unavoidable array of burgers. *Front St., Hamilton, tel. 809/292–4737. Reservations suggested for dinner. Dress: casual but neat. AE, DC, MC, V.*

Seahorse Grill. With rustic decor reminiscent of old Bermuda, this casual restaurant at the Elbow Beach Hotel in Paget is a winner. In addition to overwhelmingly large burgers and pizzas, the Seahorse's diverse menu includes breast of chicken in fruit-tinged curry sauce, lamb chops in Provencale herbs, and beef fillet in green peppercorn sauce. Don't overlook the dessert trolley. *Elbow Beach Hotel, Paget, tel. 809/236–3535. Reservations recommended. Dress: casual. AE, DC, MC, V.*

Showbizz. This colorful Hamilton hangout is not unlike the Hard Rock Cafes that have turned up around the world, except that the entire menu is a celebration of the '60s. Every dish on the large, eclectic menu fits into the theme of the music, movies, or fashion of the decade. One example is the Del Shannon ("Don't run away until you try this freshly made vegetable casserole with pilaf rice"). Some of the best items offered are the burgers, ranging from the fairly standard Beatle Burger to one built around a fish filet and named in honor of "Mamas and Papas" singer, Mama Cass. *66 King and Reid St., Hamilton, tel. 809/292–0676. Reservations not necessary. Dress: casual. AE. DC, MC, V.*

Swizzle Inn. People come to this outwardly nondescript place as much to drink as to eat. Just west of the airport near the Bermuda Perfume Factory, the inn created one of Bermuda's most hallowed drinks—the rum swizzle. Sit in the shadowy bar—plastered with business cards from all over the world—sipping one of these delightful concoctions, and watch the mopeds whiz by. If you get hungry, try a "swizzleburger." On Saturday nights, the "Dining Around the World" theme features reasonably priced international menus. *Blue Hole Hill, Bailey's Bay, tel. 809/293–9300. Reservations unnecessary. Dress: casual. AE, MC, V.*

White Horse Tavern. Set on the water's edge overlooking the harbor in St. George's, this restaurant has a great location and atmosphere. The new management's expanded menu offers a variety of local dishes not seen here before. Alongside the salads and burgers are mussel pie, cassava pie with a slice of ham, and codfish cake on a hot-cross bun. *King's Sq., St. George's, tel. 809/297–1838. Reservations unnecessary. Dress: casual. DC, MC, V.*

Wickets Brasserie & Cricket Club. Tastefully decorated with prints of the game of cricket, this restaurant offers dishes to suit most any palate. Bermuda fish chowder or the soup of the day are always good starters. The California salad of shrimp, artichoke heart, tomato, celery, heart of palm, sweet corn, and asparagus is tasty and light. At the other end of the spectrum are the Princess Triple Decker Club or the Manhattan Deli sandwiches, loaded with meat and served up on a croissant, French roll, or pita bread. Pasta pescatore is a winner with its combination of shrimp, scallops, and herbed garlic butter over linguine. Top off the meal with "Embrace by Chocolate," a concoction of dark chocolate ice cream, hot fudge, whipped cream, and mint crisps. *Southampton Princess Hotel, South Shore Rd., Southampton, tel. 809/238–8000. Reservations necessary for dinner. Dress: casual. AE, MC, V.*

Inexpensive   **Pink's.** This deli in the heart of Hamilton is certain to make your day—or at least your lunch. Salads are wide-ranging, from tabouleh to tarragon chicken and pasta; creative sandwich combinations are available. Try the country pâté. *55 Front St., Hamilton, tel. 809/295–3524. Reservations unnecessary. Dress: casual. No credit cards. Breakfast and lunch Mon.–Sat.*

Italian

Expensive   **Little Venice.** The name of this restaurant may refer to the lovely city of canals, but the atmosphere is strictly Roman—stylish, self-confident, and urbane. Bermudians head for this trattoria when they want more from Italian cooking than pizza. Little Venice can be expensive, but the food is decent enough to command higher prices and the service is expert. In particular, try the snails in tomato sauce as an appetizer, or perhaps the grilled vegetables in olive oil and balsamic vinegar. Grilled salmon served with a tomato, black olive, and caper sauce makes an excellent main course. A special early evening dinner deal is offered before 7 PM, featuring appetizer, main course, dessert, and coffee. It is available for $19.75—less than most of the à la carte entrées. *Bermudiana Rd., Hamilton, tel. 809/295–3503 or 809/295–8279. Reservations necessary. Dress: casual but neat. AE, DC, MC, V.*

Moderate   **Il Palio.** A ship's spiral staircase leads upstairs from the bar to the dining room at this West End restaurant. Some of the best pizzas on the island are served here, with all the usual trimmings. Among the other offerings are a wide range of good antipasti and pasta dishes, including cannelloni and pasta primavera. The selections of veal, chicken, and beef are straightforward. *Main Rd., Somerset, tel. 809/234–1049 or 809/234–2323. Reservations suggested. Dress: casual. AE, DC, MC, V.*

Portofino. Busy for both lunch and dinner, this popular Italian restaurant has been enlarged to seat 55, and a separate bar/waiting area accommodates patrons without reservations. A wide selection of pizza toppings is available, and customers are asked to phone 15 minutes ahead if they want their pie to go. If you're not in the mood for pizza, however, try the excellent sirloin steak with olives, capers, and tomato sauce, or the fried calamari in a delicate batter. More adventurous diners will enjoy the octopus, cooked in red sauce with olives and capers and served on a bed of rice. Risotto specials are excellent, particularly any that feature mussels and clams. *Bermudiana Rd., Hamilton, tel. 809/ 292–2375 or 809/295–6090. Reservations necessary. Dress: casual. Closed for lunch weekends. No credit cards.*

Primavera. White and burgundy dominate this pleasing Mediterranean dining room in the west end of Hamilton. Ultimately, however, it's the food that makes a visit here worthwhile. A spectacular starter is baked mushrooms in garlic butter with paprika and cream, followed by one of the house specialties: fillet of tenderloin served with white wine sauce. Guests can also choose from a wide variety of consistently good pastas. *Pitt's Bay Rd., Hamilton, tel. 809/295–2167. Reservations suggested. Dress: casual but neat. AE, DC, MC, V. No lunch weekends.*

The Red Carpet. Very popular at lunch, this tiny restaurant sports a few New York touches, such as a ravioli dish named for Frank Sinatra, but otherwise the flavor is Old World Italian. The clever use of mirrors dispels a sense of claustrophobia, while plentiful brass gives the place a stylish look. Among the culinary highlights are the veal, the fish dishes, tortellini stuffed with veal and served with a light tomato sauce, and chicken Normand (prepared with Calvados apple brandy). *Armoury Bldg., Reid St., Hamilton, tel. 809/292–6195. Reservations suggested. Dress: casual but neat. AE, DC, MC, V.*

Inexpensive **La Trattoria.** Tucked in a Hamilton alley, this comfortable trattoria is typical of every no-nonsense Italian restaurant with red-check tablecloths: Veal parmigiana is the staple, and tortellini is a typical starter. However, this restaurant also serves an interesting "diet" pizza, made with wholewheat flour and topped with zucchini and tomatoes. Early dinner special menu ($12.75) includes appetizer, main course, dessert, and coffee and is available before 7:30 PM. *Washington La., Hamilton, tel. 809/292–7059 or 809/295– 1877. Reservations suggested. Dress: casual. AE, DC, MC, V.*

★ **Pasta Basta.** A fun place to eat and a favorite of Bermudians. The brightly painted interior and colorful tables and chairs create a lively atmosphere, despite the institutional cafeteria look of the serving area. The food here is well prepared and delicious; an ever-changing menu of simple northern Italian cuisine provides astoundingly good value. Try the *penne* with chicken and pepper sauce, classic or vegetable lasagna, *orechiette* (small shells) with pesto and potato, the Caesar salad, and a nightly special. Servings are large, so order a half portion unless you're ravenous or sharing. The only drawback here is that no liquor is served, so you'll have to dine without vino. *1 Elliot St. W, Hamilton, tel. 809/295–9785. No reservations. Dress: casual. No credit cards.*

Specialty Inn. A favorite with locals, this south-shore restaurant is cheerful, clean, and cheap. The low prices are reflected in the fact that the restaurant is almost totally lacking in decoration. Try the fish chowder or the red-bean soup. Otherwise, all the dishes are just what you would expect of a family-style Italian restaurant, plus milk shakes and ice cream. *Collectors Hill, Smith's, tel. 809/236–3133. Reservations suggested. Dress: casual. No credit cards.*

Tio Pepe. You don't need to spend a lot of money for a satisfying meal at this Italian restaurant with a Mexican name. Photocopied menus and flourishes of red and green (also rather Mexican) create an easygoing atmosphere ideal for bathers returning from a day at Horseshoe Bay Beach. Try an appetizer such as spicy eggplant baked in tomato sauce and cheese, followed by a small pizza or pasta dish. *South Shore Rd., Southampton, tel. 809/238–1897 or 809/238–0572. Reservations suggested. Dress: casual. AE, DC, MC, V.*

Mexican

Moderate **Rosa's Cantina.** The island's only Tex-Mex eatery has a festive, lively atmosphere, and a predictable decor of sombreros, serapes, and south-of-the-border bric-a-brac. Despite its monopoly on the cuisine, the food here is consistently good. Nachos Unbelievable (melted cheese, refried beans, beef, onions, tomatoes, peppers, jalapeño peppers, and guacamole), fajitas, and burritos are popular favorites. Things here are generally not too spicy, although extra-hot just about anything is an option. This place has a loyal local following, and is always filled with a crowd of both Bermudians and vacationers. *Reid St., Hamilton, tel. 809/295–1912. Reservations unnecessary. Dress: casual. AE, MC, V.*

Seafood

Expensive **Lillian's.** Part of the Sonesta Beach Hotel, this elegant art nouveau restaurant gains much of its character from testimonials and mementos in honor of Aunt Lillian, whose counsel appears on the menus advising diners to "be wonderful or be horrible, but for heaven's sake, don't be mediocre." Lillian's is neither mediocre nor horrible, and it is well worth a visit for its northern Italian cuisine. Two outstanding dishes are linguine in creamy cheese sauce with applewood-smoked bacon, and broiled snapper with tomato and onion gratinée and grilled polenta. The roast rack of lamb with rosemary sautéed spinach is superb. *Sonesta Beach Hotel, Southampton, tel. 809/238–8122. Reservations suggested. Jacket required. AE, DC, MC, V. Closed Mon.*

Port O' Call. For lunch or dinner, this delightfully intimate restaurant is one of Hamilton's elegant favorites. Fresh local fish such as wahoo and red hind filet are done to a perfect turn, and the sauces are pure silk. *87 Front St., Hamilton, tel. 809/295–5373. Reservations recommended. Jacket required at dinner. AE, DC, MC, V. Closed Sun.*

Whaler Inn. Perched above the rocks and surf at the Southampton Princess, this seafood house has one of the most dramatic settings on the island. The table d'hôte menu ($35 per person, plus a 15% gratuity) entitles you to an appetizer, or soup or a salad, a main course, dessert, and coffee or tea. Try the Bermuda Triangle, an entrée of three fresh fish fillets, either deep- or panfried or chargrilled, served with three sauces—red bell pepper, butter, and lobster. Cooked the way you want, any of the selections of fresh wahoo, yellowfin tuna, barracuda, shark, or dolphinfish makes an excellent main course. *Southampton Princess Hotel, South Shore Rd., Southampton, tel. 809/238–0076. Reservations suggested. Dress: casual but neat. AE, DC, MC, V.*

Moderate **Fisherman's Reef.** Located above the Hog Penny Pub, this restaurant has a predictable nautical motif. The Reef draws a crowd of locals, who are attracted by the restaurant's high-quality seafood and steaks, for lunch and dinner. The fish chowder is excellent, as is the St. David's conch chowder. Of the wide selection of seafood entrées, the best are the Bermuda lobster, the wahoo Mangrove Bay (seasoned and broiled with slices of Bermuda onions and banana), and the Cajun-style, baked or pan-fried local catch of the day. Fresh local mussels are delicious either in curry sauce or baked with tomatoes and cheese. *Burnaby Hill, just off Front St., Hamilton, tel. 809/292–1609. Reservations recommended. Dress: casual but neat. AE, DC, MC, V.*

Harley's. Mildly nautical in theme, this pleasant restaurant in the Princess emphasizes fresh fish and simple presentation. Best bets are the grilled grouper, snapper, and dolphinfish, or the scallops en brochette. The restaurant stopped short of placing the grill in the open as entertainment, but the muted sea and sand tones bespeak a consultant's touch. *Princess Hotel, Hamilton, tel. 809/295–3000. Reservations recommended. Dress: casual. AE, DC, MC, V.*

Lobster Pot. Locals swear by this place, which serves local lobster from September through March in keeping with local fishing laws, excellent Maine lobster, and a host of other local shellfish and fish. Special Lobster Pot snails are delicious in their buttery secret sauce. Apropos its specialty, the restaurant sports a nautical decor, including shining brass instruments and sun-bleached rope. This place features some of the best versions of the local standards. *Bermudiana Rd., Hamilton, tel. 809/292–6898. Reservations suggested. Dress: casual but neat. AE, DC, MC, V. Closed Sun.*

9 Lodging

By Honey Naylor If all the accommodations available on Bermuda were reviewed here, this book would barely qualify as carry-on luggage. Visitors to this tiny island can choose from a huge array of full-service resort hotels, cottage colonies, small inns, guest houses, and housekeeping apartments. It is the beachfront cottage colonies for which Bermuda is probably most famous, however—free-standing cottages clustered around a main building housing a restaurant, a lounge, and an activities desk. Many properties, especially these cottage colonies, are sprawling affairs set in extensive grounds and connected by walkways and steps; at some of the smaller guest houses and housekeeping apartments visitors must carry their own luggage on the long walk to their rooms. Disabled visitors or anyone unwilling to climb hills may be happier at a conventional hotel with elevators and corridors.

Like everything else in Bermuda, lodging is expensive. The rates at Bermuda's luxury resorts are comparable to those at posh hotels in New York, London, and Paris. The high prices would be easier to swallow if you received first-class service in return. However, such features as 24-hour room service and same-day laundry service are rare; in most instances, you pay extra for room service when it is available. You can shave about 40% off your hotel bill by visiting Bermuda during the low or shoulder seasons. The trick is in trying to define which dates apply. Low season runs roughly from mid-November until mid-March; however, each property sets its own guidelines, and they may change even from year to year. Some hotels begin high season rates on April 1, others April 15, and a few kick in as late as May 1. Best bet is to call and ask about low- and shoulder-season rates. Temperatures rarely dip below 60°F during the winter, and the weather is ideal for tennis, golf, and shopping, although the water is a bit chilly for swimming. Low-season packages are attractively priced, and during this time a host of government-sponsored special events (many of which are free) are staged for tourists. Many of the larger hotels close each year during January and/or February in order to refurbish and prepare for the high season.

The greatest concentration of accommodations is along the south shore, in Paget, Warwick, and Southampton parishes, where the best beaches are located. If shopping is your bag, however, there are several hotels just a stone's throw from the main shopping area in Front Street in Hamilton, as well as a host of properties clustered around Hamilton Harbour, a five- to 10-minute ferry ride from the capital. The West End is a bit remote, but there is regularly scheduled ferry service across the Great Sound to Hamilton, and it is ideal for boaters, fishermen, and those who want to get away from it all. The East End has its share of nautical pursuits, too, but its major attraction is the charming, historic town of St. George. In truth, the island is so

Hotel Facilities

	Access for Disabled	On The Beach	Swimming Pool	Restaurant	Cable T.V.	Fitness Facilities	Golf Nearby	Tennis Courts	Conference Fac.	Accept Children	Children's Prog.	Access To Spa	On-Site Water-Sports	Accept Credit Cards	Air-Conditioned	Entertainment
Angel's Grotto	•				•		•			•			•	•	•	
Ariel Sands Beach Club		•	•	•			•	•		•	•		•	•	•	•
Barnsdale Guest Apts.			•		•		•			•				•	•	
Belmont Hotel	•		•	•			•	•	•	•	•			•	•	•
Cambridge Beaches		•	•	•		•	•	•	•			•	•		•	
Edgehill Manor			•		•					•					•	
Elbow Beach Hotel	•	•	•	•	•		•	•	•	•	•	•	•	•	•	•
Fourways Inn			•	•	•		•		•						•	
Grotto Bay Beach Hotel	•		•	•	•	•	•	•	•	•	•		•	•	•	•
Glencoe Harbour Club			•	•			•			•			•	•	•	•
Granaway Guest House							•			•			•	•	•	
Greenbank Cottages							•			•			•	•	•	
Harmony Club			•	•	•		•	•						•	•	•
Hillcrest Guest House							•			•					•	
Horizons & Cottages			•	•			•	•		•					•	•
Lantana Colony Club			•	•			•	•	•	•			•		•	•
Little Pomander Guest House	•				•		•			•			•	•	•	
Longtail Cliffs	•		•		•		•			•				•	•	
Loughlands Guest House			•				•			•					•	
Marley Beach Cottages		•	•		•		•			•			•	•	•	
Marriott's Castle Harbour	•		•	•	•	•	•	•	•	•			•	•	•	•
Newstead			•	•			•	•		•			•		•	•
Oxford House					•					•					•	
Palmetto Hotel			•	•			•		•	•			•	•	•	•
Paraquet Guest Apartments				•	•		•			•					•	
Pink Beach Club		•	•	•			•	•	•	•			•	•	•	•
Pompano Beach Club		•	•	•			•	•	•	•			•		•	•

	Access for Disabled	On The Beach	Swimming Pool	Restaurant	Cable T.V.	Fitness Facilities	Golf Nearby	Tennis Courts	Conference Fac.	Accept Children	Children's Prog.	Access To Spa	On-Site Water-Sports	Accept Credit Cards	Air-Conditioned	Entertainment	Boat Dock/Marina
etty Penny			•				•			•				•	•	•	
ncess, Hamilton	•		•	•	•	•	•	•	•	•			•	•	•	•	•
e Reefs	•	•	•	•			•	•	•	•			•	•	•	•	
sedon			•							•					•		
yal Palms Hotel			•	•	•					•					•	•	
George's Club	•	•	•	•	•			•	•	•			•	•	•	•	
lt Kettle House							•			•				•			•
y Top Cottages							•			•					•	•	
nesta Beach Hotel	•	•	•	•	•	•	•	•	•	•	•	•	•	•	•	•	
uthampton Princess	•		•	•	•	•	•	•	•	•	•	•	•	•	•	•	•
onington Beach Hotel		•	•	•			•	•	•				•	•	•	•	
rf Side Beach Club		•	•	•	•		•		•	•			•	•	•		
aterloo House			•	•						•	•			•	•	•	
nale Bay Inn							•			•					•		
illowbank		•	•	•			•		•	•	•				•		

small that it's possible to see and do everything you want, regardless of where you unpack your bag.

Whether or not they are officially classified as cottage colonies, a large number of guest accommodations are in cottages—usually pink with white trim and gleaming white, tiered roofs. There are some sprawling resorts, but no high rises and no neon signs. An enormous property like the Southampton Princess is hard to miss, but many hotels and guest houses are identified only by small, inconspicuous signs or plaques. The island is noted for its lovely gardens and manicured lawns, and the grounds of almost every hotel and cottage are filled with subtropical trees, flowers, and shrubs.

Return visitors to the island will notice significant improvements in virtually all properties. The Hotel Refurbishment Tax Act of 1992 substantially reduced the duty on goods imported to the island, and hotels and guest house owners have taken advantage of the tax break to spruce up their properties.

A 6% tax is tacked onto all hotel bills, and a service charge is levied in lieu of tipping: Some hotels calculate the service charge as 10% of the bill, others charge a per diem dollar amount. Some of the smaller guest houses and housekeeping units have also instituted a 5% "energy surcharge." All guests are required to make a two-night deposit two to three weeks before their arrival; those accommodations that don't take credit cards for payment—and many do not—may accept them for the deposit. Virtually every hotel on the island offers at least one vacation package—frequently some kind of honeymoon special—and many of these are extraordinarily good deals. It's worth learning about the various policies and programs at the properties that interest you before booking.

Bermuda has not traditionally been noted as a great family destination, but that has begun to change. While some hotels still discourage families from bringing small children, others now have day care and children's activities programs. The Belmont Hotel Golf and Country Club, the Elbow Beach, the Grotto Bay Beach Hotel & Tennis Club, the Sonesta Beach Hotel & Spa, the Southampton Princess, and Willowbank all offer supervised programs for children, some of which are part of attractive packages. Many hotels on the island can arrange for baby-sitters.

Most lodgings offer their guests a choice of meal plans, and the hotel rate varies according to the meal plan you choose. Under the American Plan (AP), breakfast, lunch, and dinner are included in the hotel rate; the Modified American Plan (MAP) offers breakfast and dinner; the Bermuda Plan (BP) includes a full breakfast but no dinner, while the Continental Plan (CP) features a breakfast of pastries, juice, and coffee. The rates quoted below are based on the European Plan (EP), which includes no meals at all. Many hotels also have a variety of "dine-around" plans that allow guests to eat at other restaurants on the island as part of their meal plan. The Princess and the Southampton Princess offer a Royal Dine-Around program year-round, which allows guests to eat at any of the several Princess restaurants. The six properties in the Bermuda Collection (Cambridge Beaches, Lantana, the Reefs, Glencoe Harbour Club, Stonington Beach, and the Pompano) have a similar arrangement, known as the Carousel Dine-Around program, as do Horizons, Newstead, and Waterloo House. The Belmont Hotel and the Harmony Club, both of which are Forte properties, have an exchange dining plan. Elbow Beach's dine-around plan encompasses all of that hotel's restaurants, as well as the Henry VIII. Dinner is usually formal in restaurants at hotels and cottage colonies, and men are asked to wear jackets and ties; neat but casual dress is suggested for women. Many hotels will pack a picnic lunch for those guests who want to get out and about.

Bermuda's Small Properties Ltd. is a group of small hotels and guest houses that share a toll-free information/reservations line and a fax number. The properties include Angel's Grotto, Ariel Sands Beach Club, Granaway, Greenbank, Little Pomander Guest House, Longtail Cliffs, Marley Beach Cottages, Pretty Penny, Royal Palms Hotel, and the Whale Bay Inn. To reserve at any of those properties, call 800/637–4116 or fax 809/236–1662.

Cottage colonies and hotels offer entertainment at least one night a week during high season, staging everything from calypso to classical music; barbecues and dinner dances are also popular. Afternoon tea is served daily in keeping with British tradition, and a rum-swizzle party is usually held on Monday night. Featuring the Bermudian beverage of choice, these parties present a pleasant opportunity to welcome new arrivals, get acquainted—and, of course, knock back some rum. Guest houses and housekeeping apartments do not have regularly scheduled entertainment, although informal gatherings are not uncommon.

Most of the large hotels have their own water-sports facilities where guests can rent Windsurfers, Sunfish, paddleboats, and other equipment. Even the smallest property, however, can arrange sailing, snorkeling, scuba, and deepsea fishing excursions, as well as sightseeing and harbor tours. The Coral Beach & Tennis Club and the Mid Ocean Club are posh private clubs, where an introduction by a member is necessary to gain access to their excellent beach, tennis, and golf facilities. However, many hotels have arrangements with one or the other to allow guests certain club privileges.

Highly recommended lodgings are indicated by a star ★.

Category	Cost*
Very Expensive	over $200
Expensive	$125–$200
Moderate	$90–$125
Inexpensive	under $90

*All prices are for a standard double room for two (EP) during high season, excluding 6% tax and 10% service charge (or equivalent).

The following credit card abbreviations are used: AE, American Express; DC, Diners Club; MC, MasterCard; V, Visa.

Resort Hotels

Very Expensive **Belmont Hotel, Golf & Country Club.** Occupying 110 acres between Harbour and Middle roads, this large, pink hotel was built at the turn of the century and has a distinctly British personality. As its name suggests, it's also a sports-minded resort: Golf and tennis pros are on hand to give lessons and organize golf scrambles and tennis round-robins (golf and tennis are free to hotel guests, though there is a $5 an hour fee for night tennis). Hotel guests also play free on the miniature golf range and the floodlit putting green. In 1993 the Belmont inaugurated an extensive deep sea-fishing program and a children's program. The latter, called the Kee Kee Club and costing $10 per year, allows guests to enroll their children age 2–12 in a plan that includes free meals, full day-care services, and a quarterly newsletter, among other perks. A social director coordinates a range of other activities. The enormous lobby, decorated with chandeliers and fresh flowers, bustles with the golf groups that frequent the hotel. Refurbished in 1993, the rooms are average in size (bathrooms are quite small), but their large windows admit plenty of light and create a sense of spaciousness. Mahogany Queen Anne furniture is mixed with wicker, carpets are dusty pink, and the bedspreads and drapes are in bright tropical floral patterns. With views over the harbor and the resort's gardens and pool—one of the largest on the island—the rooms on the fourth floor are probably the best. The Hamilton ferry stops at the Belmont Wharf; it's a long haul up the hill from the wharf to the hotel, but a shuttle bus makes the trip regularly. *Box WK 251, Warwick WK BX, tel. 809/236–1301 or 800/225–5843 in U.S. and Canada; fax 809/236–6867. 149 rooms, 1 suite, all with bath. Meal plans: BP, MAP. Facilities: 2 restaurants, bar, beauty salon, heated saltwater pool, 18-hole golf course, miniature golf, putting green, 3 lighted tennis courts, children's program, shops, ferry dock, water sports. AE, DC, MC, V.*

Elbow Beach Hotel. Set amid 34 acres of botanical gardens overlooking the superb south-shore beach for which it is named, this large sports-oriented resort changed ownership in 1991 and began a five-year, multimillion-dollar transformation. The first phase, completed for the 1992–93 season, was a $20 million renovation of the main building. Behind the five-story hotel's white-column facade, the lobby has been expanded to palatial proportions and paved with green marble and Oriental area rugs. Walls are paneled with white oak, and six giant crystal chandeliers hang over a gilt table, cushy furnishings, and huge, handsome arrangements of artificial flowers. The main building houses 200 rooms, suites, and junior suites, most of which have a balcony or patio and an ocean view (avoid the landside rooms, which have neither), a health club, shopping mall, gourmet restaurant, and nightclub. Other rooms and suites are in duplex cottages and multi-unit lanais set amid the gardens or by the beach. (A shuttle bus runs between the main building and the beach). Some rooms have whirlpools; all have minibars (stocked upon request), and small marble baths. Hair dryers and minirefrigerators are available on request. The pool has a shallow end, and during July and August special children's programs are held. During high season, theme parties and barbecues are frequent affairs. There is an $8-per-hour fee for the tennis courts ($3 racquet rental, $12 for night play), and $14 for use of the ball machine. Plans include an additional 100 rooms; a conference center; another, larger, pool; and the island's largest spa/ health club. Although this is an upmarket, elegant resort hotel, it lacks any uniquely Bermudian charm, and could be just about anywhere. *Box HM 455, Hamilton HM BX, tel. 809/236–3535 or 800/223–7434 in U.S. and Canada; fax 809/236–8043. 223 rooms, 75 suites, all with bath. Meal plans: BP, MAP. Facilities: 3 restaurants, 3 bars, nightclub, private beach, beauty salon, moped rental, heated freshwater pool, shopping mall, game room, playground, 5 tennis courts (2 lighted), water sports, health club with exercise room and whirlpool. AE, DC, MC, V.*

Marriott's Castle Harbour Resort. Bordered by Harrington Sound on one side and the Castle Harbour golf course on the other, this whitewashed hilltop resort is an impressive sight from the air. If "castle" conjures up images of King Ludwig, though, forget it. This is a big, busy, modern hotel geared to groups and conventions. The original Castle, which opened in 1931, was built by the Furness Withy Steamship Line as a hotel for steamship passengers traveling between U.S. and British ports. Since 1984 Marriott has spent $60 million in renovation and expansion ($1.5 million in a 1992 refurbishment), and four wings are now connected to the original building by glass-enclosed skywalks: the two-story Golf Club wing, the Bay View wing, and the two nine-story Harbour View wings, which descend in terraces to the water. Rooms throughout the hotel are identical, featuring upholstered wing-back chairs, windows dressed in ruffled valances, and heavy drapes with matching quilted bedspreads. All rooms have minifridges, and

Lodging

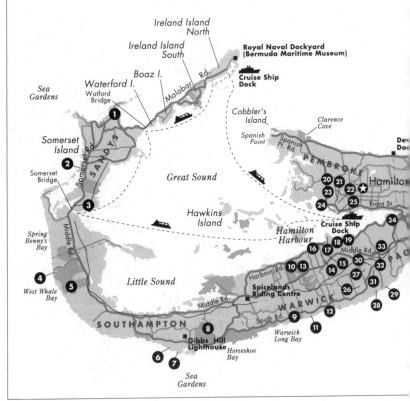

ATLANTIC OCEAN

Ireland Island North

Ireland Island South

Boaz I.

Waterford I.

Watford Bridge

Royal Naval Dockyard (Bermuda Maritime Museum)

Cruise Ship Dock

Sea Gardens

Cobbler's Island

Clarence Cove

Somerset Island

Spanish Point

Dev Do

SANDYS

Somerset Bridge

Great Sound

PEMBROKE

Hamilton

Spring Benny's Bay

Middle Rd.

Hawkins Island

Front St.

West Whale Bay

Little Sound

Hamilton Harbour

Cruise Ship Dock

PA

Harbour Rd.

Middle Rd

Spicelands Riding Centre

WARWICK

Middle Rd.

SOUTHAMPTON

South Rd.

Gibbs Hill Lighthouse

Horseshoe Bay

Warwick Long Bay

Sea Gardens

Angel's Grotto, **37**

Ariel Sands Beach Club, **35**

Barnsdale Guest Apartments, **32**

Belmont Hotel, Golf & Country Club, **13**

Cambridge Beaches, **1**

Edgehill Manor, **23**

Elbow Beach Hotel, **28**

Fourways Inn, **14**

Glencoe Harbour Club, **16**

Granaway Guest House & Cottage, **10**

Greenbank Cottages, **17**

Grotto Bay Beach Hotel & Tennis Club, **40**

Harmony Club, **33**

Hillcrest Guest House, **41**

Horizons & Cottages, **26**

Lantana Colony Club, **3**

Little Pomander Guest House, **34**

Longtail Cliffs, **9**

Loughlands Guest House & Cottage, **30**

Marley Beach Cottages, **11**

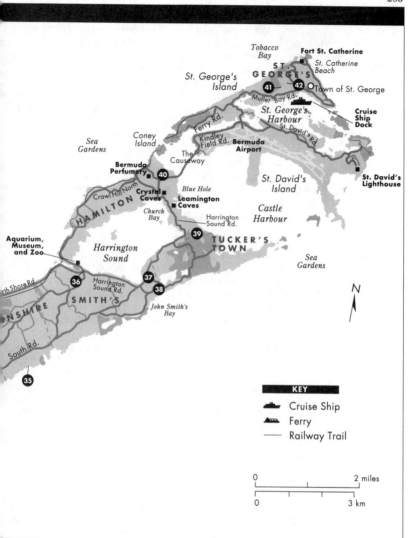

KEY

🚢 Cruise Ship

⛴ Ferry

— Railway Trail

0		2 miles
0		3 km

many have balconies. Most suites boast wet bars, refrigerators, and huge balconies. The resort's two beaches are minuscule, but guests have access to a private beach on the south shore and to three pools, including an Olympic-size lap pool and a cascading pool. Tennis courts are $10 an hour (plus $5 for racquet rental), but the well-equipped health club is free to guests. The big draw is the 18-hole Castle Harbour golf course; it is one of the best courses on the island. *Box HM 841, Hamilton HM CX, tel. 809/293–2040 or 800/228–9290 in U.S.; fax 809/293–8288. 375 rooms, 27 suites, all with bath. Meal plan: EP. Facilities: 4 restaurants; 3 bars; 2 beaches; beauty/barber shop; concierge; moped rental; 3 freshwater pools (1 heated); 6 all-weather tennis courts; 18-hole golf course; shops; business services; conference rooms; same-day laundry/dry cleaning; marina and water sports; health club with exercise room, sauna, and whirlpool. AE, DC, MC, V.*

Sonesta Beach Hotel & Spa. A sloping, serpentine drive leads through landscaped lawns to this hotel, the only property on the island where you can step directly from your room onto a sandy south-shore beach. Set on a low promontory fringed by coral reefs, the six-story modern building has a stunning ocean view and direct access to three superb natural beaches. Totally refurbished in 1992, the Sonesta caters to guests who want an action-packed vacation: An activities director coordinates bingo games, theme parties, movies, water sports, and other diversions. During high season, children's programs and family packages are offered. Vacationers seeking a quiet beachfront retreat will probably be happier elsewhere—perhaps at The Reefs (*see below*), adjacent to the Sonesta. A glass-enclosed entranceway leads to the enormous, low-ceiling lobby (where there is now a separate registration area for the large groups that often check in here). Guest rooms and suites are decorated in dark wicker and rattan furnishings upholstered with pink and green fabrics. A shuttle takes guests to the hotel's beach at Cross Bay, but beach lovers should insist on a Bay Wing minisuite that opens onto a private sandy beach. The split-level minisuites feature separate dining areas, hair dryers, and VCRs. All rooms in the 25-acre property have balconies, but standard rooms in the main building have land views only. Sports facilities include an indoor pool under a huge glass dome, a well-equipped health spa (extra charge), six tennis courts ($9 an hour; $5 for racquet rental), and the considerable facilities (extra charge) of South Side Scuba Watersports, which has an outlet at the hotel. A shuttle bus transports guests between the hotel and South Road, at the top of the hill. *Box HM 1070, Hamilton HM EX, tel. 809/238–8122 or 800/343–7170 in U.S.; fax 809/238–8463. 365 rooms, 37 suites, all with bath. Meal plans: MAP (EP and BP on request). Facilities: 3 restaurants; 3 bars; nightclub; beaches; beauty salon; concierge service; moped rental; heated indoor and outdoor freshwater pools; 6 tennis courts (2 lighted); shuttle bus; health spa with* *steam room, saunas, whirlpool, exercise and massage rooms; shopping arcade; game rooms; children's playground; water sports. AE, DC, MC, V.*

Expensive–Very Expensive

Grotto Bay Beach Hotel & Tennis Club. Only a mile from the airport, this is the smallest and most casual of the hotels in this price category. Set in 20 acres of gardens, it appeals to a young crowd that likes the hotel's informal atmosphere and the romantic coves and natural caves in the nearby enclosed bay. Also in the bay are a fish-feeding aquarium and two illuminated underground attractions: the Cathedral Cave for swimming, and Prospero's Cave, which can be seen on a guided tour. The hotel itself consists of a main building and 11 three-story pink lodges dotting a hill that slopes to the waters of Ferry Reach. The spacious, low-ceiling main building lobby has tile floors, murals in soft colors, and rattan furniture upholstered in pastel fabrics. The main dining room and small health club (with exercise machines) are near the registration area. You can avoid a long hike across the hotel grounds by requesting a room in a lodge near the main building. Each lodge contains 15–30 sunny rooms featuring light woods and fabrics, private balconies or patios, and views of the water. All rooms have a TV, coffee maker, hair dryer, and in-room safe. The three suites have two bedrooms, three bathrooms, a living room, and a balcony. Regardless of the location of your room, you will be forced to do a fair amount of walking at this sprawling resort; and the lodges don't have elevators. The hotel has its own sightseeing excursion boat and offers scuba diving and snorkeling from a private deep-water dock. The beach—not the island's best by any means—is a small strip of sand just below the pool. During high season entertainment is held poolside. Recent additions to this Bermudian-owned property included a putting green, shuffleboard, and ping pong tables. Guests can play on the resort's four tennis courts for $8 an hour ($10 for night play), and racquets can be rented for $5 an hour. There is a children's playground, and children's activities are held in season. Tipping at the Grotto Bay is at the discretion of its guests. *11 Blue Hole Hill, Hamilton Parish CR 04, tel. 809/293-8333 or 800/582-3190; fax 809/293-2306. 198 rooms, 3 suites, all with bath. Meal plans: BP, EP, MAP. Facilities: restaurant, 2 bars, nightclub, beach, 2 coves, 4 cork tennis courts (2 lighted), freshwater pool, health club, putting green, shuffleboard, ping pong, business services, meeting room, gift shop, children's playground, excursion boat, water sports. AE, MC, V.*

★ **The Princess.** Named in honor of Princess Louise, Queen Victoria's daughter who visited the island in 1883, this large pink landmark opened in 1884 and is credited with starting Bermuda's tourist industry. Refurbished in 1993, this traditional grand hotel retains a slightly formal atmosphere, and its staff provides swift, courteous service. The walls at the entrance to the Tiara Room restaurant are covered with pictures of the politicians and royals who have visited the hotel. Ideally located on Hamilton Harbour, the hotel now caters to business and professional people, convention groups, and other visitors who want to be near downtown Hamilton. The 1993 refurbishment added a health club (free to hotel guests) with exercise machines, sauna, and whirlpool; mahogany furnishings throughout the original six-story main building and the two three-story wings; and installation of in-room safes. Plush cream-colored upholstery, bedspreads, and drapes are used throughout the hotel, and most of the rooms and suites have balconies. There are several categories of suites, and all are large and sumptuous—the penthouse suite has a Jacuzzi. The Princess Club's amenities include Continental breakfast, and showers and changing facilities for travelers with late flights who want to swim after morning check-out. In high season a ferry makes regular runs across the harbor to the Southampton Princess (*see below*), which has excellent sports facilities (none of which is free to guests). The Hamilton Princess has no beach, but there are stretches of lawn with deck chairs for relaxing and sunning. In season, island revues showcasing Bermuda's top-rated entertainer, Gene Steede, are presented in the Gazebo Lounge. Details of the Royal Dine-Around plan are somewhat Byzantine, but essentially there are nine Princess restaurants from which guests can choose. *Box HM 837, Hamilton HM CX, tel. 809/295-3000, 800/223-1818 in U.S., or 800/268-7176 in Canada; fax 809/295-1914. 422 rooms, 28 suites, all with bath. Meal plans: BP, EP, MAP. Facilities: 3 restaurants; 2 bars; nightclub; beauty salon; concierge; moped rental; heated freshwater pool; saltwater pool; health club, putting green; private dock and ferry; shopping arcade; water sports; access to Southampton Princess for golf, tennis, health and beach clubs. AE, DC, MC, V.*

★ **Southampton Princess.** This hotel is much larger and livelier than its older sister, The Princess (*see above*) in Hamilton. This is not the place for those seeking a quiet retreat, but it's an excellent choice for anyone who enjoys planned activities, such as theme parties, bingo, aerobics, cooking demonstrations, and tennis matches. For families, it offers one of the island's best children's programs, including parties and baby-sitting services (children under 16 stay free, and if their parents are on MAP they also get free meals). The six-story, ultramodern main building, which contains all rooms and suites, dominates a hilltop near Gibbs Hill Lighthouse; the 300-year-old Waterlot Inn restaurant (*see Chapter 8, Dining*) occupies a dockside spot on the north side, and the Whaler Inn beach club is perched above the surf at South Shore Beach. A jitney churns over hill and dale to connect them all, and a regiment of staffers is on hand to assist you if you get lost. Rooms vary in size, but they're all decorated in soft corals and light woods, and all have in-room safes, terry-cloth robes, hair dryers, and plenty of marble in the spacious bathrooms. Obviously, oceanfront deluxe rooms are preferable; if possible, avoid rooms on the first three floors of the west and north wings, which overlook rooftops. Some of the elegant suites feature kitchens, dishwashers, and four-poster beds. Perks in the 55-room Newport Club include private check-in/out, complimentary Continental breakfast, hair dryers, bathrobes, and a business center. Guests pay a one-time $10 fee ($15 per couple) to use the health club and spa; the greens fee is $28.50, and tennis costs $10 an hour ($6 an hour for racquet rental). Major changes in 1993 included transformation of the Empire Room, erstwhile site of Vegas-style floor shows, into a high-tech international conference center; addition of a lobby bar; and conversion of the downstairs disco into a children's-activity center. _Box HM 1379, Hamilton HM FX, tel. 809/238–8000 or 800/223–1818 in U.S.; fax 809/238–8968. 598 rooms, 36 suites, all with bath. Meal plan: MAP. Facilities: 6 restaurants, 4 bars, nightclub, disco, 2 beaches, beauty salon, concierge, moped rental, heated indoor and outdoor freshwater pools, dive shop, 18-hole par-54 golf course, 11 tennis courts (3 lighted), health club, croquet, boccie court, shopping arcade, water sports. AE, DC, MC, V._

Small Hotels

Very Expensive   **Harmony Club.** Nestled in lovely gardens, this two-story pink-and-white hotel—the island's only all-inclusive resort—was built in the 1930s as a private home and extensively renovated in 1993. The hotel has a couples-only policy, but a couple can be two aunts, two friends, or any other combination. The base rate covers everything, including round-trip airport transfers, meals, alcohol, and even two-seater scooters. All meals come with the package, but food lovers who like to try other restaurants get a modest break with the 1993 inauguration of a dine-around plan between the Belmont Hotel and the Harmony Club. The spacious reception area has warm wood paneling; and the club lounge has a big-screen TV and an assortment of games, including cards, darts, and backgammon. Upon arrival, guests find complimentary champagne in their rooms, which are luxuriously decorated with Queen Anne furnishings and feature hair dryers, bathrobes, and coffee makers. All but 12 of the rooms have a patio or balcony. The hotel is not on the water, but it's only about a five-minute scooter ride to the south-shore beaches. Guests can partake of a host of activities during high season, from informal barbecues to formal dances and complimentary use of the golf course at the Belmont Hotel. _Box PG 299, Paget PG BX, tel. 809/236–3500 or 800/225–5843 in U.S.; fax 809/236–2624. 71 rooms with bath. Meal plan: AP. Facilities: restaurant, bar, freshwater pool, whirlpool, sauna, moped rental, putting green, 2 tennis courts. Not suitable for children. AE, DC, MC, V._

Pompano Beach Club. Expect a friendly, personal welcome

when you arrive at this informal seaside hotel, owned and operated by the American-born Lamb family. Located on the western end of the island, adjacent to the Port Royal Golf Club, this was the island's first fishing club before opening as a small hotel in 1956. Today, it still appeals primarily to golfers, water-sports enthusiasts, and anyone in search of a quiet, remote getaway. The main building is a crescent-shape, split-level structure of pink and white stone, containing the main dining room, a British-style pub, and a cozy lounge with a large stone fireplace. Spread across the luxuriant hillside are rooms and one-bedroom suites, all with balconies or patios, and ocean views. Following a 1993 refurbishment, rooms and suites throughout are done in a tropical motif, and feature light woods, soft pastel prints, and glass-topped tables. All guest rooms have minifridges, irons, and ironing boards; eight have kitchenettes. The "superior" rooms offer the best value, not only because the rooms are larger than in the suites, but also because guests wake in the morning to a splendid ocean view through the bedroom window (suites have an ocean view through the living room window). Perched on a hill adjacent to the main building is an attractive pool and a small conference center. Serious beachgoers should head elsewhere; there is a tiny patch of natural beach (at low tide guests can stroll 250 yards into waist-high ocean waters), and two manmade sunbathing beaches clinging to the hillside. The hotel's water-sports facility offers Sunfish, Windsurfers, paddle boats, and small glass-bottom boats for rent. The hotel's restaurant offers fine food, as well as spectacular views of the sunset. *36 Pompano Beach Rd., Southampton SB 03, tel. 809/234-0222 or 800/343-4155 in U.S.; fax 809/234-1694. 33 rooms, 21 suites, all with bath. Meal plans: BP, MAP. Facilities: restaurant, bar, heated freshwater pool, 2 outdoor whirlpools, water sports, conference center. No credit cards; personal checks accepted.*

★ **The Reefs.** The pink lanais of this small, casually elegant resort are set in cliffs above the beach at Christian Bay, adjacent to the Sonesta Beach Hotel & Spa (*see above*). The pace here is sedate, offering guests a restful stay in a spectacular beachfront setting. Vacationers looking for action are better off at such sports-oriented resorts as the Sonesta, Elbow Beach, or the Southampton Princess (*see above*). In the pink Bermuda cottage that serves as the clubhouse, the registration area opens onto a spacious, comfortable lounge, where a pianist or guitarist entertains nightly. Beyond the lounge lies the main dining room, with additional seating in a tropical glass-ceiling conservatory and on a large terrace. Dinner dances are held frequently during the high season. Another restaurant is the waterside Coconuts, which is popular for casual lunches and candlelight dinners under the stars. Two guest rooms are located in the clubhouse, but the best rooms are in the lanais around the pool and on the hillside above the sandy beach. Lanais near the beach are the most expensive. Earth tones and rattan predominate in the guest rooms; bathrooms are small, with beige-marble vanities and an adjoining dressing area. All rooms have balconies safes, robes, hair dryers, and a stunning ocean view. In addition to the lanais, there are seven secluded cottages, one a three-bedroom, three-bathroom unit. Changing rooms near the beach are available for travelers with late flights who want to swim after morning check-out. The tennis courts are free to guests. As part of the 1993 refurbishment, a health club with exercise machines was added near the beach. Reefs guests have access (for a fee) to the spa at the Sonesta. *56 South Rd., Southampton, SN 02, tel. 809/238-0222 or 800/223-1363 in U.S. and Canada; fax 809/238-8372. 58 rooms, 7 cottage suites, all with bath. Meal plans: BP, MAP. Facilities: 2 restaurants, 2 bars, beach, moped rental, heated freshwater pool, 2 tennis courts, water sports. No credit cards.*

Stonington Beach Hotel. A training ground for students of the Bermuda Department of Hotel Technology, this south-shore hotel has one of the friendliest, hardest-working staffs on the island. Like students everywhere, they make mistakes, but if you have a little patience and a sense of humor your stay here should be most enjoyable. The place has a warm, gracious atmosphere; the formal restaurant is excellent; and the beach at the bottom of the hill rivals any on the island. This is the only major south-shore property that does not tack a service charge onto the hotel bill; gratuities are included in the room rate. Set in two-story terraced lodges leading to the beach, the hotel features identical rooms (all of which were renovated and redecorated in 1993 in handsome woods and attractive fabrics) with balconies and an ocean view. The furnishings are modern, and the decor includes heavy drapes and quilted bedspreads in matching fabrics; a minibar and in-room safe are tucked into the small dressing area adjacent to the bathroom. The spacious hotel lobby gains much of its character from its beamed ceiling and large windows with graceful fanlights. The adjoining library features Regency furnishings, bookshelves, a fireplace, and large-screen TV. Weekly champagne receptions are held during the high season, and classical music is played in the attractive Norwood Dining Room. Use of the tennis courts is free. *Box HM 523, Hamilton HM CX, tel. 809/236-5416, 800/447-7462 (U.S. and Canada); fax 809/236-0371. 64 rooms with bath. Meal plans: BP, MAP. Facilities: restaurant, bar, beach, moped rental, heated freshwater pool, 2 tennis courts, library, game room, gift shop, water sports. AE, DC, MC, V.*

Waterloo House. About a three-minute walk from the Hamilton ferry and the Front Street shops, this quiet Relais et Châteaux retreat is so secluded you can easily pass by without noticing it. A pink archway and steps leading to the flower-filled patio from Pitts Bay Road were later additions to a house that predates 1815, when it was renamed in honor of the defeat of Napoleon. The white-column house faces the harbor, and a spacious harborside terrace filled with umbrellas and tables is used for outdoor dining and entertainment. The stately lounge is furnished traditionally, with oil paintings, wing chairs, and a large fireplace. The majority of the rooms are in the main house; others are in pink two-story stone buildings beside the pool and patio. The quietest rooms are on the second floor of the main house. Matching fabrics are used in the rooms' quilted bedspreads, dust ruffles, draperies, and valances. Bathrooms are large, and most have double vanities. TVs can be rented. Guests on MAP have dine-around privileges at Horizons & Cottages (*see below*) and Newstead (*see above*); the short golf course at Horizons is also open to guests. *Box HM 333, Hamilton HM BX, tel. 809/295–4480 or 800/468–4100 in U.S.; fax 809/295–2585. 28 rooms, 6 suites, all with bath. Meal plans: BP, MAP. Facilities: restaurant, bar, heated freshwater pool. AE, MC, V.*

Expensive– Very Expensive **Glencoe Harbour Club.** Located in a manor house dating to the1700s, this quiet, secluded inn on Salt Kettle Bay is a favorite of boaters. It is not a beachfront hotel, however: A tiny man-made beach offers deep-water swimming, sailing, and windsurfing, but for other beach activities guests use facilities of the Elbow Beach Hotel (*see above*), where they are welcome; Glencoe provides a complimentary shuttle between May and November. The lobby is small and unprepossessing, but a few steps away is a cozy wood-paneled lounge with a fireplace and nautical decor. Dining (and dancing in season) is in a chic room with velvet chairs, candlelight, and crisp napery. The waterside terrace is open for meals and frequent barbecues during high season. Rooms are in the main house (Number 10 has its original fireplace and Old World charm) or across the road in two-story pink-stone buildings with rambling decks. Rooms and suites are individually decorated in elegant rattan furniture with bright tropical chintz fabrics; some have cathedral ceilings. All rooms have balconies or patios, but the best rooms are those with a view of the harbor; the least expensive rooms overlook the garden. TVs can be rented. *Box PG 297, Paget PG BX, tel. 809/236–5274, 800/468–1500 in U.S., 800/463–1469 in Canada; fax 809/236–9108. 33 rooms, 8 suites, all with bath. Meal plans: BP, MAP. Facilities: 2 restaurants, 2 bars, 2 heated freshwater pools, man-made beach. AE, MC, V.*

★ **Newstead.** This renovated manor house could accommodate only 12 people when it opened as a guest house in 1923. Since then the elegant harborside hotel has expanded considerably, with brick steps and walkways now leading to several poolside units and cottages. Set amid tall trees and a profusion of flowering shrubs and plants, the main house and cottages are typically Bermudian—in fact, some of the cottages were originally private residences. The spacious drawing room boasts handsome wing chairs, traditional furnishings, fresh flowers, and a fireplace, and the less-formal lounge has large windows overlooking the harbor. A harpist entertains during dinner. The large guest rooms feature polished mahogany campaign chests with brass drawer-pulls, framed prints, and fresh flowers; sliding glass doors open onto a balcony. The units are oddly designed—the front door opens into the large dressing area adjoining the bathroom—but there is ample vanity space, as well as a coffee maker, trouser press, hair dryer, and heated towel rack. Radios and TVs can be rented. The hotel has no beach, but a private dock is available for deep-water swimming in the harbor, and guests have use of the facilities at the Coral Beach & Tennis Club, on the south shore, about 10 minutes away by cab. Men's and women's changing rooms by the pool allow guests to go straight from swimming to the Hamilton ferry at Hodsdon's Landing. Tennis costs $3.50 an hour, and tennis whites are preferred. *Box PG 196, Paget PG BX, tel. 809/236–6060 or 800/ 468–4111 in U.S.; fax 809/236–7454. 47 rooms, 3 suites, all with bath. Meal plans: BP, MAP. Facilities: restaurant, bar, freshwater pool, private dock for deep-water swimming, men's and women's saunas, putting green, 2 tennis courts. No credit cards.*

★ **Rosedon.** Notable for its spacious veranda and white iron furniture, this stately Bermuda manor attracts an older crowd—mostly of women—that appreciates the hotel's ambience, service, and proximity to Front Street shops. Some of the four rooms in the main house have leaded-glass doors and other Old World touches; all other rooms are in two-story buildings arranged around a large pool in the back garden. Rooms are rather dark, despite their white wicker furniture and bright prints and wallpaper. Each has a minifridge, a coffee maker, and a small dining table. There is no restaurant, but breakfast, sandwiches, and light meals are served either in your room or under umbrellas by the pool. Afternoon tea is served in the large lounges in the main house, where a TV and an honor bar are also located. The hotel has no beach of its own, but use of the beach and tennis courts at the Elbow Beach Hotel (*see above*) is free; complimentary transportation is provided for the 15–20 minute drive. *Box HM 290, Hamilton HM AX, tel. 809/ 295–1640 or 800/225–5567 in U.S. and Canada; fax 809/ 295–5904. 43 rooms with bath. Meal plans: BP, EP. Facilities: 2 lounges, heated freshwater pool, complimentary shuttle to beach, same-day laundry service. No credit cards.*

Willowbank. On a high promontory overlooking Ely's Harbour, this former home was converted to a hotel by a Christian trust. Morning devotionals are held in a lounge, for those who wish to attend, and grace is said before meals, which are announced by an ancient ship's bell and are served family-style. There is no proselytizing, however, and no pressure to participate in religious activities. The hotel is simply a serene alternative to the glitzy resorts; anyone who likes plenty of action will not be happy here. With their cedar paneling and fireplaces, the two large lounges in the main building are the focal point for quiet conversations, TV viewing, and afternoon tea; there are also a restaurant and library. Guests may have liquor in their rooms, but there is no bar. Located in one-story white cottages, the guest rooms are large and simply furnished—they have neither phones nor TVs. Rooms with an ocean or harbor view are the most desirable and expensive. The hotel has instituted a summer children's program that includes, among other things, crafts workshops and trips to the aquarium. No service charge is added to the bill and tipping is not expected, but the staff is friendly and helpful nonetheless. *Box MA 296, Sandys MA BX, tel. 809/234–1616 or 800/752–8493; fax 809/234–3373. 60 rooms with bath; 2 double rooms share bath. Meal plan: MAP. Facilities: restaurant, 2 lounges, 2 small beaches, 2 tennis courts, heated freshwater pool. No credit cards.*

Expensive **Palmetto Hotel & Cottages.** Set amid tall shade trees on the banks of Harrington Sound, this casually elegant property was once a private home. The main building is a sprawling two-story pink-and-white structure typical of Bermuda. Adjoining the small reception area is the Ha'Penny, a very British pub. Afternoon tea is served in a small but attractive lounge which has a tile floor, Oriental area rug, cushy furnishings, and green plants. Twenty-four rooms are located in the main building, but the 16 rooms in cottages on the banks of the sound are the most luxurious. All rooms have balconies, coffee makers, and many have a good view of the water. The beach is small, but the hotel provides guests complimentary bus fare to the south shore. In addition, guests can swim or snorkel off the hotel's private dock; windsurfing lessons are available. *Box FL 54, Flatts FLBX, tel. 809/293–2323 or 800/982–0026; fax 809/293–8761. 42 rooms with bath. Meal plans: EP (BP and MAP on request). Facilities: restaurant, bar, beach, private dock, saltwater pool. AE, MC, V.*

Royal Palms Hotel. The Richard Smiths (his parents own and operate nearby Oxford House) have transformed this typical Bermudian cottage into a chic, upscale hotel. It's on a quiet residential street, on a hill above Pitt's Bay Road and the Hamilton Princess Hotel. Front Street's shops are within an easy walk. The house dates from 1903, and is aptly named, surrounded as it is by tall palms and lush gardens; the terrace, with its white wicker furniture, is a favorite spot for guests to read quietly. The fully air-conditioned hotel has polished wood floors and Oriental rugs in some rooms, and wall-to-carpeting in others; drapes and bedspreads are in matching fabrics. All the rooms (a mix of doubles, triples, and quads) have private baths, TV, radio, and phones; some have marble-topped dressers. Ascots restaurant, quite popular with locals, is a charmer, with white-clothed tables and high–backed upholstered chairs. A complimentary Continental breakfast of scones, cereal, and fruit is served. *Box HM 499, Hamilton HM CX, tel.*

809/292–1854; fax 809/292–1946. 11 rooms, 1 suite, all with private bath. Meal plan: CP. Facilities: restaurant, lounge, outdoor pool. AE, MC, V.

Cottage Colonies

Very Expensive **Ariel Sands Beach Club.** This most informal of the cottage colonies surrounds Cox's Bay in Devonshire Parish, not far from the Edmund Gibbons Nature Reserve. The beach here is large and sandy, and a graceful statue of Ariel perches on a rock in the sea. The one-story white-limestone clubhouse, designed in Bermudian cottage style, contains the dining room and a lounge. A grand piano, a fireplace, hardwood floors, and Oriental rugs give the resort an air of distinction. The large patio is ideal for outdoor dining, dancing, and barbecues in season. Two- to eight-unit white cottages are set in the sloping, tree-shaded grounds. Redecorated in 1993 to the tune of just under $1 million, the rather small guest rooms have Mexican tile floors, matching drapes and quilted spreads, in-room safes, and tea and coffee makers. Shakespeare's Dream has two bedrooms, one of which has a single bed. Rooms in the lowest price bracket have no ocean view. Tennis is free to guests. During summer the cottage colony offers a children's day-care program. *Box HM 334, Hamilton HM BX, tel. 809/236–1010 or 800/468–6610 in U.S.; fax 809/236–0087. 48 rooms with bath. Meal plans: BP, MAP. Facilities: restaurant, bar, meeting room and business services, beach, freshwater pool, saltwater lagoon, 3 tennis courts (2 lighted), putting green, volleyball, water sports. AE, MC, V.*

★ **Cambridge Beaches.** Within walking distance of Somerset Village in the West End (*see* Chapter 4, Exploring Bermuda), this outstanding resort occupies a beautifully landscaped peninsula edged with private coves and six pink-sand beaches. The original cottage colony (it opened in 1947), it remains a favorite among British and Saudi royalty, as well as a host of commoners. Many guests return year after year, attracted by the elegant style, superior watersports facilities, and those unsurpassed pink-sand beaches. Registration is in a Bermuda-style clubhouse with large, elegantly furnished lounges. Candlelight dining and dancing take place in the lower-level restaurant and on the terrace, which has a splendid view of Mangrove Bay. A wide range of accommodations is offered—the entire peninsula is dotted with cottages—and prices vary considerably. On the high end, Pegem is a 300-year-old, two-bedroom Bermuda cottage with a cedar-beam ceiling, English antiques, a den, and a sunporch. On the other end of the spectrum the least expensive units are those that have land rather than water views. The decor differs from cottage to cottage, but antiques and fireplaces are common throughout. Many units have whirlpools, and suites have bidets as well. A $1-million renovation in 1993 included construction of eight new units. Don't fret about being far from Front Street: A shopping launch ($4) makes trips three times a week from the resort's private dock. Ferry tokens are complimentary, in the off-season. Guests have complimentary use of the putting green, croquet lawn, exercise room, and tennis courts. Children under five must be accompanied by a nanny or nurse. *Somerset MA 02, tel. 809/234-0331 or 800/468-7300 in U.S.; fax 809/234-3352. 62 rooms, 20 suites, all with bath. Meal plan: MAP. Facilities: restaurant, 2 bars, 6 beaches, heated saltwater pool, private marina, ferry, 3 tennis courts (1 lighted), putting green, exercise room, croquet lawn, health spa, conference room, business services, water sports. No credit cards.*

Fourways Inn. About a five-minute ride from the ferry landing and the south-shore beaches, this luxury hotel has a sedate, formal ambience. Look elsewhere if you want exciting nightlife or if you plan to bring the kids—children under 16 are discouraged at the inn, and nothing here would interest them anyway. The architecture is typically Bermudian: The main building is a one-time family home that dates from 1727; the five cottages, set in a profusion of greenery and flowers, each contain a poolside suite and a deluxe upper-floor room. Marble floors and marble bathrooms are common throughout, and plenty of flowers give the rooms a bright freshness. In addition, each room has a balcony or terrace, a stocked minibar, a bar/kitchenette, and large closets paneled with full-length mirrors. Amenities in the suites include hair dryers, bath phones, bathrobes, and slippers. Guests receive a complimentary bottle of champagne on arrival, and homemade pastries and the morning paper are delivered daily to the door. The hotel serves a sumptuous Sunday brunch. *Box PG 294, Paget, PG BX, tel. 809/236-6517 or 800/962-7654 in U.S.; fax 809/236-5528. 5 rooms, 5 suites, all with bath. Meal plan: CP. Facilities: restaurant, bar, freshwater pool, business services. AE, DC, MC, V.*

★ **Horizons & Cottages.** Oriental rugs, polished wood floors, cathedral ceilings, and knee-high open fireplaces are elegant reminders of the 18th century, when the main house in this resort was a private home. A Relais et Châteaux property, the cottage colony had a multimillion-dollar refurbishment in 1993 that included new baths and sprucing up the private nine-hole golf course. It consistently maintains a formal atmosphere that appeals to an upscale crowd. Horizons Restaurant is a chic place for intimate candlelight dining; in pleasant weather, tables are set on the terrace. (The hotel has an exchange dining arrangement with Waterloo House and Newstead.) Monday-night rum swizzling is done downstairs in a wood-panel pub, where Austrian-born manager Wilhelm Sack makes every effort to see that guests (many of whom are European) are introduced. Guest cottages dot the terraced lawns, and each cottage has a distinct personality and decor: Most have two or three rooms and a large common room with a fireplace, library, and shelves of board games. Some of the spacious guest rooms feature white wicker furnishings, and others have an Old European flavor. Most cottages also have a kitchen, where a maid prepares breakfast before bringing it to your room. The hotel has no beach of its own, but guests may use the facilities of the Coral Beach & Tennis Club, within walking distance along South Road. Tennis courts cost $3.50 per hour and the greens fee for the short nine-hole golf course is also $3.50. *Box PG 198, Paget,PG BX, tel. 809/236–0048 or 800/468–0022 in U.S.; fax 809/236–1981. 45 rooms, 5 suites, all with bath. Meal plans: BP, MAP (combination also available). Facilities: restaurant, bar, heated freshwater pool, 3 tennis courts, 9-hole golf course. No credit cards.*

Lantana Colony Club. A short walk from the Somerset Bridge ferry landing in the West End, this cottage colony is known for its lavish gardens, delightful topiary, and impressive, museum-quality objets d'art. Several life-size sculptures by Desmond Fountain are dotted through the grounds, including a delightful rendering of a woman seated on a bench reading a newspaper. The solarium dining area in the main house is dazzling, with hanging plants and wall brackets of frosted Bohemian glass grapes. All accommodations are spacious and airy suites, and come in a variety of configurations: lanais, split-levels, garden cottages, and family cottages with two bedrooms, two bathrooms, and a living/dining room. All units have sliding glass doors that open onto private balconies or patios; some have cedar doors, beams, and trim, and vivid Souleaido prints. Waterfront split-level suites have Mexican tile floors on the lower level, carpeting in the sleeping area, fridges, and wet bars; waterview suites have fireplaces, separate men's and women's dressing areas, and kitchens. About half of the suites are in garden settings; one of those is a cottage where guests have use of the owner's private pool. On the downside, the beach is small, and man-made. Lunch is a featured attraction here, something to bear in mind when you're tooling around the West End. *Box SB 90, Somerset Bridge SB BX, tel. 809/234–0141, 800/468–3733 in U.S., or 800/463–0036 in Canada; fax 809/234–2562. 56 suites, 6 cottages, all with bath. Meal plans: BP, MAP. Facilities: 2 restaurants, 2 bars, man-made beach, heated freshwater pool, private dock, 2 tennis courts, putting green, croquet lawn, shuffleboard, water sports. No credit cards.*

Pink Beach Club & Cottages. With its two pretty pink beaches, this secluded, relaxing colony is a favorite of international celebrities. The location is a bit remote, however, and might not appeal to those who want to be near the shops of Front Street or the swinging resorts. Built as a private home in 1947, the main house has a clubby ambience derived from its dark-wood paneling, large fireplace, and beamed ceilings. Paved paths lace the attractively landscaped grounds and lead to 25 pink cottages and to the beaches. Some cottages contain a single unit, while others are comprised of several units, and accommodations range from single rooms to two-bedroom suites with two bathrooms and twin terraces. Seventy-three rooms and suites front on the ocean. Each spacious unit has maple furnishings upholstered in rich flame-stitch fabrics, two double beds, extensive use of marble, and sliding glass doors that open onto a balcony or terrace. All are equipped with safes, hair dryers and pants pressers. The best accommodations are, of course, those near the beach. Breakfast is prepared by a maid and served on your terrace or in your room. Use of the tennis courts is free. *Box HM 1017, Hamilton HM DX, tel. 809/293–1666, 800/422–1323 in U.S., or 800/338–8782 in Canada; fax 809/293–8935. 14 rooms, 67 suites, all with bath. Meal plan: MAP. Facilities: restaurant, bar, 2 beaches, saltwater pool, 2 tennis courts, water sports. MC, V.*

The St. George's Club. Within walking distance of King's Square in St. George's, this ultramodern time-share property adjoins an 18-hole golf course designed by Robert Trent Jones. The sleek, three-story main building contains the office, activities desk, a game room, a restaurant, a pub, and the Club Shop, where you can buy everything from champagne to suntan lotion. In two-story white cottages sprinkled over 18 acres, the individually decorated apartments are huge and filled with sunlight. In some, stark white walls are offset by bright accent pieces and fabrics in muted colors. In others, sweeping bold designs draw upon the entire spectrum of colors. Each apartment has a full kitchen with dishwasher, fine china, and crystal. Bathrooms are large and lined with marble; some feature double Jacuzzis in dramatic settings. *Box GE 92, St. George's GEBX, tel. 809/297–1200; fax 809/297–1022. 61 suites with bath. Meal plan: EP. Facilities: 2 restaurants, bar, 3 freshwater pools (1 heated), 18-hole golf course, putting green, tennis court, private beach club, meeting rooms, convenience store. AE, DC, MC, V.*

Housekeeping Cottages and Apartments

Expensive– Very Expensive
★

Marley Beach Cottages. Scenes from the films *Chapter Two* and *The Deep* were filmed here, and it's easy to see why— the setting is breathtaking. Near Astwood Park on the south shore, the resort sits high on a cliff overlooking a lovely beach and dramatic reefs; a long path leads down to the sand and the sea. If you plan to stay here, pack light—there are a lot of steep steps, and you may have to carry your own luggage. The price is also steep for one couple, but this is an excellent choice for two couples vacationing together (and who don't mind preparing their own meals); there is ample space here, and splitting the cost brings it down to a moderate price for each pair. Each cottage contains a suite and a studio apartment, which can be rented separately or together, by families or friends. This is not a good place for children, and there's little to occupy them except the pool and the beach. Refurbished in 1993, the units are individually decorated; all have large rooms, superb ocean views, private porches or patios, phones, and fully equipped kitchens. Heaven's Above, the deluxe suite, is a spacious affair with two wood-burning fireplaces, tile floors, upholstered rattan furniture, and ample kitchen facilities. TVs can be rented, and groceries delivered. Daily maid service is provided. *Box PG 278, Paget PG BX, tel. 809/236–1143 (ext. 42), 800/637–4661 in U.S.; fax 809/236–1984. 7 suites, 6 studios, all with bath. Meal plan: EP. Facilities: private beach, heated freshwater pool, whirlpool. AE, MC, V.*

Expensive **Longtail Cliffs.** Don't be put off by the small office and the concrete parking lot that serves as the front yard of this motel-like establishment. Although it may not have the personality or splendid beach views of Marley Beach Cottages (*see above*), its relatively flat setting makes it much more suitable for elderly people or anyone who doesn't want to do a lot of climbing. Housed in a modern, two-story building, guest apartments are large, light, and airy, with balconies and ocean views. Each has two bedrooms and two spacious bathrooms decorated with brightly colored tiles. A small but well-equipped kitchen features a microwave oven, a coffee maker, an iron, and an ironing board. Italian-tile floors grace the living areas and are accented by scatter rugs and high-quality white wicker furniture. Many units have beamed ceilings and some have fireplaces. There's a coin-operated laundry, cable TV, and a gas barbecue grill for cookouts. Despite its location on the south shore, the complex does not have a beach; however, Astwood Cove is nearby. *Box HM 836, Hamilton HM CX, tel. 809/236–2864, 809/236–2822, 800/637–4116 in U.S.; fax 809/236–5178. 13 apartments with bath. Meal plan: EP. Facilities: freshwater pool. AE, MC, V.*

Surf Side Beach Club. This is another option for couples looking to share a space on the South Shore. The wood-paneled reception area with upholstered chairs is sizeable enough to be a small conversation area. Cottages are on terraced levels, and each has a view of the ocean and the long stretch of sandy beach below. There are spacious studios and suites; each has a fully equipped kitchenette (with microwaves), cable TV, telephone, and porch. Some are decorated with dark wood furnishings, bright yellow spreads, and wall-to-wall carpeting; others have tile floors and light rattan furnishings. There is a barbecue grill, a poolside coffee shop (open April–October, room service at extra charge), and weekly rum swizzle parties. *Box WK 101, Warwick WK BX, tel. 809/236–7100 or 800/553–9990, fax 809/236–9765. 10 apartments, 23 studios, 2 penthouse units, all with bath. Meal plan: EP. Facilities: coffee shop; cable TV; meeting room and business services; cycle rental; sun deck with freshwater pool, sauna, and Jacuzzi; coin-operated laundry. AE, MC, V.*

Moderate– **Angel's Grotto.** Some 30 years ago this was a swinging
Expensive nightclub and one of the hottest spots on the island. Now,
★ it's a quiet residential apartment house close to Devil's

Hole Aquarium on the south shore of Harrington Sound. Since the 1992–93 refurbishments, this rather simple property has blossomed into a real charmer. New curtains and spreads are in cool, pretty pastels; all rooms have TVs, radios, and phones, and kitchens are fully equipped. Owner Daisy Hart and her efficient staff maintain these apartments in shipshape condition. There is no beach, but the pink sands of John Smith's Bay on the South Shore are about a five-minute walk. Other South Shore beaches are less than ten minutes away by moped. Most of the guests are couples; the secluded Honeymoon Cottage is particularly appealing to those who want privacy. The two-bedroom, two-bath apartment in the main house is a good buy for two couples traveling together. A large patio is ideal for cocktails in the evening, and there is also a barbecue. Deep-water swimming is possible in Harrington Sound. *Box HS 62, Smith's HS BX, tel. 809/295–6437 daytime, 809/293–1986 evening, or 800/637–4116, in U.S.; fax 809/292–1243. 7 apartments with bath. Meal plan: EP. Facilities: swimming in Harrington Sound. AE, MC, V.*

Moderate **Greenbank Cottages.** Located on a quiet dead end two minutes' walk from the Salt Kettle ferry landing, these one-story green cottages nestle among tall trees beside Hamilton Harbour. This is not a grand hotel—it's small and family-owned—but guests can count on plenty of personal attention from the Ashton family. In the 200-year-old main house, the guests' lounge has Oriental rugs, hardwood floors, a TV, and a grand piano. There are three guest rooms in the main house; all other units are self-contained, with private entrances and shaded verandas. Most units have fully equipped kitchenettes for preparing light meals. The waterside cottages are the best choice, especially Sea Foam (formerly called the Pink One)—the view of the harbor from the dining table in the kitchen is lovely. Rooms are rather simply furnished; none has a phone, but all are air-conditioned. There is no beach, but there is a private dock suitable for deep-water swimming, and Salt Kettle Boat Rentals is located on the property. The fine dining room at Glencoe is a minute's walk from here. *Box PG 201, Paget PG BX, tel. 809/236–3615 or 800/637–4116 in U.S.; fax 809/236–2427. 3 rooms and 7 apartments, all with bath. Meal plans: CP, EP. Facilities: private dock for deep-water swimming, billiards room. AE, MC, V.*

Paraquet Guest Apartments. These apartments (pronounced "parakeet") are in an ideal location—a mere five-minute walk from Elbow Beach. A real find for budget travelers, they are spartan but spic-and-span. Each is spacious and well-lit, and contains a TV, clock/radio, and small fridge; nine units have kitchens. Rooms are done in simple furnishings, with white-painted dressers and chests and plain white spreads. Efficiency units have full baths, while the rest have only shower baths. The three units in the Paraquet Cottage share a patio. There is a market nearby for supplies, and the fine restaurants at Horizons and the Stonington Beach Hotel are within walking distance. The bus stops right in front of the Paraquet's counter-service restaurant. *Box PG 173, Paget PG BX, tel. 809/236–5842; fax 809/236–1665. 12 rooms with bath. Meal plan: EP. Facilities: restaurant. No credit cards.*

★ **Pretty Penny.** A three-minute walk from the ferry dock at Darrell's Wharf and 10 minutes by scooter from the south-shore beaches, this upscale lodging has one of the friendliest, most helpful staffs on the island. The grounds are small and offer no good views, but guest cottages are surrounded by trees and shrubs. Each room is brightened by a colorful tile floor and has a dining area and private patio. A small kitchen area features a microwave oven, refrigerator, and cupboards well-stocked with china, cooking utensils, and cutlery. TVs can be rented. The property was completely refurbished in 1993; the Shilling, a newly renovated room in a quaint cottage across from the main building, is a charmer. If you want absolute privacy ask for the Play Penny, which is tucked away by itself. Owner Steve Martin throws frequent cocktail parties so guests can get acquainted. *Box PG 137, Paget PG BX, tel. 809/236–1194 or 800/637–4116 in U.S.; fax 809/236–1662. 9 apartments with shower bath. Meal plan: EP. Facilities: freshwater pool. AE, MC, V.*

Inexpensive– Moderate **Barnsdale Guest Apartments.** Budget travelers who want to be near the south-shore beaches would do well to consider the small apartments in this two-story white cottage. The setting may not be spectacular, and the amenities are less than luxurious, but the units are clean and neat, and each has a private entrance. The 1993 sprucing up included installation of TVs in all units, and tasteful spreads, dust ruffles, drapes, and upholstery fabrics. Apartments with sofa beds can sleep four, but the four people must be able to get along well—the quarters are close. Kitchenettes have sufficient utensils to prepare light meals, and each has an iron and ironing board. Apartment Number 5 is a charmer—a somewhat larger, light, airy room decorated with colorful prints—but it's next to the pool area, which can become noisy. *Box DV 628, Devonshire DV BX, tel. 809/236–0164 or 800/441–7087 in U.S.; fax 809/236–4709. 7 apartments with bath. Meal plan: EP. Facilities: freshwater pool. AE, MC, V.*

★ **Sky Top Cottages.** The smooth paving that has replaced the crumbling stone driveway makes ascent to this hilltop property much less formidable; still, it is aptly named, and guests will be happy to make the climb in a scooter or taxi—especially if they're hauling grocery bags. The ascent is worthwhile, though, because the views of the ocean from here are spectacular. Neat sloping lawns, paved walks bordered by geraniums, and a nearby citrus grove provide a pleasant setting for studio and one-bedroom apartments that are only five minutes by scooter from Elbow Beach. Although the furnishings are basic, the individually decorated units do have character. The friendly owners, **Marion Stubbs** and **Susan Harvey**, have decorated the rooms with attractive prints and carefully coordinated colors, and the property is freshened up annually and well-maintained. Studio apartments have full kitchens and shower baths; one-bedroom apartments have limited kitchen facilities and full baths. Frangipani is furnished in white wicker and rattan and has an eat-in kitchen, a king-size bed, and a sofa bed. Honeysuckle is a three-level apartment with a sitting room, kitchen, dining room, and a bedroom and bathroom upstairs; each room is small but decorated in bright colors. All units have phones; TVs can be rented. A barbecue grill is available for guests' use. *Box PG 227, Paget PG BX, tel. 809/236–7984. 11 apartments with bath. Meal plan: EP. No facilities. MC, V.*

Inexpensive **Whale Bay Inn.** Golfers approaching the 14th hole of the Port Royal course are sometimes baffled to find golf balls other than their own dotting the green. Little do they know that it's a mere chip shot from the front lawn of this inn, and some guests can't resist the challenge to play through. Vacationers who want to be near good beaches or Hamilton's shops are better served elsewhere, however. The friendly Metschnabel family owns, operates, and lives on the premises of this small, attractive property in the remote West End. New tile floors in all units, and extensive landscaping were part of the 1992–93 refurbishments. The ocean is visible beyond beds of flowers and the rolling lawn that surrounds the Bermuda-style pink building. At the bottom of the hill, a tiny patch of pink beach is tucked under the rugged cliff; it's pretty and private, but you'll have to do a fair amount of climbing to reach it. The decor of the guest rooms is contemporary, relying on rattan and muted prints. All five ground-floor units have a bedroom, a separate sitting room with sofa beds, phone, and a private entrance. The two end units have larger bathrooms and are better-suited to families. Small, modern kitchens are equipped with microwave ovens, two-burner stoves, small refrigerators, cutlery, dinnerware, and cooking utensils. Groceries can be delivered from nearby markets. TVs can be rented. *Box SN 544, Southampton SNBX, tel. 809/238–0469 or 800/637–4116, fax 809/238–1224. 5 apartments with bath. Meal plan: EP. Facilities: small beach, use of barbecue grill. No credit cards.*

Guest Houses

Moderate **Edgehill Manor.** Atop a high hill surrounded by gardens and shrubs, this large colonial house is within easy walking distance of downtown Hamilton. Anyone wanting to spend a lot of time on the beach should stay elsewhere, however— the best south-shore beaches are 15–20 minutes away by scooter. The staff is friendly and helpful, and guests are guaranteed plenty of personal attention. In the morning, feast on home-baked muffins and scones in the cheery breakfast room, which is decorated with white iron chairs, glass-top tables, and vivid wallpaper. The individually decorated guest rooms feature French provincial furniture, colorful quilted bedspreads, large windows, and terraces. If you want air-conditioning be sure to request it—the four upstairs rooms have ceiling fans only. A large poolside room has a kitchen and is suitable for families. Anyone traveling alone on a tight budget should ask for the small ground-level room that offers a kitchen and private terrace. *Box HM 1048, Hamilton HM EX, tel. 809/295–7124; fax 809/295–3850. 9 rooms with bath. Meal plan: CP. Facilities: freshwater pool. No credit cards.*

Granaway Guest House & Cottage. In the 18th and 19th centuries, this 1734 manor house on Hamilton Harbour was used as a storehouse for pirate's booty. Surrounded by mounds of shrubbery, the house is a bit hard to find even today. Guests come and go through a side entrance, where there is a coffee maker, honor-system phone, and colored cups that correspond to each guest room (pink, red, and so on). A Continental breakfast is served in the garden with antique silver and Herend china. The large Pink Room, in the main house, has a king-size bed, white wicker furniture, and soft prints. The Strawberry Room was once the kitchen of the main house. The old hearth remains, and the room is now decorated with a patchwork quilt and scarred cedar beams; the walls and rafters are adorned with ceramic strawberries and other gifts from repeat guests. The Cottage, formerly the slave quarters, has a fully equipped modern kitchen, a phone, hand-painted tile floors, and its own entrance and lawn. The other guest rooms are nondescript. There is no beach—south-shore beaches are 10–15 minutes away by scooter—but the waterside patio can be used for deep-water swimming and snorkeling. In the evening, guests gather on the patio for cocktails. *Box WK 533, Warwick WK BX, tel. 809/236–1805 or 800/637–4116 in U.S.; fax 809/236–0609. 4 rooms, 1 cottage, all with bath. Meal plans: CP, EP. Facilities: waterside patio, TVs provided on request. AE, MC, V.*

★ **Little Pomander Guest House.** A little jewel in a quiet residential area near Hamilton Harbour, this is a find for budget travelers seeking accommodations near Hamilton. The two cottages were professionally decorated with a keen eye for detail—nothing here is out of place. Soft colors, fresh flowers, and tastefully arranged sofas and chairs make the registration area spacious and airy. In the main house, guest rooms are decorated in French provincial style: Plump pastel-colored comforters cover the beds, and the shams, dust ruffles, drapes, headboards, and shower curtains are made of matching fabrics. Continental breakfast is served family-style to guests in the main house in a sunny room where tables are set with china in a blue-and-white floral design. There are three apartments in the neighboring cottage; of particular interest is the spacious Captain's apartment, with its white wicker furniture, coordinated blue-and-white decor, and balcony overlooking Hamilton Harbour. All units have microwaves, cable TV, phones, and refrigerators. Guests may use the backyard barbecue grill. For a $10 fee, guests can play tennis across the road at the Pomander Tennis Club. *Box HM 384, Hamilton HM BX, tel. 809/236–7635 or 800/637–4116 in U.S.; fax 809/236–8332. 5 rooms, 3 apartments with bath. Meal plan: CP. No facilities. AE, MC, V.*

★ **Oxford House.** This is the closest you can get to downtown Hamilton without pitching a tent. The two-story establishment is popular with older people and is an excellent choice for shoppers. It is family-owned and operated, and guests receive friendly, personal attention. Just off the small entrance hall a fireplace and colorful floral tablecloths lend warmth to the breakfast room, where guests sample scones, English muffins, fresh fruit, and cereal in the morning. The rooms (doubles, triples, and quads) are bright and airy and are decorated with white rattan and bold fabrics. Each room has a coffee maker. Two of the rooms have shower baths only. A small bookcase in the upstairs hall is crammed with paperbacks and serves as a library for guests. *Box HM 374, Hamilton HM BX, tel. 809/295–0503 or 800/548–7758 in U.S.; fax 809/295–0250. 12 rooms with bath. Meal plan: CP. No facilities. No credit cards.*

Inexpensive– Moderate **Loughlands Guest House & Cottage.** Built in 1920, this stately white mansion sits on a green hill above South Road, a mere five-minute ride by scooter from the best beaches. The house contains an eclectic collection of fine antiques and flea-market bric-a-brac. Lladro figurines grace the mantelpiece in the formal parlor; grandfather clocks stand in corners; and handsome breakfronts display Wedgwood and cut glass. There are an Empire chaise lounge, an elegant pink-satin prie-dieu, and a refrigerator for guests' use in the upstairs hallway. A Continental breakfast of cereals, fresh fruit, croissants, and coffee is served in the enormous, well-appointed dining room. The guest rooms are not nearly as interesting as the public rooms, however. No two are alike—there are singles, doubles, triples, and quads— though most include large overstuffed chairs and chenille spreads. There are additional rooms in a large cottage near the main house. *79 South Rd., Paget PG 03, tel. 809/236–1253. 18 rooms with bath, 7 with shared bath. Meal plan: CP. Facilities: freshwater pool, tennis court. No credit cards; personal checks accepted.*

Inexpensive **Hillcrest Guest House.** Set back from Nea's Alley in St. George's, behind a gate and gardens, this green double-gallery house dates to the 18th century. It's been a guest house since 1961, but owner Mrs. Trew Robinson says her father took in shipwrecked sailors in 1914, when this was a private home. Today, Mrs. Robinson offers personal attention and helpful advice to budget travelers. The upstairs and downstairs lounges are spacious and homey, decorated with Oriental rugs, treasured family pictures, and heir-looms. Guest rooms are spotlessly clean, but they lack the charm of the public rooms. No meals are served, but guests can keep refreshments in the refrigerator. The house is far from Hamilton and the best beaches, but St. George's golf course is almost within putting distance. *Box GE 96, St. George's GE BX, tel. 809/297–1630, fax 809/297–1630. 10 rooms with bath. No facilities. No credit cards.*

★ **Salt Kettle House.** Set behind a screen of palm trees on Hamilton Harbour, this small secluded guest house attracts plenty of repeat visitors and is popular with boating enthusiasts. Just to the left of the entrance is a cozy lounge with a fireplace where guests gather for cocktails (BYOB) and conversation. A hearty English breakfast is served family-style in the adjacent dining room. Two guest rooms are located in the main house, and an adjoining apartment features a double bedroom, bathroom, living room, and kitchen. The best accommodations are in the waterside cottages, which have shaded patios and lounge chairs. Two of the cottages have a bed/sitting room and a kitchen. The Starboard, which accommodates four people, is a two-bedroom, two-bathroom unit with a living room, fireplace, and kitchen. Guest rooms overall are small, however, and are arranged haphazardly. Nonetheless, owner Mrs. Hazel Lowe makes improvements every year; those made in 1993 included better kitchen equipment and electric blankets for all beds. All of the units are air-conditioned. *10 Salt Kettle Rd., Paget PG 01, tel. 809/236–0407; fax 809/236–8639. 6 rooms with bath. Meal plan: BP. Facilities: deep-water swimming, lounge. No credit cards.*

10 The Arts and Nightlife

The Arts

By Honey Naylor   Available in all hotels and tourist information centers, *This Week in Bermuda*, *Preview Bermuda*, and *Bermuda Weekly*, are free publications that list what's happening around the island. *The Bermudian* ($4) is a glossy monthly magazine that also carries a calendar of events. The Bermuda Channel (Channel 4), a local television station, broadcasts a wealth of information about sightseeing, restaurants, cultural events, and nightlife on the island. Tourist-related information can also be heard on an AM radio station, VSB-1160, between 7 AM and 12:30 PM. Or you can dial 974 for a phone recording that details information about nature walks, tours, cultural events, afternoon teas, and seasonal events. The island is so small, however, that virtually everyone knows what's going on—taxi drivers, in particular, have a good idea of what's hot and what's not. In truth, the arts scene in Bermuda is not extensive, and many of the events and performing groups listed below operate on a casual or part-time basis. **City Hall Theatre** (City Hall, Church St., Hamilton) is the major venue for a number of top-quality cultural events each year, although performances and productions are sometimes staged elsewhere on the island. Contact the **Box Office** (Visitors Service Bureau, tel. 809/295–1727) for reservations and information about all cultural events on the island. American Express, MasterCard, and Visa are accepted.

In January and February the **Bermuda Festival** brings internationally renowned artists to the island for a series of performances. The two-month program includes classical and jazz concerts and theatrical performances. Recent festivals have included appearances by classical and jazz trumpeter Wynton Marsalis, the Dance Theatre of Harlem, the Royal Shakespeare Company, and the Flying Karamazov Brothers. Most of the performances take place in City Hall, although some are held in major hotels. Ticket prices range from $18 to $35 ($13 for students). For information and reservations, contact Bermuda Festivals, Ltd. (Suite 480, 48 Par-la-Ville Rd., Hamilton HM 11, tel. 809/295–1291) or the Bermuda Department of Tourism (*see* Government Tourist Offices in Chapter 1, Essential Information).

Concerts

The Bermuda Philharmonic Society presents several programs throughout the year, including classical music concerts by the full Philharmonic and by soloists. Students of the Menuhin Foundation, established in Bermuda by virtuoso violinist Yehudi Menuhin, sometimes perform with the orchestra. Concerts take place either in City Hall Theatre (*see above*) or the Cathedral of the Most Holy Trinity in Hamilton (*see* Chapter 4, Exploring Bermuda).

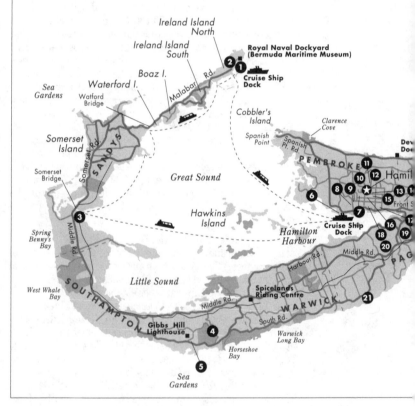

The Gilbert & Sullivan Society of Bermuda mounts a musical production each year, usually in October. In addition to Gilbert and Sullivan operettas, the group occasionally does Broadway shows.

Dance

The **Gombey Dancers,** a Bermudian dance group, perform each week as part of the off-season (mid-November–March 31) festivities. Gombey (pronounced "gum-bay") dancing is a blend of African, West Indian, and American Indian influences. The Gombey tradition in Bermuda dates to the mid-18th century, when costumed slaves celebrated Christmas by singing and marching through the streets. The masked male dancers move to the accompaniment of skin-covered drums, called gombeys, and the shrill whistle commands of the captain of the troupe. The ritualistic, often frenetic movements of the dancers, the staccato drum accompaniment, and the whistle commands are passed from generation to generation. Dancers wear colorful costumes that include tall headdresses decorated with peacock feathers and tiny mirrors. On all major holidays the Gombeys dance through the streets, attracting large crowds of followers. It's traditional to toss coins at the feet of the dancers.

The Bermuda Civic Ballet performs classical ballets at various venues during the year. Internationally known artists sometimes appear as guests.

Movies

Bermuda has three cinemas showing first-run movies—two are in Hamilton and the third is in the West End. Check the listings in the *Royal Gazette* for movies and show times.

Neptune Cinema (The Cooperage, Dockyard, tel. 809/234–2923) is a 250-seat cinema that shows feature films at night. Features are usually shown at 6:30 and 10:30.

The Little Theatre (Queen St., Hamilton, tel. 809/292–2135) is a 173-seat theater across the street from Casey's Bar. Show times are usually 2:15, 7:15, and 9:30 daily.

Liberty Theatre (corner Union and Victoria Sts., Hamilton, tel. 809/292–7296) is a 270-seat cinema located in an unsavory section of Hamilton. The area is safe during the day, but visitors should avoid it after dark. Show times are usually at 2:30, 5:30, 7:30, and 9:30.

Theater

Bermuda is the only place outside the United States where **Harvard University's Hasty Pudding Theatricals** are performed. For almost 30 years, the satirical troupe has performed on the island during Bermuda College Weeks (March–April). Produced by the estimable Elsbeth Gibson, an American-born actress/producer who lives in Bermuda, each show incorporates political and social themes and issues of the past year. The Hasty Pudding Theatricals are staged in the City Hall Theatre (*see above*); ticket prices are about $20.

Nightlife

During high season all hotels and cottage colonies feature entertainment—barbecues, steel bands, dinner dancing, and other diversions. Otherwise, the island's nightlife is fairly subdued; there are no casinos and only a few nightclubs and discos. Much of the action occurs in the pubs and lounges, which range from hotel bars to local hangouts. Some places close during the off-season, so check *This Week in Bermuda* and *Preview Bermuda* (*see above*) for the latest information about what's happening each night. As a general rule, men should wear a jacket and tie to clubs; for women the dress code is smart but casual. Pubs and discos begin to fill up around 9:30 or 10.

The music scene is dominated by local acts and bands playing the island's hotel and pub circuits. Occasionally, outside performers are billed, particularly during the Bermuda Festival (*see above*). The island superstar is **Gene Steede,** a guitarist, singer, and comedian who has been described as Tony Bennett, Harry Belafonte, and Johnny Carson rolled into one. Among the other popular entertainers to watch for are the **Talbot Brothers,** calypso singers and instrumentalists, the **Coca-Cola Steel Band,** and the **Bermuda Strollers. Jimmy Keyes** is a popular pianist/comedian who holds forth at Henry VIII. **Bermuda** (formerly the Electronic Symphony) is a glitzy show band that performs an eclectic selection of pop, country, gospel, rock, and island music. **Jimmy O'Connor** heads a band that plays Kenny Rogers and Neil Diamond tunes, as well as island music and '50s hits. The **Shinbone Alley Cats** play Dixieland jazz, and the flamboyant trio of **Tino and Friends** plays a mix of classics and standards. **Sharx** is a rock band; the **Travellers** straddle country and rock music.

Around 3 AM, when the bars and discos close, head for the **Ice Queen** (Middle Rd., Paget, tel. 809/236–3136). This place is like a drive-in movie without the movie—the parking lot is jammed with cars and mopeds. The main attraction is the $3.50 burgers, which are probably the best on the island. You don't sit down here—there's just a take-out window where you line up to place your order—but it's *the* place to be after hours. It's also open during the day, and a good place to stop for an ice-cream cone break.

Other after-hours spots are **After Hours** (117 South Rd., Paget, tel. 809/236–8563), and the **Green Lantern** (Serpentine Rd., Pembroke Parish, tel. 809/295–6995). Both are informal spots that serve sandwiches and supper until the wee hours.

Bars and Lounges

Almost anyone will tell you that **Casey's** (Queen St., across from the Little Theatre, Hamilton, tel. 809/293–9549) is the best bar on the island. It's not fancy, nor is it touristy by any means. It's just a bar—a narrow room with a juke box and a few tables—but the place packs them in, especially on Friday night. It's open 10–10 every day except Sunday. **The Colony Pub** (The Princess, Pitts Bay Rd., Hamilton, tel. 809/295–3000), where the lights are low and the piano music is soft and soothing, is a popular meeting place for young professionals. **Henry VIII** (South Shore Rd., Southampton, tel. 809/238–1977) is a wildly popular place with a devoted following of locals of all ages, who like its piano player, Jimmy Keyes, its sing-alongs, and its British ambience. **Ye Olde Cock & Feather** (Front St., Hamilton, tel. 809/295–2263), which draws locals and tourists, hosts happy hour Monday through Saturday from 5 to 7, a mixed bag of live entertainment weeknights, and Sat. night dancing to a DJ's spins. **Loyalty Inn** (Somerset Village, tel. 809/234–0125) is a very casual neighborhood bar, where laid-back locals sometimes dare to do the karaoke bit. The big attraction at **Showbizz** (King and Reid Sts., Hamilton, tel. 809/292–0676) is the Wurlitzer jukebox bursting with sixties rock 'n' roll. There's no cover, and four-course meals ($18.50) are served nightly. In the Bailey's Bay area, the **Swizzle Inn** (Middle Rd., Hamilton Parish, tel. 809/293–9300) is strictly for the young, with a dart board, a juke box that plays soft and hard rock, and business cards from all over the world tacked on the walls, ceilings, and doors. The yachting crowd gathers at the **Wharf Tavern** (Somers Wharf, St. George's, tel. 809/297–1515) for rum swizzling and nautical talk.

The Club Scene

Cabaret The posh and nautical-theme **Neptune Lounge** (Southampton Princess, South Rd., Southampton Parish, tel. 809/238–8000) presents a lively cabaret show that draws a chic crowd of all ages. High-season cover is $12.

Calypso Bermuda legend **Gene Steede** is top banana for an island revue at the 280-seat **Gazebo Lounge** (Hamilton Princess, Pitts Bay Rd., Hamilton, tel. 809/295–3000). The $35 cover includes two drinks and the show. The **Clayhouse Inn** (North Shore Rd., Devonshire, tel. 809/292–3193) is a dark dive that packs in locals and tourists for a rowdy show involving limbo dancers, calypso singers, fire eaters, steel bands, and an occasional top-name entertainer. Shows are at 10:15 Monday, Tuesday, Wednesday, and Friday; $22.50 covers admission, two drinks, and tip.

Jazz **Jazz Club 21** (16 Ireland Island, Sandys, Dockyard, tel. 809/
234–7037 or 809/234–2721) is a sophisticated spot where the
lights are low and the live jazz is loud. High season shows
are Tuesday through Saturday at 9:30 and 11:30, and there
are Sunday jam sessions from 9 PM to 2 AM. $12 cover. **Os-
car's** (9 Victoria St., Hamilton, tel. 809/292–0348) has daily
happy hour from 5–8, live jazz every Friday from 9 PM to 1
AM, a casual local clientele, and no cover.

Discos

A snappy canopy covers the entrance to **Scandal** (119 Front
St., Hamilton, tel. 809/292–4040), where the decor is shock-
ing pink and black, and a sophisticated crowd pays $15 to
sip wine and champagne and dance nightly till the wee
small hours. **The Club** (Bermudiana Rd., Hamilton, tel. 809/
295–6693) is a ritzy room with red velvet, brass, and mirrors, that attracts an older professional crowd. Open for
dancing every night from 10 PM to 3 AM, the disco also hosts
Club Hour, on Friday from 5 to 7 PM. The $12 admission fee is
waived if you have dinner at The Harbourfront, La Trattoria,
Tavern on the Green, or Little Venice beneath the disco (*see*
Chapter 8, Dining). **The Oasis** (Emporium Bldg., Front St.,
Hamilton, tel. 809/292–4978 or 809/292–3379) is a hot spot
with a karoake bar and disco, and a slightly younger crowd
that gladly pays the $12 cover charge. Dancing is done
nightly in the chic **Palm Court** at the Sonesta Beach Hotel &
Spa (off South Rd., Southampton, tel. 809/238–8122). At
the elegant Elbow Beach Hotel (South Shore Rd., Paget,
tel. 809/236–3535), **Caesar's** is the place to dance to an R&B
band. It's open nightly; cover is $12. **The Caribbean Lounge**
(on the wharf east of King's Sq., St. George's, tel. 809/293–
9715) is a laid-back local spot with disco dancing Friday and
Saturday for a $5 cover.

Index

Personal Itinerary

Departure *Date*

Time

Transportation

Arrival *Date*   *Time*

Departure *Date*   *Time*

Transportation

Accommodations

Arrival *Date*   *Time*

Departure *Date*   *Time*

Transportation

Accommodations

Arrival *Date*   *Time*

Departure *Date*   *Time*

Transportation

Accommodations

Personal Itinerary

Arrival *Date*   *Time*

Departure *Date*   *Time*

Transportation

Accommodations

Arrival *Date*   *Time*

Departure *Date*   *Time*

Transportation

Accommodations

Arrival *Date*   *Time*

Departure *Date*   *Time*

Transportation

Accommodations

Arrival *Date*   *Time*

Departure *Date*   *Time*

Transportation

Accommodations

Personal Itinerary

Arrival *Date*   *Time*

Departure *Date*   *Time*

Transportation

Accommodations

Arrival *Date*   *Time*

Departure *Date*   *Time*

Transportation

Accommodations

Arrival *Date*   *Time*

Departure *Date*   *Time*

Transportation

Accommodations

Arrival *Date*   *Time*

Departure *Date*   *Time*

Transportation

Accommodations

Personal Itinerary

Arrival   *Date*   *Time*

Departure   *Date*   *Time*

Transportation

Accommodations

Arrival   *Date*   *Time*

Departure   *Date*   *Time*

Transportation

Accommodations

Arrival   *Date*   *Time*

Departure   *Date*   *Time*

Transportation

Accommodations

Arrival   *Date*   *Time*

Departure   *Date*   *Time*

Transportation

Accommodations

Personal Itinerary

Arrival   *Date*   *Time*

Departure   *Date*   *Time*

Transportation

Accommodations

Arrival   *Date*   *Time*

Departure   *Date*   *Time*

Transportation

Accommodations

Arrival   *Date*   *Time*

Departure   *Date*   *Time*

Transportation

Accommodations

Arrival   *Date*   *Time*

Departure   *Date*   *Time*

Transportation

Accommodations

Personal Itinerary

Arrival *Date*   *Time*

Departure *Date*   *Time*

Transportation

Accommodations

Arrival *Date*   *Time*

Departure *Date*   *Time*

Transportation

Accommodations

Arrival *Date*   *Time*

Departure *Date*   *Time*

Transportation

Accommodations

Arrival *Date*   *Time*

Departure *Date*   *Time*

Transportation

Accommodations

Addresses

Name	*Name*
Address	*Address*
Telephone	*Telephone*
Name	*Name*
Address	*Address*
Telephone	*Telephone*
Name	*Name*
Address	*Address*
Telephone	*Telephone*
Name	*Name*
Address	*Address*
Telephone	*Telephone*
Name	*Name*
Address	*Address*
Telephone	*Telephone*
Name	*Name*
Address	*Address*
Telephone	*Telephone*
Name	*Name*
Address	*Address*
Telephone	*Telephone*
Name	*Name*
Address	*Address*
Telephone	*Telephone*

Addresses

Name	*Name*
Address	*Address*
Telephone	*Telephone*
Name	*Name*
Address	*Address*
Telephone	*Telephone*
Name	*Name*
Address	*Address*
Telephone	*Telephone*
Name	*Name*
Address	*Address*
Telephone	*Telephone*
Name	*Name*
Address	*Address*
Telephone	*Telephone*
Name	*Name*
Address	*Address*
Telephone	*Telephone*
Name	*Name*
Address	*Address*
Telephone	*Telephone*
Name	*Name*
Address	*Address*
Telephone	*Telephone*

Notes

Notes

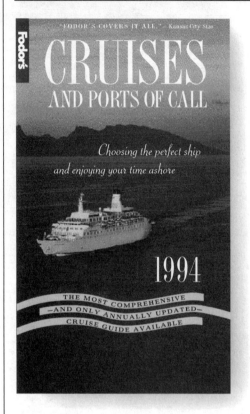

Announcing the only guide to explore
a Disney World you've never seen before:

The one for grown-ups.

This terrific new guide is the only one written specifically for the millions of adults who visit Walt Disney World each year <u>without</u> kids. Upscale, sophisticated, packed full of facts and maps, *Walt Disney World for Adults* provides up-to-date information on hotels, restaurants, sports facilities, and health clubs, as well as unique itineraries for adults, including: a Sporting Life Vacation, Day-and-Night Romantic Fantasy, Singles Safari, and Gardens and Natural Wonders Tour. Get essential tips and everything you need to know about reservations, packages, annual events, banking service, rest stops, and much more. With *Walt Disney World for Adults* in hand, you'll get the most out of one of the world's most fascinating, most complex playgrounds.

At bookstores everywhere, or call 1-800-533-6478

Fodor's

Fodor's Travel Guides

Available at bookstores everywhere, or call 1–800–533–6478, 24 hours a day.

U.S. Guides

Alaska

Arizona

Boston

California

Cape Cod, Martha's Vineyard, Nantucket

The Carolinas & the Georgia Coast

Chicago

Colorado

Florida

Hawaii

Las Vegas, Reno, Tahoe

Los Angeles

Maine, Vermont, New Hampshire

Maui

Miami & the Keys

New England

New Orleans

New York City

Pacific North Coast

Philadelphia & the Pennsylvania Dutch Country

The Rockies

San Diego

San Francisco

Santa Fe, Taos, Albuquerque

Seattle & Vancouver

The South

The U.S. & British Virgin Islands

The Upper Great Lakes Region

USA

Vacations in New York State

Vacations on the Jersey Shore

Virginia & Maryland

Waikiki

Walt Disney World and the Orlando Area

Washington, D.C.

Foreign Guides

Acapulco, Ixtapa, Zihuatanejo

Australia & New Zealand

Austria

The Bahamas

Baja & Mexico's Pacific Coast Resorts

Barbados

Berlin

Bermuda

Brazil

Brittany & Normandy

Budapest

Canada

Cancun, Cozumel, Yucatan Peninsula

Caribbean

China

Costa Rica, Belize, Guatemala

The Czech Republic & Slovakia

Eastern Europe

Egypt

Euro Disney

Europe

Europe's Great Cities

Florence & Tuscany

France

Germany

Great Britain

Greece

The Himalayan Countries

Hong Kong

India

Ireland

Israel

Italy

Japan

Kenya & Tanzania

Korea

London

Madrid & Barcelona

Mexico

Montreal & Quebec City

Morocco

Moscow & St. Petersburg

The Netherlands, Belgium & Luxembourg

New Zealand

Norway

Nova Scotia, Prince Edward Island & New Brunswick

Paris

Portugal

Provence & the Riviera

Rome

Russia & the Baltic Countries

Scandinavia

Scotland

Singapore

South America

Southeast Asia

Spain

Sweden

Switzerland

Thailand

Tokyo

Toronto

Turkey

Vienna & the Danube Valley

Yugoslavia

Special Series

Fodor's Affordables

Caribbean

Europe

Florida

France

Germany

Great Britain

London

Italy

Paris

Fodor's Bed & Breakfast and Country Inns Guides

Canada's Great Country Inns

California

Cottages, B&Bs and Country Inns of England and Wales

Mid-Atlantic Region

New England

The Pacific Northwest

The South

The Southwest

The Upper Great Lakes Region

The West Coast

The Berkeley Guides

California

Central America

Eastern Europe

France

Germany

Great Britain & Ireland

Mexico

Pacific Northwest & Alaska

San Francisco

Fodor's Exploring Guides

Australia

Britain

California

The Caribbean

Florida

France

Germany

Ireland

Italy

London

New York City

Paris

Rome

Singapore & Malaysia

Spain

Thailand

Fodor's Flashmaps

New York

Washington, D.C.

Fodor's Pocket Guides

Bahamas

Barbados

Jamaica

London

New York City

Paris

Puerto Rico

San Francisco

Washington, D.C.

Fodor's Sports

Cycling

Hiking

Running

Sailing

The Insider's Guide to the Best Canadian Skiing

Skiing in the USA & Canada

Fodor's Three-In-Ones (guidebook, language cassette, and phrase book)

France

Germany

Italy

Mexico

Spain

Fodor's Special-Interest Guides

Accessible USA

Cruises and Ports of Call

Euro Disney

Halliday's New England Food Explorer

Healthy Escapes

London Companion

Shadow Traffic's New York Shortcuts and Traffic Tips

Sunday in New York

Walt Disney World and the Orlando Area

Walt Disney World for Adults

Fodor's Touring Guides

Touring Europe

Touring USA: Eastern Edition

Fodor's Vacation Planners

Great American Vacations

National Parks of the East

National Parks of the West

The Wall Street Journal Guides to Business Travel

Europe

International Cities

Pacific Rim

USA & Canada

WHEREVER YOU TRAVEL, *H*ELP IS NEVER FAR AWAY.

From planning your trip to replacing lost cards, American Express® Travel Service Offices* are always there to help.

BERMUDA

L.P. Gutteridge, Ltd.
34 Bermudiana Road
Hamilton
809-295-4545

INTRODUCING

AT LAST, YOUR OWN PERSONALIZED LIST OF WHAT'S GOING ON IN THE CITIES YOU'RE VISITING.

KEYED TO THE DAYS WHEN YOU'RE THERE, CUSTOMIZED FOR YOUR INTERESTS, AND SENT TO YOU BEFORE YOU LEAVE HOME.

EXCLUSIVE FOR PURCHASERS OF FODOR'S GUIDES...

Fodor's WORLDVIEW
TRAVEL UPDATE

Introducing a revolutionary way to get customized, time-sensitive travel information just before your trip.

Now you can obtain detailed information about what's going on in each city you'll be visiting <u>before</u> you leave home—up-to-the-minute, objective information about the events and activities that interest you most.

This is a special offer for purchasers of Fodor's guides – a customized Travel Update to fit your specific interests and your itinerary.

Travel Updates contain the kind of time-sensitive insider information you can get only from local contacts – or from city magazines and newspapers once you arrive. But now you can have the same information before you leave for your trip.

The choice is yours: current art exhibits, theater, music festivals and special concerts, sporting events, antiques and flower shows, shopping, fitness, and more.

The information comes from hundreds of correspondents and thousands of sources worldwide. Updated continuously, it's like having your own personal concierge or friend in the city.

You specify the cities and when you'll be there. We'll do the rest — personalizing the information for you the way no guidebook can.

It's the perfect extension to your Fodor's guide and the best way to make the most of your valuable travel time.

Your Itinerary:
Customized repor
available for 160
destinations

K
7
in
dom
tion a
worthw
the perfe
Tickets are
venue. Alt
mances are ca
given. For mor
Open-Air Theatre
NW1 4NP Open
Tel: 935-5756. Ends:
International Air Tatto
Held biennially, the wor
military air display i
demostra-
tions, mili-
band,

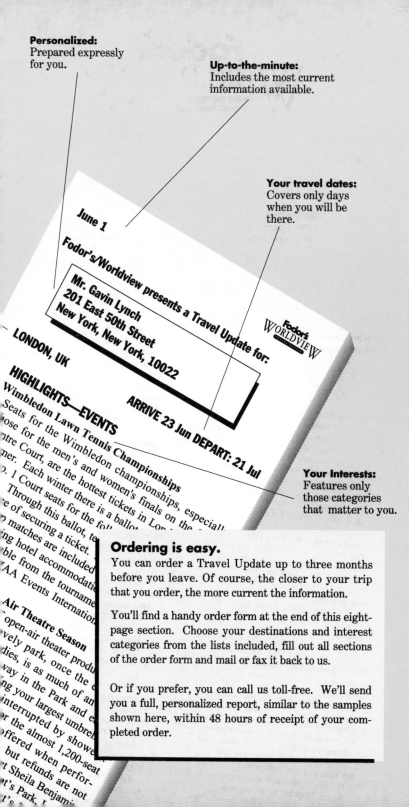

Personalized:
Prepared expressly
for you.

Up-to-the-minute:
Includes the most current
information available.

Your travel dates:
Covers only days
when you will be
there.

June 1

Fodor's/Worldview presents a Travel Update for:

Mr. Gavin Lynch
201 East 50th Street
New York, New York, 10022

Fodor's
WORLDVIEW

LONDON, UK

ARRIVE 23 Jun DEPART: 21 Jul

HIGHLIGHTS—EVENTS

Wimbledon Lawn Tennis Championships
Seats for the Wimbledon championships, especiall
ose for the men's and women's finals on the
ntre Court, are the hottest tickets in Lo
ner. Each winter there is a ballo
o. 1 Court seats for the foll
Through this ballot, te
e of securing a ticket.
o matches are included
ng hotel accommodati
ble from the tourname
AA Events Internationa

Your Interests:
Features only
those categories
that matter to you.

Air Theatre Season
open-air theater produ
vely park, once the
dies, is as much of an
way in the Park and e
ng your largest umbrel
interrupted by showe
or the almost 1,200-seat
offered when perfor-
but refunds are not
t Sheila Benjami
t's Park, r

Ordering is easy.
You can order a Travel Update up to three months
before you leave. Of course, the closer to your trip
that you order, the more current the information.

You'll find a handy order form at the end of this eight-
page section. Choose your destinations and interest
categories from the lists included, fill out all sections
of the order form and mail or fax it back to us.

Or if you prefer, you can call us toll-free. We'll send
you a full, personalized report, similar to the samples
shown here, within 48 hours of receipt of your completed order.

Fodor's WORLDVIEW
TRAVEL UPDATE

Special concerts—
who's performing
what and where

One-of-a-kind,
one-time-only events

Special interest,
in-depth listings

Children — Events

Angel Canal Festival

The festivities include a children's fun
entertainers, a boat rally and displays on
water. Regent's Canal. Islington. N1. T
Angel. Tel: 267 9100. 11:30am-5:30pm. 7/

Blackheath Summer Kite Festival

Stunt kite displays with parachuting te
bears and trade stands. Free admission. S
BR: Blackheath. 10am. 6/27.

Megabugs

Children will delight in this infestation
giant robotic insects, including a pray
mantic 60 times life size. Mon-Sat 10a
6pm; Sun 11am-6pm. Admission 4.
pounds. Natural History Museum, Cromw
Road. SW7. Tube: South Kensington. T
938 9123. Ends 10/01.

Childminders

This establishment employs only wome
providing nurses and qualified nannies to

Music — Jazz & Blues

Tito Puente's Golden Men of Latin Jazz

The father of mambo and Cuban rumba king
comes to town. Royal Festival Hall. South Bank.
SE1. Tube: Waterloo. Tel: 928 8800. 8pm. 7/15.

Georgie Fame and The New York Band

Riding a popular tide with his latest album, the
smoky-voiced Fame and his keyboard are on a
tour yet again. The Grand. Clapham Junction.
SW11. BR: Clapham Junction. Tel: 738 9000.
7:30pm. 7/07.

Jacques Loussier Play Bach Trio

The French jazz classicist and colleagues.
Kenwood Lakeside. Hampstead Lane.
Kenwood. NW3. Tube: Golders Green, then bus
210. Tel: 413 1443. 7pm. 7/10.

Tony Bennett and Ronnie Scott

Royal Festival Hall. South Bank. SE1. Tube:
Waterloo. Tel: 928 8800. 8pm. 7/11.

Santana

Royal Festival Hall. South Bank. SE1. Tube:
Waterloo. Tel: 928 8800. 8pm. 7/12.

Count Basie Orchestra and Nancy Wilson Trio

Royal Festival Hall. South Bank. SE1. Tube
Waterloo. Tel: 928 8800. 8pm. 7/14.

King Pleasure and the Biscuit Boys

Royal Festival Hall. South Bank. SE1. Tube
Waterloo. Tel: 928 8800. 6:30 and 9pm. 7/16.

Al Green and the London Community Gospel Choir

Royal Festival Hall. South Bank. SE1. Tube
Waterloo. Tel: 928 8800. 8pm. 7/13.

BB King and Linda Hopkins

Mother of the blues and successor to Bessi
Smith, Hopkins meets up with "Blues Boy
Royal Festival Hall. South Bank. SE

Music — Classical

Marylebone Sinfonia

Kenneth Gowen conducts music by
and Rossini. Queen Elizabeth Hall
Bank. SE1. Tube: Waterloo. Tel: 92
7:45pm. 7/16.

London Philharmonic

Franz Welser-Moest and George F
conduct selections by Alexande
Messiaen, and some of Benjamin's C
positions. Queen Elizabeth Hall. So
SE1. Tube: Waterloo. Tel: 928 8800

London Pro Arte Orchestra and Fore

Murray Stewart conducts sele
Rossini, Haydn and Jonathan Willoc
Queen Elizabeth Hall. South B
Tube: Waterloo. Tel: 928 8800. 7:4

Kensington Symphony Orchestra

Russell Keable conducts Dvorak

Here's what you get . . .

Detailed information about what's going on — precisely when you'll be there.

**Show openings
during your visit**

**Reviews by
local critics**

Exhibitions & Shows—Antique & Flower
Westminster Antiques Fair
Over 50 stands with pre-1830 furniture and other Victorian and earlier items. Thu-Fri 11am-8pm; Sat-Sun 11am-6pm. Admission 4 pounds, children free. Old Royal Horticultural Hall. Vincent Square. SW1. Tel: 0444/48 25 14. 6-24 thru 6/27.

Royal Horticultural Society Flower Show
The show includes displays of carnations, summer fruit and vegetables. Tue 11am-7pm; Wed 10am-5pm. Admission Tue 4 pounds, Wed 2 pounds. Royal Horticultural Halls. Greycoat Street and Vincent Square. SW1. Tube: Victoria. 7/20 thru 7/21.

ampton Court Palace International Flower Show
Major international garden and flower show king place in conjunction with the British

ter — Musical
unset Boulevard
In June, the four Andrew Lloyd Webber musicals which dominated London's stages in the 1980s (Cats, Starlight Express, Phantom of the Opera and Aspects of Love) are joined by the composer's latest work, a show rumored to have his best music to date. The 1950 Billy Wilder film about a helpless young writer who is drawn into the world of a possessive, aging silent screen star offers rich opportunities for Webber's evolving style. Soaring, aching melodies, lush technical effects and psychological thrills are all expected. Patti Lupone stars. Mon-Sat at 8pm; matinee Thu-Sat at 3pm. In-person sales only at the box office; credit card bookings, Tel: 344 0055. Admission 15-32.50 pounds. Adelphi Theatre. The Strand. WC2. Tube: Charing Cross. Tel: 836 7611. Starts: 6/21

Leonardo A Portrait of Love
A new musical about the great Renaissance arti and inventor comes in for a London premier tested by a brief run at Oxford's Old Fire Stati autumn. The work explores the relations Vinci and the woman

ectator Sports — Other Sports
Greyhound Racing: Wembley Stadium
This dog track offers good views of greyhound racing held on Mon, Wed and Fri. No credit cards. Stadium Way. Wembley. HA9. Tube: Wembley Park. Tel: 902 8833.

Benson & Hedges Cricket Cup Final
Lord's Cricket Ground. St. John's Wood Road. NW8. Tube: St. John's Wood. Tel: 289 1611. 11am. 7/10.

ess-Fax & Overnight Mail
ost Office, Trafalgar Square Branch
Offers a network of fax services, the Intelpost system, throughout the country and abroad. Mon-Sat 8am-8pm, Sun 9am-5pm. William IV Street. WC2. Tube: Charing Cross. Tel:

Alberquerque • Atlanta • Atlantic City • Ne
Baltimore • Boston • Chicago • Cincinnati
Cleveland • Dallas/Ft.Worth • Denver • De
• Houston • Kansas City • Las Vegas • Los
Angeles • Memphis • Miami • Milwaukee •
New Orleans • New York City • Orlando •
Springs • Philadelphia • Phoenix • Pittsburg
Portland • Salt Lake • San Antonio • San Di
San Franc • Seattle • St Louis • Tamp
Oslo • Wash • Louis • Tamp
Hawaii • Kauai • Maui • lu • Island
Ex • Bimini
Ber Countryside • Hamilton • lar
Antigua & B • vis • orto

Fodor's WORLDVIEW TRAVEL UPDATE

Gorda • Barbados • Dominica • Gren
cia • St. Vincent • Trinidad &Tobago
ymans • Puerto Plata • Santo Doming
Aruba • Bonaire • Curacao • St. Ma
ec City • Montreal • Ottawa • Toror
Vancouver • Guadeloupe • Martiniqu
helemy • St. Martin • Kingston • Ixta
o Bay • Negril • Ocho Rios • Ponce
n • Grand Turk • Providenciales • S
St. John • St. Thomas • Acapulco •
& Isla Mujeres • Cozumel • Guadal
a • Los Cabos • Manzinillo • Mazatl
City • Monterrey • Oaxaca • Puerto
do • Puerto Vallarta • Veracruz • Ix
dam • Athens • B

Interest Categories

For <u>your</u> personalized Travel Update, choose the categories you're most interested in from this list. Every Travel Update automatically provides you with *Event Highlights* – the best of what's happening during the dates of your trip.

1.	**Business Services**	Fax & Overnight Mail, Computer Rentals, Photocopying, Secretarial , Messenger, Translation Services

Dining

2.	**All Day Dining**	Breakfast & Brunch, Cafes & Tea Rooms, Late-Night Dining
3.	**Local Cuisine**	In Every Price Range—from Budget Restaurants to the Special Splurge
4.	**European Cuisine**	Continental, French, Italian
5.	**Asian Cuisine**	Chinese, Far Eastern, Japanese, Indian
6.	**Americas Cuisine**	American, Mexican & Latin
7.	**Nightlife**	Bars, Dance Clubs, Comedy Clubs, Pubs & Beer Halls
8.	**Entertainment**	Theater—Drama, Musicals, Dance, Ticket Agencies
9.	**Music**	Classical, Traditional & Ethnic, Jazz & Blues, Pop, Rock
10.	**Children's Activities**	Events, Attractions
11.	**Tours**	Local Tours, Day Trips, Overnight Excursions, Cruises
12.	**Exhibitions, Festivals & Shows**	Antiques & Flower, History & Cultural, Art Exhibitions, Fairs & Craft Shows, Music & Art Festivals
13.	**Shopping**	Districts & Malls, Markets, Regional Specialities
14.	**Fitness**	Bicycling, Health Clubs, Hiking, Jogging
15.	**Recreational Sports**	Boating/Sailing, Fishing, Ice Skating, Skiing, Snorkeling/Scuba, Swimming
16.	**Spectator Sports**	Auto Racing, Baseball, Basketball, Football, Horse Racing, Ice Hockey, Soccer

Please note that interest category content will vary by season, destination, and length of stay.

Destinations

The Fodor's/Worldview Travel Update covers more than 160 destinations world-wide. Choose the destinations that match your itinerary from this list. (Choose bulleted destinations only.)

United States (Mainland)
- Albuquerque
- Atlanta
- Atlantic City
- Baltimore
- Boston
- Chicago
- Cincinnati
- Cleveland
- Dallas/Ft. Worth
- Denver
- Detroit
- Houston
- Kansas City
- Las Vegas
- Los Angeles
- Memphis
- Miami
- Milwaukee
- Minneapolis/ St. Paul
- New Orleans
- New York City
- Orlando
- Palm Springs
- Philadelphia
- Phoenix
- Pittsburgh
- Portland
- St. Louis
- Salt Lake City
- San Antonio
- San Diego
- San Francisco
- Seattle
- Tampa
- Washington, DC

Alaska
- Alaskan Destinations

Hawaii
- Honolulu
- Island of Hawaii
- Kauai
- Maui

Canada
- Quebec City
- Montreal
- Ottawa
- Toronto
- Vancouver

Bahamas
- Abacos
- Eleuthera/ Harbour Island
- Exumas
- Freeport
- Nassau & Paradise Island

Bermuda
- Bermuda Countryside
- Hamilton

British Leeward Islands
- Anguilla
- Antigua & Barbuda
- Montserrat
- St. Kitts & Nevis

British Virgin Islands
- Tortola & Virgin Gorda

British Windward Islands
- Barbados
- Dominica
- Grenada
- St. Lucia
- St. Vincent
- Trinidad & Tobago

Cayman Islands
- The Caymans

Dominican Republic
- Puerto Plata
- Santo Domingo

Dutch Leeward Islands
- Aruba
- Bonaire
- Curacao

Dutch Windward Island
- St. Maarten/ St. Martin

French West Indies
- Guadeloupe
- Martinique
- St. Barthelemy

Jamaica
- Kingston
- Montego Bay
- Negril
- Ocho Rios

Puerto Rico
- Ponce
- San Juan

Turks & Caicos
- Grand Turk
- Providenciales

U.S. Virgin Islands
- St. Croix
- St. John
- St. Thomas

Mexico
- Acapulco
- Cancun & Isla Mujeres
- Cozumel
- Guadalajara
- Ixtapa & Zihuatanejo
- Los Cabos
- Manzanillo
- Mazatlan
- Mexico City
- Monterrey
- Oaxaca
- Puerto Escondido
- Puerto Vallarta
- Veracruz

Europe
- Amsterdam
- Athens
- Barcelona
- Berlin
- Brussels
- Budapest
- Copenhagen
- Dublin
- Edinburgh
- Florence
- Frankfurt
- French Riviera
- Geneva
- Glasgow
- Interlaken
- Istanbul
- Lausanne
- Lisbon
- London
- Madrid
- Milan
- Moscow
- Munich
- Oslo
- Paris
- Prague
- Provence
- Rome
- Salzburg
- St. Petersburg
- Stockholm
- Venice
- Vienna
- Zurich

Pacific Rim Australia & New Zealand
- Auckland
- Melbourne
- Sydney

China
- Beijing
- Guangzhou
- Shanghai

Japan
- Kyoto
- Nagoya
- Osaka
- Tokyo
- Yokohama

Other
- Bangkok
- Hong Kong & Macau
- Manila
- Seoul
- Singapore
- Taipei

Fodor's WORLDVIEW TRAVEL UPDATE **Order Form**

THIS TRAVEL UPDATE IS FOR (Please print):

Name			
Address			
City	State		ZIP
Country	Tel # ( ) -		

Title of this Fodor's guide:

Store and location where guide was purchased:

INDICATE YOUR DESTINATIONS/DATES: Write in below the destinations you want to order. Then fill in your arrival and departure dates for each destination.

		Month Day	Month Day
(Sample) LONDON	From:	6 / 21	To: 6 / 30
1	From:	/	To: /
2	From:	/	To: /
3	From:	/	To: /

You can order up to three destinations per Travel Update. Only destinations listed on the previous page are applicable. Maximum amount of time covered by a Travel Update cannot exceed 30 days.

CHOOSE YOUR INTERESTS: Select up to eight categories from the list of interest categories shown on the previous page and circle the numbers below:

1 2 3 4 5 6 7 8 9 10 11 12 13 14 15 16

CHOOSE HOW YOU WANT YOUR TRAVEL UPDATE DELIVERED (Check one):

❑ Please mail my Travel Update to the address above **OR**

❑ Fax it to me at **Fax #** ( ) -

DELIVERY CHARGE (Check one)

	Within U.S. & Canada	Outside U.S. & Canada
First Class Mail	❑ $2.50	❑ $5.00
Fax	❑ $5.00	❑ $10.00
Priority Delivery	❑ $15.00	❑ $27.00

All orders will be sent within 48 hours of receipt of a completed order form.

ADD UP YOUR ORDER HERE. *SPECIAL OFFER FOR FODOR'S PURCHASERS ONLY!*

	Suggested Retail Price	Your Price	This Order
First destination ordered	$13.95	$ 7.95	$ 7.95
Second destination (if applicable)	$ 9.95	$ 4.95	+
Third destination (if applicable)	$ 9.95	$ 4.95	+
Plus delivery charge from above			+
		TOTAL:	$

METHOD OF PAYMENT (Check one): ❑ AmEx   ❑ MC   ❑ Visa   ❑ Discover
❑ Personal Check   ❑ Money Order

Make check or money order payable to: Fodor's Worldview Travel Update

Credit Card # _____   **Expiration Date:** _____

Authorized Signature _____

SEND THIS COMPLETED FORM TO:
Fodor's Worldview Travel Update, 114 Sansome Street, Suite 700, San Francisco, CA 94104

OR CALL OR FAX US 24-HOURS A DAY
Telephone **1-800-799-9609** • Fax **1-800-799-9619** (From within the U.S. & Canada)
(Outside the U.S. & Canada: Telephone 415-616-9988 • Fax 415-616-9989)

(Please have this guide in front of you when you call so we can verify purchase.)

Offer valid until 12/31/94